AMERICA'S
MONUMENTS, MEMORIALS, AND HISTORIC SITES

Yvette La Pierre

**Consultant:
Jane Bangley McQueen**

PUBLICATIONS INTERNATIONAL, LTD.

Yvette La Pierre is former associate editor of *National Parks* magazine and a writer specializing in travel, science, and environmental issues. She is the author of numerous articles on the national park system, and two books for young readers, *Native American Rock Art: Messages from the Past* and *Mapping a Changing World.*

Jane Bangley McQueen is director of communications for the National Park Foundation, the nonprofit partner of the National Park Service. A former newspaper editor and reporter, she is also a writer and publication consultant who edits *The Complete Guide to America's National Parks* for the National Park Foundation.

Louis Weber, C.E.O.
Publications International, Ltd.
7373 North Cicero Avenue
Lincolnwood, Illinois 60646

Manufactured in USA.

8 7 6 5 4 3 2 1

ISBN 0-7853-1243-9

Library of Congress Catalog Card Number 95-72806

Contents
America's Monuments, Memorials, and Historic Sites

Hopewell Furnace National Historic Site

Statue of Liberty National Monument

WASHINGTON, D.C.

The White House

THE SOUTH

Fort Pulaski National Monument

Chimney Rock National Historic Site

THE MIDDLE WEST

THE SOUTHWEST

Organ Pipe Cactus National Monument

Golden Spike National Historic Site

THE NORTHWEST

Devils Tower National Monument

INTRODUCTION

While the crown jewels of the National Park System may be the big national parks, many smaller gems can be counted among our country's treasures. These are our national monuments, memorials, and historic sites.

National monuments are an eclectic grouping. Intended to preserve what are termed "nationally significant resources," they include natural areas, historic military fortifications, prehistoric ruins, fossil sites, and even the Statue of Liberty.

National memorials are primarily commemorative, but the various sites and structures so designated do not have to be directly connected with their subjects. Thus, Abraham Lincoln's former home in Springfield, Illinois, is a national historic site, while the Lincoln Memorial in Washington, D.C., is a national memorial.

Abandoned wagons decorate Utah's Golden Spike National Historic Site, where America's first transcontinental railroad was completed in 1869.

More than half of the sites administered by the National Park Service commemorate people, events, and activities important in our nation's history. National historic sites, which range from remnants of prehistoric civilizations to the homes and workplaces of modern Americans, generally focus on a single point in history, that being the moment of their greatest historical significance.

Historic sites weren't always under the aegis of the National Park System. Originally, military and other historic sites were controlled by the War Department and other government agencies. In 1930, Horace Albright, the second director of the Park Service, argued that his agency could manage historic sites better than the War Department. Congress agreed, establishing the George Washington Birthplace National Monument and placing it under the Park System's care. A few years later,

Congress transferred all national monuments and historic sites managed by the federal government to the Park Service, making it a truly national system of significant scenic, historic, and scientific sites.

With its illuminating text and more than 300 photos, this book will introduce you to all of the national monuments and historic sites, as well as the handful of locales managed by other agencies or groups in conjunction with the Park Service. It also includes several of our most popular national memorials, as well as a special section on Washington, D.C.

If you are planning to visit any of the monuments, historic sites, or other attractions featured in this book, the Appendix beginning on page 334 provides addresses and phone numbers, hours of operation, fees if any, and other useful information.

Wintertime view of the San Francisco Mountain Range, as seen from Sunset Crater National Monument in northern-central Arizona.

The Northeast

National Monuments and Historic Sites

It is no surprise that the Northeast, birthplace of the United States, is rich in historic sites. The region contains many settings that trace America's transformation from a colony to an independent nation. But here one will also find sites that commemorate important people and celebrate milestones in our economic, cultural, and social development, including advances in industry, the rise of American art and literature, and the struggle for racial equality and women's rights.

The national monuments of the Northeast, while fewer in number than can be found in other regions, likewise provide an intimate look at important landmarks in American history.

The Statue of Liberty, now a national monument, lit the way for millions of immigrants arriving in New York Harbor.

The Salem Maritime National Historic Site recalls the glory days of the eighteenth-century seaport, located on Massachusetts Bay.

Castle Clinton

National Monument

The fortress that became a civic garden

Castle Clinton, at the tip of Manhattan, has had a long and varied existence. The circular fortress was built between 1807 and 1811 as one of a series of forts to protect New York City from potential British aggression.

Originally known as the Southwest Battery, its name was changed after the War of 1812 to Castle Clinton in honor of DeWitt Clinton, a former mayor of the city and later governor of New York State. No longer needed to defend New York, Castle Clinton was turned into a civic garden in 1824.

A newspaper described Castle Garden as a "fanciful garden, tastefully ornamented with shrubs and flowers." It was the setting for fireworks, gala concerts, an occasional balloon ascension, and scientific demonstrations. A month after its opening, the Marquis de Lafayette began his year-long tour of America at the Garden. Castle Garden served as a theater for more than a quarter century.

In 1855, Castle Garden became the depot for immigrants entering the country. For the first time, immigrants were protected from people who roamed the wharves looking for gullible newcomers to cheat.

After Ellis Island became the immigration center in 1892, Castle Clinton became an aquarium and then finally a museum and information center for National Park Service sites in metropolitan New York. The walls of the original fort remain intact; inside, exhibits trace the evolution of Castle Clinton.

This circular fortress was originally built in 1811 to protect New York harbor from British attack. Today, Castle Clinton serves as the embarkation point for ferry trips to Liberty and Ellis Islands.

Fort McHenry
National Monument and Historic Shrine

A battle here stirred a songwriter's imagination

Fort McHenry National Monument and Historic Shrine is the birthplace of our national anthem.

On September 13, 1814—during the War of 1812—the British Navy attacked Fort McHenry, which protected Baltimore's inner harbor. For 25 hours, British troops bombarded the fort with an estimated 1,500 to 1,800 rockets and shells. The next morning, still unable to capture the strategic city, the British sailed away as American soldiers hoisted a large flag over the fort and musicians played "Yankee Doodle."

From a vessel offshore, Francis Scott Key saw the Stars and Stripes still waving and began penning the lines to "The Star-Spangled Banner" on the back of a letter. Key later described how he felt that morning: "Through the clouds of the war, the stars of that banner still shone in my view . . . Then, in the hour of deliverance, and joyful triumph, my heart spoke; and 'Does not such a country and such defenders of their country deserve a song?' was its question." Key's tribute became the national anthem in 1931. That war was the last time Britain challenged America's independence.

A reproduction of the famous flag, made by Baltimore resident Mary Pickersgill, still flies at Fort McHenry (the original is in the Smithsonian's Museum of American History). Exhibits, films, and historic reenactments tell the story of Fort McHenry's significant role in establishing America's military reputation.

After the British attack in 1814, Fort McHenry never again came under enemy fire, although it continued as an active military post for the next 100 years.

Fort Stanwix

National Monument

Where the Stars and Stripes first flew in battle

In 1777, the well-built fortress survived a three-week siege by British troops, who eventually withdrew to Canada.

■ ■ ■

*I*n colonial times, a traveler could journey all the way from New York City to Canada and back again by water, except for a short portage across nearly level ground between the Mohawk River and Wood Creek in what is now Rome, New York.

Indians had used the portage, which they called *De-O-Wain-Sta*, for centuries. The British, realizing that the portage was crucial for commerce, settlement, and military activity in the area, built Fort Stanwix in the summer of 1758 to protect the land passage. The new log and earth fort replaced three smaller forts that had protected the portage during the early years of the French and Indian War. The fort was abandoned by the military after the British conquest of Canada in 1763, but it continued to serve as a center for Indian affairs.

The importance of Fort Stanwix for defense purposes was not realized again until after the American Revolution began in

Fort Stanwix in Rome, New York, has been reconstructed to approximate its 1777 appearance.

■ ■ ■

The Stars and Stripes, quickly sewn up from clothes, reportedly flew for the first time in battle during the siege of Fort Stanwix in 1777.

■ ■ ■

the spring of 1775, and patriot leaders began to rebuild the fort, which was by then in ruins. In 1777, two forces of British troops marched toward New York in an attempt to occupy the colony and disrupt the major supply and communications route between New England and the Middle Colonies. Fort Stanwix survived a three-week siege by one British force, which finally withdrew to Canada.

According to legend, the Stars and Stripes, hastily sewn up from garments, flew for the first time during this battle. The other British force, surrounded and cut off from reinforcements, surrendered in Saratoga. These two British defeats marked a turning point in the Revolution and led to the formal French, Dutch, and Spanish alliances that helped the patriots gain independence.

Fort Stanwix, a national monument since 1935, was carefully reconstructed in time for the 1976 Bicentennial, with earthworks, a cannon platform, barracks, and officers' quarters. Artifacts recovered during excavations shed light on the garrison life of the time.

A BLUFF SAVES THE FORT

Fort Stanwix survived the three-week British siege with the help of a little trickery engineered by Benedict Arnold, who was still a patriot at the time.

Arnold and his troops were sent to relieve Fort Stanwix, but Arnold knew he didn't have enough men to take on the British army outside the fort, more than half of whom were Indian. So Arnold sent Hon Yost Schuyler, a loyalist whose family was being held hostage by the patriots, to spread the word that an American force numbering as many as "the leaves on the trees" was coming. The Indians deserted, and the British were left without enough troops to capture the fort. "Arnold's Bluff" saved Fort Stanwix.

■ ■ ■

Statue of Liberty

National Monument

The "Lady with the Lamp" is a symbol of Freedom

For millions of new Americans, the first glimpse of their new country was the colossal "Lady with the Lamp," standing 152 feet tall and weighing in at 2,225 tons. She holds high the torch of freedom in New York Harbor.

The Statue of Liberty, completed in 1884, was a gift from France to celebrate "the alliance of the two nations in achieving the independence of the United States of America . . . . " The French historian Edouard Laboulaye and sculptor Frederic-Auguste Bartholdi designed the statue, and Gustave Eiffel, who engineered the Eiffel Tower, designed the interior iron support structure.

The only condition of the gift was that America provide the statue's base. Hungarian immigrant and publisher Joseph Pulitzer headed a fundraising campaign, and American schoolchildren donated pennies to help pay for the 89-foot-high pedestal. One hundred years later, a team of French and American craftsmen refurbished "Lady Liberty" in time for her centennial celebration.

The Statue of Liberty National Monument, designated in 1924, is one of the country's most visited monuments—a trip to the Lady's crown can mean a several-hour wait in line and a strenuous climb. The monument, however, has other attractions, including a museum and exhibit in the pedestal where visitors can learn more about immigration and the story behind the statue. The promenade, colonnade, and top levels of the pedestal offer spectacular views of New York Harbor, including Ellis Island.

A gift from the French people, the Statue of Liberty has been greeting ships in New York harbor for more than a century.

In preparation for Lady Liberty's centennial celebration in 1986, the statue was restored to its original glory—at a cost of $30 million.

■ ■ ■ ■ ■

French craftsmen began building the statue in 1875. Sculptor Frederic-Auguste Bartholdi's design was said to be inspired by the giant statues, called colossi, that were popular in ancient Egypt and Rome.

■ ■ ■

By the time Ellis Island closed in 1954 after 62 years of operation, 20 million immigrants had passed through its doors.

■ ■ ■

Ellis Island was the first stop for some 12 million immigrants between 1892 and 1924. On one day alone—April 17, 1907—11,747 people were processed there. The descendants of the Ellis Island immigrants account for nearly 40 percent of the country's population.

Their contribution to twentieth-century America was recognized in part in 1965 when Ellis Island became part of the Statue of Liberty National Monument. Full recognition came nearly 30 years later when the Ellis Island Immigration Museum was opened in time for the immigration depot's centennial in 1992.

The museum is in the refurbished Main Building, a graceful Beaux-Arts-style structure with four copper domes. More than 30 galleries featuring artifacts, historic photos, maps, and oral histories tell the story of the people who helped settle America.

Visitors can climb the stairs to the Registry Room, as the immigrants did, and see the place where doctors determined in less than ten seconds if an immigrant was healthy enough to proceed. The old railroad ticket office now houses an exhibition that traces immigration before and after Ellis Island, and the "Treasures from Home" exhibit displays artifacts that immigrants brought from home, including jewelry, clothes, and toys. An innovative oral history collection fills the museum with voices of immigrants.

HOW THE STATUE WAS CREATED

Sculptor Frederic-Auguste Bartholdi first created Liberty as a 1.25-meter clay model. Then he enlarged the model in plaster several times until he had 300 full-sized sections. Thin copper sheets were hammered into shape against wooden forms matching the contours of the plaster sections to form the statue.

Gustave Eiffel designed a huge central wrought-iron pylon to support a secondary framework, to which the statue's "skin" was attached with flexible iron bars. The skin, therefore, "floats" on the pylon and is strong enough to withstand high winds, yet is able to expand and contract with changes in temperature.

The statue was completed in June of 1884 in Paris, where it stood until it was dismantled and sent to America early in 1885.

■ ■ ■

Adams
National Historic Site

Birthplace and home of two former Presidents

*J*ust south of Boston, in the small city of Quincy, is the Adams National Historic Site, former home to five generations of the Adams family, including two Presidents. Unlike most presidential homes, "The Old House," as the Adamses called it, never passed out of family hands, and its furnishings never had to be sought out or replaced.

Included in the 10-acre park are the modest birthplaces of the country's only father-and-son Presidents, John Adams and John Quincy Adams. John Adams bought the 22-room mansion, the centerpiece of the park, in 1787, after he had become a successful lawyer and politician. He helped draft the Declaration of Independence and later served as the American envoy to Great Britain. After serving as

John Adams bought this house in 1787 as the Constitution was being written. Five generations of Adamses lived here, including the only father-son Presidents.

The eighteenth-century formal gardens at the Adams National Historic Site brighten the grounds with seasonal displays of blooming plants.

George Washington's Vice President—a job he described as "... the most insignificant office that ever the invention of man contrived or his imagination conceived"—he became the second President of the United States.

During John Adams' diplomatic missions, his son, John Quincy, gained a firsthand education in foreign affairs, serving as an interpreter for the foreign service in Russia when he was only 14 years old. In 1825, when he was 58 years old, he became our nation's sixth President.

Other Adamses that called "The Old House" home included Charles Francis Adams, who served as U.S. Minister to Great Britain,

The separate birthplaces of John Adams and his son John Quincy are preserved as part of the Adams National Historic Site.

and writers Henry Adams and Brooks Adams. Throughout the years, family members enlarged the mansion and filled it with acquisitions from trips and missions around the globe.

Rangers lead visitors through 15 of the rooms, including John Adams' study, which he used during the summers of his presidency and where he later composed many of his letters to Thomas Jefferson. It was in this room also that he died on July 4, 1826—on the fiftieth anniversary of Independence Day and just hours after Jefferson himself passed away.

John Quincy's son, Charles Francis, added the impressive Stone Library, filled to the brim with the books, papers, and mementos of

John Quincy's son Charles Francis, minister to Great Britain during the Civil War, added the Stone Library in 1870. It contains nearly 12,000 volumes from the collected works of the Adams family, whose motto was, "Whatever you write, preserve."

the family. On opposite ends of the room stand the desks used by John Adams when he was President and John Quincy when he was a state representative. Dominating the room is an oak library table at which generations of Adamses sat to read, write, and study. On the fireplace mantel are John Quincy's "Household Gods"—the busts of classical authors.

This one site, officially established in 1946, helps bring to life the fascinating story of one of our country's most influential early families. As an added attraction, a walk through the grounds reveals one of the best-kept eighteenth-century formal gardens in New England.

A LIBRARY THAT SPEAKS VOLUMES

On display at the Stone Library are books that testify to John Quincy Adams' long crusade against slavery.

In 1839, John Quincy argued on behalf of a boatload of slaves who had mutinied aboard the ship taking them to Haiti. He won their freedom, and in thanks they presented him with an inscribed Bible, now on display at the library.

The library also contains John Quincy's copy of *Poems on Various Subjects, Religious and Moral* (1773) by ex-slave Phillis Wheatley, considered the first African-American poet.

Allegheny Portage Railroad

National Historic Site

The first train to cross the Allegheny Mountains

The Allegheny Portage Railroad, completed in 1834, was a system of tracks on inclined planes that crossed the summit of Allegheny Mountain, reducing the travel time from Pittsburgh to Philadelphia to four days instead of 23. The railroad linked the eastern and western canals of the Pennsylvania system in an attempt to compete with the Erie Canal for commerce.

Charles Dickens took a trip on the line in 1842 and later wrote down his impressions of the experience: "It was pretty traveling thus at a rapid pace along the heights of the mountain and with a keen wind, to look down into a valley full of light and softness and catching glimpses through the treetops . . . and we riding onward high above them like a whirlwind."

In the early 1800s, steam engines weren't very powerful, so this ingenious railroad system was devised to "walk" cars uphill. Railroad cars were attached by thick hemp ropes to a cable that was pulled from level to level by a stationary steam engine.

Despite this new technology, more powerful locomotives and dependable railroads made the portage railroad obsolete, and it was abandoned after 23 years.

Four of the ten original inclined planes are visible at Allegheny Portage Railroad National Historic Site, in addition to excavated engine-house foundations, a bridge that was built without mortar, and the first railroad tunnel in the country. Near the summit is Lemon House, a restored tavern that once served as a rest stop for travelers.

Lemon House, originally built in 1832 as a tavern and rest stop for travelers on the railroad, now serves as a visitor center.

Boston African-American
National Historic Site

A look at black life in post-Colonial America

The Black Heritage Trail includes the Phillips School, one of Boston's first integrated schools.

A one-and-a-half-mile walking tour through Boston's Beacon Hill district transports visitors back to the time when African Americans struggled for independence and citizenship.

The Boston African-American National Historic Site, which includes 15 pre-Civil War structures linked by the Black Heritage Trail, focuses on the political, social, and educational aspects of black life during this time.

Rangers from the National Park Service lead the guided tour, which begins at the Boston Common. There, at the corner of Park and Beacon streets, is a statue sculpted by Augustus Saint-Gaudens and dedicated to the Massachusetts 54th, the first black regiment to fight in the Civil War. The next stop is the 1797 George Middleton House, the oldest home built by African-Americans on Beacon Hill. George Middleton was a veteran of the Revolutionary War and is said to have led a company known as the "Bucks of America."

The elite of Boston's black community first built and owned the homes in this area. Beacon Hill became a safe

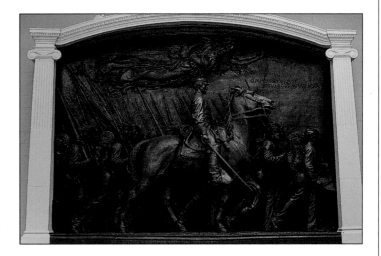

The Robert Gould Shaw 54th Regiment Memorial in Boston Common memorializes the first black regiment to be recruited by the North during the Civil War.

The African Meeting House, dedicated in 1806, is the oldest black church in the country. Still used as a community center, it also marks the beginning of the Black Heritage Trail.

haven for runaway slaves and was a major point along the Underground Railroad.

Other stops along the trail include the Phillips School, one of Boston's first integrated schools (1855); the home of abolitionist John J. Smith; Abel Smith School, a grammar school organized by black parents in 1808, when their children were denied access to the public school system; and several homes typical of those owned by black Bostonians in the nineteenth century.

The trail also includes the Lewis and Harriet Hayden House, home to an escaped slave and his wife and a station along the Underground Railroad. The Haydens reportedly kept kegs of gunpowder under their front stoop. When bounty hunters came to their house looking for escaped slaves, they met them at the door with burning candles, saying they would rather drop the candles and blow up the house than turn in the ex-slaves in their care.

The tour ends at the African Meeting House, the oldest black church still standing in the United States. It was formed in 1805 and built almost entirely by black labor. The structure served as a house of worship as well as a political meeting place, and it helped bind together the free black community in Boston as it struggled to find its place in the new nation.

The Abel Smith School, dedicated in 1835, was named after a white businessman who left an endowment of $2,000 to the city of Boston for the education of black children.

■ ■ ■

BOSTON'S BLACK COMMUNITY

The first Africans arrived in Boston in 1638 as slaves purchased in Providence Isle, a Puritan colony off the coast of Central America. By 1705, there were more than 400 slaves in the city, and a small community of free blacks was just forming in the North End.

The American Revolution proved to be a turning point for that small community, and by the end of the war there were more free blacks than slaves. When the first federal census was taken in 1790, Massachusetts was the only state in the Union to record no slaves. Blacks in Boston were already struggling with some of the issues—finding decent housing, educating their children, earning equal pay—that would be addressed by the civil rights movement more than 150 years later.

■ ■ ■

Clara Barton

National Historic Site

Honoring the founder of the American Red Cross

Clara Barton defied antifeminist prejudices of her day. She tended the wounded on Civil War battlefields, established an office to locate missing soldiers, and founded the American Red Cross.

■ ■ ■

The Clara Barton National Historic Site in Maryland preserves the home of the founder of the American Red Cross and famous "Angel of the Battlefield"—a woman who went far beyond the traditional role of a nineteenth-century female.

Clara Barton was born in 1821 and worked as a schoolteacher and Patent Office clerk before she devoted her energy to the care of the sick and wounded during the Civil War. She tended the wounded at the Second Battle of Manassas, Antietam, the Wilderness, Fredericksburg, and Spotsylvania.

Barton tended the soldiers for humanitarian, not patriotic, reasons. "Men have worshipped war till it has cost a million times more than the earth is worth . . . ," she said. After the war, she spent the next several years helping to locate missing soldiers and identifying the graves of unknown soldiers at Andersonville Prison.

In 1868, after suffering a nervous breakdown, Barton went to Europe, intending to rest. Instead, she nursed the wounded of the Franco-Prussian War and learned for the first time about the International Red Cross. Back home, she battled bureaucracy until the U.S. Senate established the Red Cross in the United States in 1882. One of the American Red Cross's first efforts was aiding victims of the Johnstown flood of 1889.

The house where Barton lived from 1897 until her death in 1912 at age 90 displays some of her furniture and personal possessions. The structure was originally built as a warehouse for Red Cross supplies. It also served as the first permanent headquarters of the American Red Cross.

The Maryland house where Clara Barton lived for the last 15 years of her life served as a warehouse for disaster-relief supplies, then became the first permanent headquarters of the American Red Cross.

■ ■ ■

Edgar Allan Poe
National Historic Site

Where a great writer wrestled with his demons

Sometime between the fall of 1842 and June of 1843, Edgar Allan Poe, his wife Virginia, his mother-in-law Maria Clemm, and their cat Catterina moved into this house on Philadelphia's North Seventh Street.

Edgar Allan Poe is best known for his gripping tales of terror, but he also had a gift for romantic poetry. Visitors to the Edgar Allan Poe National Historic Site in Philadelphia can contemplate both sides of the talented writer as they explore one of the places where he lived and worked.

Of Poe's several homes in Philadelphia, only this small brick house on North Seventh Street remains. It is not known exactly how long he lived here, so it is difficult to say which stories he produced while living in this house. But it is likely he wrote, among others, "The Gold Bug," "The Fall of the House of Usher," and "The Murders in the Rue Morgue."

Because little is known about Poe's furniture and belongings, the Park Service has chosen to leave the house empty. Rather than point to artifacts, rangers discuss Poe's life and writings. Ranger-guided tours begin at the visitor center, which has exhibits, photographs of Poe's family, and an eight-minute slide presentation.

Poe was born in Boston in 1809 and raised by foster parents. When he was 22, Poe lost the support of his foster father, and from that time on he struggled to make a living. Poe was able to keep himself out of debt by selling stories and poems, and he eventually became the editor of a literary magazine, *Southern Literary Messenger.*

In 1836, Poe married his cousin Virginia Clemm and enjoyed his most productive years with her in Philadelphia. The couple, Virginia's mother, and their cat Catterina moved into this rental house in 1842 or 1843.

Following Virginia's death in 1847, Poe's health began to disintegrate, and he died less than three years later in Baltimore of "acute congestion of the brain."

THE FIRST MYSTERY WRITER

Poe is credited with being the inventor of the modern detective mystery.

In 1841, he published "Murders in the Rue Morgue," which features an intelligent but eccentric detective, Cesar A. Dupin, who systematically solves crimes using rational thinking, or what Poe called "ratiocination."

This detective, who appears again in "The Purloined Letter" and "The Mystery of Marie Roget," is the unmistakable ancestor of Arthur Conan Doyle's Sherlock Holmes, Agatha Christie's Hercule Poirot, and Earl Stanley Gardener's Perry Mason.

Edison
National Historic Site

The invention factory of an American genius

Sickly and hard of hearing, young Thomas Alva Edison was not much of a student and left school when he was just a teen. Despite this rocky beginning, Edison went on to become a highly successful inventor with hundreds of patents to his name. He is still the all-time record holder of U.S. patents with 1,093.

As a boy, Edison spent a lot of time in his "laboratory" in the basement of his home doing scientific experiments. At age 29, he built the world's first private research and development lab, which was later moved to West Orange, New Jersey. According to Edison, he stocked it with everything "from an elephant's hide to the eyeballs of a United States senator."

At this "invention factory," Edison and his workers cranked out the movie camera, an improved storage battery, the fluoroscope, and rubber from the goldenrod plant.

Despite being deaf, Edison's favorite invention was the phonograph. In 1877, while working on a device for recording messages over the telephone, Edison was inspired to invent a talking machine. The world's first recorded words were "Mary had a little lamb."

In 1886, Edison and his wife Mina moved into this 23-room mansion, called Glenmont. While Edison managed his labs down the hill, Mina ruled the estate.

■ ■ ■

Despite being partially deaf since childhood, Edison's favorite invention was the phonograph. He built his first in 1877.

■ ■ ■

BRINGING AN OLD IDEA TO LIGHT

Many people mistakenly think that Edison invented the light bulb. Actually, what he did was bring an old idea "to light."

For 50 years, scientists had been trying and failing to produce a reliable source of light by sending an electric current through a material inside a vacuum, causing it to glow. Scientists had been using a high current and low-resistance material. Edison discovered that highly resistant material would glow with a lower current and last longer. In 1879, he produced an incandescent lamp that burned for more than 13 hours, ushering in the age of electric light.

■ ■ ■

Edison National Historic Site

In the spring of 1878, Edison introduced his phonograph to the world at a National Academy of Sciences meeting in Washington, D.C. Edison had someone speak into the machine, then had another man crow like a rooster. When the machine repeated their voices, two women in the audience fainted. That night, President Hayes asked to hear the phonograph. He and the First Lady sat up until early morning listening to the marvelous machine.

At Edison National Historic Site, one can visit the ten buildings that make up the West Orange laboratory complex. Though urban sprawl has changed the once-pastoral setting of the lab, the interiors of the buildings look much as they did in Edison's time, and many original inventions are on display, including a tinfoil phonograph and early electric light and power equipment. A half-mile away is Edison's Victorian mansion Glenmont, restored with original furnishings and family possessions. A tour of the 23-room red brick and wood house includes Edison's two-story library, containing some 10,000 books and the inventor's desk.

Edison was 84 when he hung up his lab coat for the last time in 1931; it still hangs there in his laboratory.

A monument marks the site of Edison's Menlo Park laboratory. While not part of the historical site, it is believed to be the world's first private research and development lab.

Edison set up an "invention factory" in West Orange, New Jersey, in 1887, preserved now as the Edison National Historic Site. The grounds include a replica of the world's first motion-picture studio where movies were made in the 1890s.

Eisenhower
National Historic Site

The simple farm where "Ike" and Mamie retired

After 50 years of public service, the former President and his wife retired to this modest farmhouse at Gettysburg, Pennsylvania.

Unlike many Presidents, Dwight D. Eisenhower owes his rise to the presidency more to his accomplishments than to family wealth.

Eisenhower attended the U.S. Military Academy, perhaps in part because his family couldn't afford to send him to college. He steadily rose in rank, and in 1943 he was named Supreme Allied Commander for the cross-Channel invasion. His wartime success made him a favorite of the American people, who elected him President in 1952. Anticipating retirement, the Eisenhowers had purchased a small Pennsylvania dairy farm two years earlier. Nearly ten years later, Eisenhower finally retired after serving the country for 50 years.

A tour through "Ike" (a nickname from childhood) and Mamie Eisenhower's farmhouse on the edge of Gettysburg battlefield in Pennsylvania helps illustrate his place in middle-class America. The couple rarely used the formal living room, except when the thirty-fourth President was entertaining dignitaries, because it was too stuffy. Their favorite room was the glassed-in porch overlooking southern Pennsylvania's rolling hills. There they ate breakfast, played cards, read, and simply relaxed.

In 1967, Ike and Mamie gave their home to the U.S. government under the agreement that they would reside there for the rest of their lives. Ike died two years later at age 78; Mamie stayed on until her death in 1979.

Dwight D. Eisenhower, who earned the nickname "Ike" in grade school, was a World War II military hero and the thirty-fourth President of the United States.

Eleanor Roosevelt

National Historic Site

The favorite retreat of an influential First Lady

Widely recognized as the most influential woman of her time, Eleanor Roosevelt is the only First Lady with a park site dedicated to her memory. Eleanor Roosevelt National Historic Site, authorized in 1977, preserves Eleanor's personal retreat, which President Franklin D. Roosevelt carved out of a remote corner of his family's Hyde Park estate.

A bumpy country lane, passing through fields and woods and over a noisy plank bridge, leads visitors to the two main buildings of the site. Eleanor shared the little fieldstone cottage, built in 1925, with her friends Marion Dickerman and Nancy Cook. A skilled cabinetmaker, Cook designed and built most of the cottage's furniture.

The Eleanor Roosevelt National Historic Site, which preserves Mrs. Franklin D. Roosevelt's beloved retreat Val-Kill, is the only national historic site dedicated to the memory of a First Lady.

■ ■ ■ ■ ■

Eleanor Roosevelt (left) was the first wife of any President to hold press conferences. Here she addresses delegates at the YWCA Convention in Philadelphia in 1934.

■ ■ ■

The project was so successful that the trio built a larger building nearby to house a small furniture factory. Until it closed during the Great Depression, Val-Kill Industries hired local people to make handmade furniture. After Franklin's death, Eleanor converted the factory into her private home, and Val-Kill Cottage became a central gathering place for her family.

Today, Val-Kill Cottage is a museum of Eleanor's furnishings and belongings. The original Stone Cottage is the headquarters of the Eleanor Roosevelt Center and is open to the public when not in other use. Highlights of a tour of the grounds include the rose garden, playhouse, swimming pool, and Val-Kill Pond.

The site is a memorial to a woman who, though extremely shy, became a powerful voice for human rights. She went far beyond the traditional role of White House hostess and traveled extensively, representing her husband and pushing for legislation to help the weak and disadvantaged. She was the first wife of a President to hold press conferences and write a syndicated column.

When Franklin died, Eleanor told a reporter, "The story is over." But her own story continued. She served as a delegate to the United Nations, and her work earned her the title "First Lady of the World."

ADVANCING THE ROLE OF WOMEN

Eleanor Roosevelt was the first First Lady to hold press conferences, but she only allowed female reporters to attend those candid meetings.

Eleanor believed that the American public had a right to know what the people in the White House were thinking and doing. By inviting only women, however, she helped many female journalists break into the male-dominated world of political reporting.

■ ■ ■

Ford's Theatre

National Historic Site

Where a President fell to an assassin's bullet

While the country was celebrating the end of the Civil War, President Abraham Lincoln decided to go to the theater and take a break from the burdens of the office. On the night of April 14, 1865, the Lincolns attended a performance of a popular comedy called *Our American Cousin* at Ford's Theatre in downtown Washington. Clara Harris, daughter of New York Senator Ira Harris, and her fiancé Major Henry Reed Rathbone joined the Lincolns in the presidential box.

At about 10:15 P.M., while the audience was laughing, John Wilkes Booth entered the presidential box and shot Lincoln. A well-known actor and Southern sympathizer who saw Lincoln as the

The interior of Ford's Theatre is decorated just as it was the last time the Lincolns occupied the presidential box.

Ford's Theatre, which began as a Baptist Church, was turned into a theater not long before Abraham Lincoln was assassinated there on April 14, 1865.

source of the South's problems, Booth had been planning for months to kidnap Lincoln and had recruited several conspirators, including John Surratt, whose mother, Mary, ran a boardinghouse where the group often met. The kidnapping plan had failed, but the assassination plot succeeded.

Lincoln was carried across the street to the back bedroom of a tailor's home. Several doctors attended Lincoln; one held his hand all night, knowing that if the President awoke he would be blind, and the doctor wanted him to know that a friend was nearby. At 7:22 the next morning, Abraham Lincoln died.

In the chaos following the shooting, Booth leapt from the presidential box to the stage, but he tripped in the bunting that decorated the box and landed off balance, breaking a small bone in his left leg. He limped across the stage to the theater's back door, mounted his horse, and rode south. On April 26, he was shot and killed by Union

This portrait of Lincoln was taken on April 9, 1865—a mere four days before he was murdered.

While Lincoln and his wife Mary Todd enjoyed a performance of Our American Cousin, *John Wilkes Booth crept into the presidential box at Ford's Theatre and shot Lincoln from behind. He died the next morning.*

The National Park Service doesn't shy away from the grisly details of Lincoln's assassination and exhibits graphic reminders of the tragedy, including the diary of assassin John Wilkes Booth and these pistols and knives, which once belonged to him.

troops while hiding in a barn near Port Royal, Virginia. Booth's alleged conspirators were soon arrested, and four were eventually sentenced to death, including Mary Surratt, the first woman hanged by the government.

The theater where Lincoln was shot and the house where he died are preserved today as Ford's Theatre National Historic Site. Both buildings have been restored to look as they did the night of the assassination. Graphic reminders of that evening are on display, including a bloody pillow upon which Lincoln rested, hoods worn by the conspirators during their trial, and Booth's .44-caliber single-shot derringer. The bed in the back room of the house is similar to the original, which was not long enough for Lincoln, who had to be laid diagonally across it. The front parlor is where Mary Todd Lincoln and her eldest son spent the night.

Ford's Theatre is a memorial to Lincoln, but it lives on as an active theater, putting on a full schedule of plays during the year.

A TRAGIC END FOR ALL

The Lincolns had originally invited General and Mrs. Grant to Ford's Theatre, but the Grants were unable to attend. At the last minute, the Lincolns asked Clara Harris and Major Rathbone to join them.

Tragedy seemed to follow the people who had shared the presidential box that night. Clara Harris Rathbone was shot by her insane husband in 1883. Rathbone was committed to an insane asylum, where he died in 1911.

Mary Todd Lincoln fared no better. Three of her four sons died during her lifetime, and in 1875 she was judged insane and admitted to a sanitarium for several months. She died in her sister's home in Springfield, Illinois, in 1882.

Frederick Douglass
National Historic Site

Recognizing a defender of equal rights for all

Frederick Douglass, born a slave and never formally educated, was one of the country's most eloquent spokesmen in the struggle against slavery.

He was born Frederick Augustus Washington Bailey around 1817. His mother, a slave, was forced to leave him as an infant, and he never knew his father. At an early age he discovered that education was the key to freedom, and he learned to read and write by trading bread for lessons.

Douglass escaped to freedom when he was 20 and became an active abolitionist. He founded an abolitionist newspaper, helped convince Lincoln to sign the Emancipation Act, and was appointed ambassador to Haiti. A defender of equal rights for all, he also supported women's rights.

When he moved into Cedar Hill, a Victorian mansion overlooking the U.S. Capitol, he was the first black man in the District's Anacostia neighborhood. Part of the National Park System since 1962, Cedar Hill is little changed from when Douglass lived there, and it shows that while Douglass advocated changes in society, he was comfortable being a part of its upper strata.

Much of the furniture in the elegant home is original, and Douglass' belongings indicate his wealth and success: Abraham Lincoln's cane, given by Mrs. Lincoln after the assassination; a leather rocking chair from the people of Haiti; and his greatest treasure, a library of 1,200 books.

In 1877, when Frederick and Anna Douglass moved into this Washington, D.C., home, they were the only blacks in the neighborhood.

Frederick Douglass, a former slave who never went to school, rose to prominence as a newspaper editor, minister to Haiti, and one of the nation's most eloquent spokesmen against slavery.

Frederick Law Olmsted

National Historic Site

A tribute to the father of landscape architecture

Unlike most historic homes, the Frederick Law Olmsted National Historic Site is more a monument to Olmsted's work than his life. Olmsted is the father of American landscape architecture, and his legacy of green spaces, wilderness areas, and urban parks—the most famous of which is New York's Central Park—helps define the way America looks today.

In 1883, Olmsted bought a small farm near downtown Boston. In the old farmhouse, he established his home and office. In 1979, the 36-room house and office complex, sitting on two acres landscaped by Olmsted, became a national historic site.

It is fitting that visitors enter the house through what had been the conservatory or plant room. It opens into the living room, which serves as the site's information center. An excellent film describing the life and work of Olmsted and his role in the park movement is shown in the dining room. Displayed in the north parlor—which was originally Olmsted's office, then that of his stepson, and finally his son—are plans, photographs, and models of some 5,000 landscape projects of the firm. It is a rare look at the body of work produced by a single professional office from 1860 to 1980.

A tour through the grounds, with its varied shrubs, meandering paths, and broad meadows, provides a firsthand glimpse of Olmsted's landscaping principles at work.

Frederick Law Olmsted's estate in Brookline, Massachusetts, is a monument to the father of American landscape architecture and urban planning.

41

Friendship Hill

National Historic Site

The home of a forgotten American patriot

Hidden in Fayette County, Pennsylvania, is one of the best-kept secrets of the National Park System—Friendship Hill National Historic Site, home of Albert Gallatin from 1789 to 1825. Though little-known today, Gallatin, a Swiss immigrant to America, was an influential man who joined Thomas Jefferson, James Madison, and James Monroe in shaping the philosophy of this nation.

In 1783, when he was a young man, Gallatin visited the Revolutionary leader Patrick Henry. After that one visit, Henry declared him "a most astonishing man!" Gallatin advised Presidents on foreign and economic affairs, reduced the national debt, and arranged financing for the Louisiana Purchase and the Lewis and Clark expedition. His influence as a member of the U.S. diplomatic corps helped

Friendship Hill National Historic Site preserves the country estate of a man who helped shape the United States.

Albert Gallatin, a Swiss immigrant to America, served as Secretary of the Treasury for Presidents Jefferson and Madison.

bring about the end of the War of 1812. He also devised a system by which the executive branch held Congress fiscally accountable. Gallatin is best known, however, as Secretary of the Treasury for Presidents Jefferson and Madison.

In 1789, Gallatin began building a plain brick house on what was then the edge of the frontier; it would be his home for forty years. On a bluff overlooking the Monongahela River, Friendship Hill was expanded over the years to accommodate Gallatin's growing family. He also established a general store, gristmill, sawmill, glassworks, and gun factory in the area.

A trip to Friendship Hill National Historic Site, authorized in 1978, offers a rare opportunity to learn more about Gallatin—a man who has been curiously lost in history. A self-guided tour of the house features exhibits and mementos of his career, including a campaign poster from his 1796 bid for Congress, an Annual Report to the House Ways and Means Committee from his tenure as Treasury Secretary, and manuscripts and pamphlets written in his later years.

Ten miles of hiking trails wind through the woods and meadows of Friendship Hill. One of them takes visitors past the memorial grave of Gallatin's first wife, Sophia.

Gallatin built his plain brick house on a bluff overlooking the Monongahela River.

The grave of Gallatin's first wife Sophia lies in a wooded glen not far from the statesman's house.

Gloria Dei Church

National Historic Site

One of our oldest houses of worship

Gloria Dei Episcopal Church, the oldest church in Pennsylvania and among the oldest in the country, still rings with the voices of worship after almost 300 years. Although designated a national historic site in 1942, Old Swedes' Church, as it is also known, is owned and maintained by its congregation.

In 1643, Swedish colonists arriving on the ships *Fogel Grip* and *Kalmar Nyckel* settled along the Delaware River. Hanging from the ceiling of Gloria Dei Church today are models of those two ships.

The first church the Swedish settlers built was a modified log house at Tinicum Island. The baptismal font that was used in the Tinicum church—and in Old Swedes' Church today—came from the old country, as did several decorations, including the golden sprays on the lectern and pulpit and the Cherubim below the organ.

Several years later, the congregation decided to move the church to Wicaco, a Native American name meaning "peaceful place" and what is now known as South Philadelphia.

Between 1698 and 1700, the permanent church was built of Flemish bond and black-header brick. Gloria Dei may have been the first church in America to use an organ, perhaps as early as 1703 (the current organ was bought in 1902). The bronze church bell still calls worshippers to service with the clapper from the old log church.

Gloria Dei Church, built around the turn of the eighteenth century, is the oldest church in Pennsylvania and one of the oldest still operating in the nation.

44

Hampton
National Historic Site

Former plantation recalls two centuries of history

Hampton Hall, one of the country's largest and most ornate Georgian mansions, represents the social and economic history of one family for nearly two centuries. The national historic site includes the Ridgely family home, slave quarters, and 24 other buildings on a 63-acre estate.

Colonel Charles Ridgely bought the original 1,500-acre tract of land, called Northhampton, in 1745. Between 1783 and 1790, his youngest son, Captain Charles Ridgely, built Hampton Hall, the 33-room showpiece of the estate. The mansion was built on a grand scale, from the massive cupola on top to the gargantuan Great Hall at the center of the house.

The mansion was built of locally quarried stone and covered with stucco, an unusual choice for the time. Its design is classic Georgian, in which symmetry is the ideal.

The furniture, paintings, silver, glassware, and decorative objects that fill the house represent the changing tastes and styles of America's wealthy from the 1760s to the late 1880s. The parlor reflects the early period, from 1790 to 1829. The 1830s-style drawing room includes an original set of Baltimore painted furniture, large gilt mirrors, a Chinese gaming table, and a family portrait painted by Rem-

Hampton National Historic Site includes a magnificent Georgian-style mansion, as well as slave quarters, various farm buildings, and landscaped gardens.

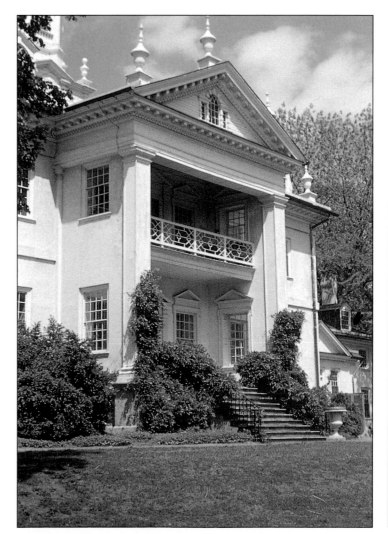

GEORGIAN STYLE

The architectural style known as Georgian combines balance and symmetry with ornate details. Hampton Hall is a classic example of a five-part Georgian home. The main part of the house, called the block, is flanked by two wings. Two enclosed passages, or hyphens, connect the wings to the central structure.

brandt Peale in 1797. The music room is decorated in the later Victorian style, with a Steinway piano made of rosewood and a Rococo Revival set of chairs, love seat, couch, and table.

The grounds of the estate are every bit as elegant as the home. A walking tour leads visitors through the landscaped grounds and formal gardens that evolved during the family's occupancy. Highlights of the tour include a reconstructed orangery from about 1825, an herb garden, natural English parks, and terraced flower gardens called *parterres.* At one time the gardens boasted 4,000 roses. The estate also has more than 200 different kinds of trees, including 200-year-old catalpa trees, a purple European beech, and an imported cedar of Lebanon.

In marked contrast to the mansion and gardens are the slave quarters. Until 1864, slaves did most of the hard labor on the estate; after the slaves were freed, the farm struggled financially.

The Ridgely family kept the house until 1948, when it was acquired by the National Park Service to be preserved for its historical and architectural significance.

Filled with trappings of wealth, the 63-acre site illustrates the life and times of a well-to-do early American family.

Nine of the mansion's 33 rooms have been decorated with period pieces in the styles popular during the two centuries that the Ridgely family lived here.

Home of Franklin D. Roosevelt

National Historic Site

Showcase of a President's remarkable career

Franklin D. Roosevelt was born into the luxurious surroundings of Hyde Park on January 30, 1882. He grew up here in the family home, returned here to raise his own children, and is buried here, with his wife Eleanor, under a simple monument in the rose garden.

Roosevelt was an immensely popular President, and this house is filled with the history of his lengthy political career. The 35-room mansion was just a large farmhouse when FDR's father bought it in 1867, but they slowly turned it into something much grander. The family added wings and a tower, and replaced the clapboard siding with stucco and fieldstone.

Roosevelt used the house as his election headquarters, greeting well-wishers from the terrace on four consecutive election nights. In the first-floor office, he often conducted the business of the presidency. It was here, in 1942, that Roosevelt and British Prime Minis-

FDR was born and lived much of his life in the Hyde Park home known as Springwood. Roosevelt often used the home as his election day headquarters.

47

Home Of Franklin D. Roosevelt National Historic Site

Franklin Delano Roosevelt and his wife Eleanor are buried among their favorite flowers in a rose garden near the house. The white marble monument was cut from the same Vermont quarry from which the marble for the Jefferson Memorial in Washington was taken.

ter Winston Churchill signed the historic agreement that led to the creation of the atomic bomb. The casual living room was the setting for several of his "fireside chats." In the main hall are his boyhood collection of stuffed birds and a bronze sculpture of him in 1911 when he was serving his first term in the New York State Senate.

Upstairs is Roosevelt's bedroom, his favorite room in the house; the Birth Room, with the bed in which he was born; and his Boyhood Bedroom, later used by each of his sons.

The nearby presidential library and museum displays a collection of items that details Roosevelt's long tenure as President, from the Great Depression to World War II and the development of the atomic bomb. The collection includes Roosevelt's model boats and naval prints, more than 15 million pages of historic documents, and his desk from the White House, complete with his favorite pipes and knickknacks.

Among the papers displayed here are his "Day of Infamy" message to Congress declaring war against Japan, as well as a letter from Albert Einstein about the atomic bomb.

Roosevelt had a lifelong interest in nature, and he planted many varieties of trees on the grounds, eventually turning sections into an experimental forestry station. As President, he set up the Civilian Conservation Corps, which was responsible for the development and maintenance of many of the country's public parks and forests.

Springwood is furnished in a comfortable mid- to late-Victorian style, with furniture and memorabilia that belonged to the former President and his family.

OVERCOMING ADVERSITY

In 1921, at the age of 39, Franklin D. Roosevelt was stricken with polio, which left him unable to walk and almost cut short his political career. With the support of Eleanor, FDR labored through years of physical therapy.

Eleanor, shy by nature, worked to keep his political career alive by writing letters, meeting with people, and traveling around the world. She became her husband's eyes and ears in the places he could no longer go.

Roosevelt reclaimed the political spotlight in 1924 with his memorable nominating speech for Al Smith at the Democratic national convention. In 1933, he became the thirty-second President of the United States.

Hopewell Furnace
National Historic Site

An early American ironmaking community

Hopewell Furnace National Historic Site in eastern Pennsylvania is one of the finest examples of a nineteenth-century, rural American ironmaking community. Using restored buildings and costumed interpreters, the site demonstrates the operation of a cold-blast furnace to produce iron goods, including making charcoal, firing the furnace, and casting the molten iron into stove plates.

Mark Bird built Hopewell Furnace in 1771 on the edge of French Creek. The setting provided all he needed to run the furnace: an abundance of iron ore, hardwood forests to turn into charcoal, and limestone to help separate the impurities from the iron ore. From the day Bird opened the furnace until it made its final blast in 1883, Hopewell

The ironmaster's mansion, begun in 1771, was home to the director of the ironmaking enterprise. A successful ironmaster had to be a financier, technician, bill collector, personnel director, and purchasing agent.

produced pig iron, iron cookware and tools, and more than 80,000 iron stoves, its specialty.

During the Revolutionary War, Bird, an American patriot who was active in politics, became a steady supplier of cannon and shot to the Continental Army and Navy. By 1789, Hopewell was the state's second largest producer. Eventually, anthracite coal and later, coke—which produced iron more economically—replaced the cold-blast furnace, and Hopewell was abandoned.

In the 1930s, Civilian Conservation Corps workers began the task of restoring Hopewell Furnace. The Park Service got involved when it was named a national historic site in 1938. Using old records, pho-

Hopewell Furnace, an "iron plantation," has been restored to look as it did in 1820. Founded around 1770, the primitive ironworks produced cannon and shot during the Revolutionary War.

Hopewell Furnace National Historic Site

In the cast house, molten iron was converted into iron bars or into products such as iron stoves, a Hopewell specialty.

■ ■ ■

tographs, artifacts, and interviews with former workers, the Park Service restored the furnace to its mid-1800s appearance. Some structures, such as the ironmaster's mansion and blacksmith shop, were in fairly good condition, but others had to be almost completely rebuilt, including the waterwheel and blast machinery.

Eleven buildings comprise the site, including a charcoal hearth, one of hundreds where workers turned 5,000 to 6,000 cords of wood a year into charcoal; the cooling shed, where smoldering charcoal was dumped before being moved to the charcoal house; the waterwheel, which drove the blast machinery; tenant houses; and a boarding house.

Hopewell Furnace National Historic Site rekindles scenes of early ironmaking in Pennsylvania.

■ ■ ■

John Fitzgerald Kennedy
National Historic Site

The house where JFK spent his early years

John F. Kennedy was a war hero, Pulitzer prize-winner in history, and the nation's youngest—and first Roman Catholic—President.

John F. Kennedy, our nation's thirty-fifth President, was born in a house at 83 Beals Street in the Boston suburb of Brookline. Kennedy's mother, Rose, supervised the restoration and refurnishing of the house, which was made a national historic site in 1967, to its appearance when Jack was born in 1917.

The piano that was a wedding present to Rose Kennedy sits in the living room, where the family often gathered to sing. Much of the dining room furniture is original, and even the napkin rings, forks, and spoons on the children's table are the very ones used by Joseph Jr. and John (the utensils are marked with their initials). Hanging in Rose Kennedy's study are a framed Mother's Day poem from her children, family photographs, and wedding and birth announcements.

Upstairs, the master bedroom is arranged as it was the spring day that John F. Kennedy was born. The bassinet in the nursery held Rose Kennedy's babies, as well as many of her visiting grandchildren.

Within a short walk from the house are other sites associated with John Kennedy: the Naples Road Residence where he lived from ages four to ten; St. Aidan's Catholic Church, where the children were baptized and Joseph Jr. and John were altar boys; and the Dexter School, attended by the Kennedy boys.

Joseph P. Kennedy purchased this home on Beals Street in Brookline, Massachusetts, shortly before his marriage to Rose Fitzgerald in 1914. The couple lived in the home for seven years.

Longfellow
National Historic Site

A loving tribute to a widely read American poet

In the mid-nineteenth century, American literature blossomed in New England, and Brahmin, Transcendentalist, and abolitionist writers in the area helped to create the literary tradition of the nation. One member of this group, Henry Wadsworth Longfellow, was the most widely read American poet in the world during his lifetime.

In 1837, Longfellow's new father-in-law gave the newlyweds a house in Cambridge, now maintained and operated by the Park Service as Longfellow National Historic Site. Before Longfellow lived there, the historic house served as General George Washington's headquarters during the siege of Boston. Longfellow wrote most of his best-known works at this house, using Washington's former of-

The Henry Wadsworth Longfellow House, built in 1759, was George Washington's residence in 1775 and 1776.

The Longfellow home is furnished today as it was in the poet's day, with family furnishings and memorabilia.

■ ■ ■

fice as his study. On the far side of the room is the armchair Longfellow pulled up to the fire to write "Evangeline" in 1847. This was Longfellow's first long narrative poem and remained one of his best-known works. Longfellow lived in the house until he died here in 1882.

The Longfellows also raised their five children in this Georgian mansion and entertained literary friends, such as Nathaniel Hawthorne and Ralph Waldo Emerson. The house is furnished as it was in Longfellow's time and contains many of the writer's personal belongings. A sentimental favorite is the armchair given to Longfellow by Cambridge schoolchildren on his seventy-second birthday. The chair is made from the wood of the "spreading chestnut tree," which Longfellow referred to in his poem, "The Village Blacksmith."

The house also features some reminders of the former occupant. Facing the entrance door is a bust of George Washington, and beside it is the Washington family coat-of-arms, whose stars and stripes are said to have influenced the American flag.

Though not as widely read today, Longfellow was immensely popular in his time. His admirers ranged from President Lincoln and Queen Victoria to all the schoolchildren who grew up reciting "The Song of Hiawatha."

The site includes a beautiful formal garden where outdoor concerts and poetry readings are held.

A MAN OF HIS WORD

"Under the spreading chestnut tree
The village smithy stands;
The smith a mighty man is he
With large and sinewy hands."

—from "The Village Blacksmith"

■ ■ ■

Despite scathing criticism by Edgar Allan Poe, Longfellow was the most popular American poet of the nineteenth century.

■ ■ ■

Martin Van Buren

National Historic Site

The stylish country estate of our eighth President

After his White House years, Martin Van Buren came back to Kinderhook, New York, home to his family for more than 150 years. He retired to Lindenwald, a large red brick house on land that once belonged to his ancestors. In 1976, the National Park Service acquired the house, along with 22 acres of land.

Van Buren was a man accustomed to stylish surroundings, and he bought the Georgian-style mansion in 1839, intending to renovate it. He turned the grounds into a gentleman's farm, complete with 220 acres of cropland, formal flower gardens, and ornamental fishponds.

The former President filled the house with fine furniture, Brussels carpets, and portraits of his friends Thomas Jefferson, Henry Clay, and Andrew Jackson. The downstairs hall was decorated with elaborate wallpaper panels, imported from France, that formed a mural of a hunt. The house changed hands many times, and most of the Van Buren family's belongings were sold, but the wallpaper mural remains, as does some of the furniture.

Van Buren's son, Smith, helped him turn the house into a replica of a grand Italian villa, adding a four-story brick tower, a Victorian-Gothic central gable, and Renaissance-style bay windows to the otherwise simple, square dwelling.

Van Buren enjoyed the pleasures of rural life at Kinderhook until his death in 1862. In the 1850 census, the eighth President of the United States listed his occupation as "farmer."

Martin Van Buren enjoyed a long and successful career, beginning with his apprenticeship with an attorney at age 14 and ending with his election to the presidency.

Lindenwald, Martin Van Buren's retirement home, was a rather plain Georgian-style mansion until Richard Upjohn, whom Van Buren called the "great architectural oracle," added Romanesque and Gothic touches.

Mary McLeod Bethune House

National Historic Site

The home of a former slave who became a presidential adviser

Starting with only her "faith and a dollar-and-a-half," Mary McLeod Bethune, born in 1875 to freed slaves on a cotton and rice plantation, founded, in 1904, a teacher-training school for African-American girls in Daytona Beach, Florida. The school, which she presided over for more than 30 years, became Bethune-Cookman College.

In addition to receiving worldwide recognition as an educator, Bethune was also President Franklin D. Roosevelt's only black female adviser and a close friend of First Lady Eleanor Roosevelt. She worked tirelessly on Capitol Hill to improve the lives of young African Americans during the Great Depression. In 1935, she founded the National Council of Negro Women and became its first president.

The Mary McLeod Bethune Council House National Historic Site, established in 1991, is the headquarters of the National Council of Negro Women and the last home of Bethune. The site consists of two buildings: a fully restored nineteenth-century townhouse and a carriage house. Galleries within the house display photographs, manuscripts, paintings, and artifacts concerning the black women's rights movement.

The Bethune Museum and Archives was organized 14 years ago to centralize the records of Bethune and other black female leaders. The archives and house pay tribute to Bethune and all black women who have made significant contributions to America and the world.

The National Council of Negro Women, which Mary McLeod Bethune founded in 1935, dedicated this statue to the famous educator in July of 1974.

Pennsylvania Avenue
National Historic Site

The street that links the Capitol to the White House

Every step of Pennsylvania Avenue, which links the White House to the Capitol, is steeped in history. For Pierre L'Enfant, who designed Washington, D.C., in 1791, the broad boulevard was a symbol for the separate yet interrelated roles of the nation's executive and legislative branches.

Throughout the years, buildings sprang up between the two seats of democracy, and the area generally deteriorated. In 1965, the Pennsylvania Avenue National Historic Site was formed to revitalize this stretch of avenue, known as "America's Main Street." It is now a place for people to stroll, shop, dine, and follow history.

The Commerce Building on 14th Street has information for tourists. Also at this site is the National Aquarium, featuring a dazzling display of freshwater and saltwater fish.

Across Pershing Park, which honors General John J. Pershing, commander of U.S. forces in World War I, is the historic Willard Hotel, restored to its original elegance. Down the avenue, at 12th Street, is the Old Post Office. This large, turn-of-the-century building now contains some 80 shops and vendors, along with a food gallery, performing arts stage, miniature golf course, and observation tower.

Lining the avenue from the Old Post Office to the Capitol are the buildings that keep our government functioning, including the I.R.S., the F.B.I., and the National Archives.

Major Pierre L'Enfant, designer of Washington, D.C., envisioned a broad avenue linking the Capitol and the White House. His plan was foiled when President Jackson allowed the Treasury Building to be erected between them.

The United States Capitol was begun in 1793. Before that, the nation's capital had shuttled among many Eastern cities, including Philadelphia, Baltimore, Annapolis, New York, and Trenton.

Sagamore Hill
National Historic Site

Theodore Roosevelt's "Summer White House"

*N*o President has ever enjoyed himself as much as I have enjoyed myself....," Theodore Roosevelt once said, and everything about Sagamore Hill reflects his enthusiasm for life.

Theodore Roosevelt spent summers at Sagamore Hill on Long Island—the "Summer White House"—with his wife and six children. While there, Roosevelt had time to run the country's affairs as well as hike, swim, climb, and lead funerals for family pets with his children. The pet cemetery is on the estate's grounds.

Roosevelt helped design the three-story, 23-room Victorian mansion, and it has been restored to the period of his presidency (1901 to 1909). The first two floors are furnished mainly with original artifacts, including Roosevelt's often large and exotic furniture, elephant tusks and stuffed buffalo heads, and the President's Rough Rider hat, sword, and binoculars.

All the furniture in the nursery—and most of the toys—belonged to the Roosevelt family. The teddy bear that sits in a small chair was a gift from the man whose father made the first teddy bear and asked to name it after Mr. Roosevelt.

The home also contains memorabilia of Roosevelt's varied careers and hobbies. In addition to being President, Roosevelt was a Spanish-American War hero, police commissioner, cowboy, assistant secretary of the Navy, New York governor, Vice President, hunter, conservationist, author, and, in 1905, a Nobel Peace Prize winner.

Sagamore National Historic Site, established in 1962, also includes the Old Orchard Museum. Originally the home of General Theodore Roosevelt, Jr., it now contains exhibits and a film relating to Theodore Roosevelt's life and career.

Known as "that damned cowboy" to Conservative Republicans, Roosevelt was an energetic man with a big appetite for life.

At Sagamore Hill, Theodore Roosevelt's Long Island estate, the twenty-sixth President held news conferences, met with foreign dignitaries, negotiated the end of the Russo-Japanese war, and planned the construction of the Panama Canal.

Saint-Gaudens
National Historic Site

The home of America's most noted sculptor

The home, studio, and gardens of America's most noted sculptor are preserved at the Saint-Gaudens National Historic Site in Cornish, New Hampshire. The 150-acre site, dotted with casts of some of his sculptures, offers a crash-course in the career of an important artist, as well as a glimpse into the life of a wealthy, artistic couple of the late nineteenth century.

Augustus Saint-Gaudens came to the rolling hills and dark pines of the upper Connecticut River Valley in the summer of 1885. He was already well-known for the Farragut Monument in New York's Madison Square Park, private commissions in the interiors of the Vanderbilt and Villard houses in New York, and Trinity Church in Boston.

In the summer of 1885, American sculptor Augustus Saint-Gaudens bought an old wayside inn in the upper Connecticut River valley of New Hampshire and turned it into a home, studio, and informal center for the arts.

Saint-Gaudens National Historic Site

Saint-Gaudens won the grand prize at the 1900 Paris Exposition with Amor Caritas *and other beautiful works. A gilded bronze cast of the statue, now owned by the Louvre, decorates the artist's retreat.*

He bought the old Wayside Inn in Cornish and transformed the rural home into a replica of an Italian villa; the outbuildings were turned into studios.

Other artists soon joined Saint-Gaudens and his wife at their rural retreat, including painter Maxfield Parrish, poet Percy MacKaye, and actress Ethel Barrymore. Saint-Gaudens' home became the center of a lively group of painters, writers, and musicians known as the Cornish Art Colony.

The pastoral setting of Cornish inspired some of Saint-Gaudens' most familiar works, including "The Standing Lincoln" in Chicago and "Diana," which once graced the tower of Stanford White's Madison Square Garden (but is now in the Philadelphia Museum of Art). While in Cornish, Saint-Gaudens also sculpted the haunting memorial to historian Henry Adams's wife in Washington, D.C.'s Rock Creek Cemetery and the equestrian statue of William Tecumseh Sherman, which stands near New York's Central Park. This work won the Grand Prix in the Paris Salon of 1900.

Seven years later, Saint-Gaudens died. His son and wife, Augusta Homer, and later a board of trustees, maintained the property for tourists until the National Park Service acquired it in 1965.

Saint-Gaudens transformed the inn's grounds into a work of art, with terraced flower beds, tall hedges, and beautiful statues.

Saint-Gaudens' vine-covered studio is the only one of his workshops to survive to this day.

■ ■ ■

The interior of the house, decorated with American, English, Arabic, Flemish, and Japanese furnishings and objects, reflects Augusta Homer's eclectic tastes. Works by Augusta and members of the Cornish Art Colony can be found throughout the house.

Fire eventually destroyed two of the studios, but the Little Studio, as Saint-Gaudens called it, remains. An exhibition gallery displays originals, casts, and replicas of the sculptor's works. The artistic skills of Saint-Gaudens can also be found in the colorful gardens, reflecting pool, and evergreen hedges of the grounds.

MASTERPIECE IN BRONZE

Saint-Gaudens' masterpiece is a Civil War monument that stands on Boston Common. In 1884, he was asked to create a memorial to Robert Gould Shaw and the 54th Massachusetts Volunteer Infantry, the first African-American regiment to fight during the Civil War. The regiment became famous for leading an assault on Fort Wagner as part of the plan to capture the Confederate city of Charleston, South Carolina. In the battle, Shaw and many members of his regiment were killed.

The memorial was made possible by a fund established by Joshua B. Smith, a fugitive slave from North Carolina who became a state representative from Cambridge. It took Saint-Gaudens 13 years to complete the high-relief bronze statue, which was dedicated on May 31, 1897.

■ ■ ■

Saint Paul's Church
National Historic Site

The only surviving colonial church in New York

Saint Paul's Church National Historic Site has a two-fold claim to historic fame. Not only is it the only surviving colonial church in New York City, but the site on which it stands is associated with the fight for freedom of the press.

In 1773, John Peter Zenger began the *New York Weekly Journal* and published an account of a controversial election that was held in front of the church, outlining the misdeeds of certain officials. He continued to publish satirical articles about corrupt officials and was eventually tried for libel in 1735.

Zenger's lawyer, Andrew Hamilton, argued that Zenger could not be found guilty of libel because he had published the truth. The jury agreed and found him innocent, and this ruling was the basis for the First Amendment, adopted in 1791 to guarantee freedom of the press. The Bill of Rights Museum, in the former parish hall, has exhibits on the Zenger trial, the First Amendment, and church history.

St. Paul's, completed in 1787, is an outstanding example of Georgian architecture. It is home to the twin of the famous Liberty Bell, and it houses one of the oldest working church organs built in this country.

Of additional interest, the church contains an altarpiece by architect Pierre L'Enfant, who designed Washington, D.C., and the pew that George Washington sat in when he attended services here after his inauguration as President in 1789.

New meets old in New York City where the spires of St. Paul's Church, established in the seventeenth century, rise between the modern twin towers of the World Trade Center.

Buried in the picturesque cemetery at St. Paul's Church are soldiers from the French and Indian War, the American Revolution, the Civil War, and both World Wars.

Salem Maritime

National Historic Site

Recalling the glory days of a thriving port town

Three wharves, the Custom House, and several historic residences and stores are the only remnants of Salem's glory days as a prosperous eighteenth-century maritime center on Massachusetts Bay.

The Salem Maritime National Historic Site, designated in 1938 to recognize Salem's contribution to the fledgling U.S. economy, recalls the time when Salem was a lively port with 50 wharves. When a ship returned from a trip to the Far East, Salem's streets filled with sailors, businessmen, tradesmen, and fancy women, breathing in the heady smells of cinnamon, pepper, cloves, coffee, and tea.

The nation's third-oldest settlement, Salem began as a fishing village in the 1630s. Shipowners soon realized that shipping goods was much more profitable than catching fish, and by 1643, Salem ships were carrying English cod and lumber to the West Indies and returning with molasses, rum, and exotic goods. Among the most profitable goods unloaded at Salem's wharves were spices, tea, sugar, ivory, and coffee. Luxuries such as fans, ivory carvings, cotton fabrics from India, and Chinese silks were found in many Salem homes.

Salem's shipping industry was so successful that it was known as the "Venice of the New World," and some foreign traders thought the city was a sovereign nation. During the Revolutionary War, Salem privateers harassed British ports and pirated weapons and supplies for the

Globe-circling sea captains docked at Derby Wharf, then reported to the Custom House at Salem to receive permits and pay customs taxes. The 1819 building had a clear view of ships arriving in Salem Harbor.

The West India Goods Store, built around 1800, stocked sugar, molasses, and tropical fruits from the Caribbean Islands, as well as locally produced dried cod, nails, and fishhooks.

■ ■ ■

Continental Army. Salem was one of the few important ports never to fall into British hands.

Salem's boom years ended when Jefferson imposed an embargo on shipping to and from England and France in 1807. Salem never recovered from the loss of business and was unable to compete as many new ports entered the market. The last square-rigger left Derby Wharf in the early 1890s.

That historic wharf still extends into Salem Harbor, with an 1871 lighthouse at its tip. At one time, 14 warehouses lined the wharf. Several Salem warehouses survive, including the Bonded Warehouse, where visitors can see original barrels of rum and chests of tea, and the Central Wharf Warehouse, which is now the visitor center.

Government workers, including American writer Nathaniel Hawthorne, collected taxes and issued permits at the two-story brick Custom House, built in 1819. The 1829 Scale House contains antique devices used for weighing and measuring goods from ships.

Three historic houses are open for tours, including Hawkes House, used as a warehouse for goods captured by privateers during the Revolutionary War; Narbonne-Hale House, built in the seventeenth century as a home and shop for craftsmen and tradesmen; and Derby House, built for wealthy merchant Elias Hasket Derby in 1762. Visitors can shop for teas, spices, Chinese porcelain, Indian fabrics, and other goods representative of 1830s trade at the restored West India Goods Store.

AMERICA'S FIRST MILLIONAIRE

Elias Hasket Derby, born in 1739, was Salem's most prominent merchant and perhaps America's first millionaire.

His ship, *Grand Turk,* was the first Salem ship to sail beyond the Cape of Good Hope, opening up the East to China. As new trade markets were opened, American farmers, fishermen, and tradesmen produced more goods to keep up with world demand, and former luxuries such as tea, coffee, and pepper became common American household goods.

Merchants like Derby touched the lives of all Americans by bringing the goods of the world back home.

■ ■ ■

Saugus Iron Works

National Historic Site

Celebrating the rise of American industry

As the Massachusetts Bay Colony grew in the seventeenth century, colonists needed iron to build ships and houses. At first the iron came from England, but it was expensive and slow in coming. By the 1640s, America's first successful ironworks on the Saugus River was pouring "pigs" (pig iron) and forging wrought iron.

At its peak in 1648, the ironworks employed approximately 185 ironworkers, miners, woodcutters, and boatmen, housing them in the company town of Hammersmith. In the 1950s, the American Iron and Steel Institute reconstructed several of the buildings at Hammersmith, and in 1969 it was designated the Saugus Iron Works National Historic Site.

After three decades of neglect, only the ironmaster's house remained at Saugus. Since then, several buildings have been reconstructed, including the forge, slitting mill, and ironhouse.

Saugus was America's first successful ironworks. Before it was built, colonists had to rely on England for all of their iron goods.

Saugus Iron Works National Historic Site

By touring the collection of rustic buildings, visitors can learn how iron was made and forged. Charcoal from nearby trees, iron ore from the marshy Saugus River, and flux from the Nahant peninsula were dumped into the top of the furnace and heated. The flux helped separate the impurities, which were skimmed off the top, and the pure molten iron ran into a sand furrow where it hardened into a long bar, or "sow." Some of the liquid iron was ladled into molds to make pots, kettles, and replacement parts for the ironworks.

The forge—where waterwheels still turn and hammers ring as they hit anvils—was the busiest of the ironworks buildings. Here,

In the seventeenth century, Saugus rang with the sound of this 500-pound hammer as it forged wrought iron.

workers hammered and pounded the ingots into refined merchant bars that could be made into tools and building materials. Some of the merchant bars were taken to the slitting mill, where they were heated in an oven and made into flats or rods. The rods could then be made into nails, and many of them were used in the construction of the community of Hammersmith.

The finest home in Hammersmith was the Iron Works House. Built around 1646, it was the social and business center of the community. The site also has a nature trail through the surrounding marsh and woodland.

At Saugus, skilled craftsmen still work white-hot iron into bars, pots, kettles, and other marketable items.

Sewall-Belmont House

National Historic Site

A shrine to the women's movement

In an old brick house on Capitol Hill hangs a faded yellow and purple banner that proclaims: "We demand an amendment to the United States Constitution enfranchising women." With this banner, women marched for equal rights under the leadership of a young woman named Alice Paul.

The Sewall-Belmont House National Historic Site is a monument to Paul, who founded the National Woman's Party in 1913. She and other suffragettes chained themselves to the White House fence and staged hunger strikes to attract national attention. Paul's determination led to ratification of the 19th Amendment to the Constitution in 1920, assuring women the right to vote. In 1923, Paul drafted the Equal Rights Amendment to end legal and economic discrimination against women. More than 70 years later, it has yet to be adopted.

Robert Sewall built the house in 1799 and later rented it to Albert Gallatin, secretary of the treasury from 1801 to 1813 for Presidents Madison and Jefferson. Gallatin probably drafted the Louisiana Purchase here.

In 1929, the National Woman's Party bought the house and named it the Alva Belmont House in honor of a party benefactress. The house contains memorabilia of the suffrage movement and a collection of portraits and marble busts of female leaders, including a life-size statue of Joan of Arc.

The Sewall-Belmont House is a memorial to Alice Paul, a leader in the women's suffrage movement and founder of the National Women's Party.

Springfield Armory
National Historic Site

An incredible collection of firearms and ammunition

Springfield Armory National Historic Site preserves a facility significant to both the production of military small arms and the adoption of the U.S. Constitution.

In 1777, General George Washington chose the small village of Springfield as the site of the first United States arsenal to keep weapons and ammunition safe from the British. Over the next 190 years, the armory grew into one of the most important facilities for the production of military small arms in the world.

In 1787, a farmer named Daniel Shays led a group of 1,100 men in an attempt to seize arms at Springfield. They intended to use the weapons to force the closure of state and county courts that were taking their land for debt repayment; Shays had lost his land over a $12 debt. The local militia put down the rebellion, but many wealthy citizens feared for their lives and property. As a result, the Federal Constitution was drafted, creating a stronger central government.

The site encompasses several buildings and the original armory complex on some 55 acres. The Main Arsenal, which houses the Springfield Museum, displays the world's largest collection of military small arms. Among the 10,000 guns are long-barreled muskets of 1795, the M-1 rifle used in World War II, and a collection of firearms donated by Presidents Kennedy, Eisenhower, Roosevelt, and Wilson.

The eighteenth-century Springfield Armory designed and built weapons for American soldiers in wars ranging from the American Revolution to the Vietnam conflict.

73

Steamtown

National Historic Site

Preserving the era of the steam locomotive

Steamtown National Historic Site in Pennsylvania is a working railroad that recalls the era of the steam locomotive, which helped spur America's westward settlement.

Not long after Lewis and Clark crossed the continent by foot, railroads duplicated the effort with tracks. In the mid-1800s, settlers pushed westward as railroads opened up new areas. Railroad companies often distributed maps printed in foreign languages to new immigrants to encourage them to settle along their rail lines.

Between the Civil War and World War I, steam locomotives helped transform the United States from an agricultural to an industrial nation. They brought raw materials to factories and carried away the finished products to supply the growing nation. Trains were the primary mode of transportation for products and people during this time.

After World War I, however, trains faced increased competition from cars and trucks. By the 1950s, railroads, which by then had replaced coal-burning steam engines with cleaner diesel engines, were closing rail lines due to lack of freight and passengers.

Steamtown, which was officially added to the Park System in 1986, occupies about 40 acres of the former Scranton Yards, housing the largest collection of steam-era locomotives and freight and passenger cars in the country. The oldest locomotive in the collection is a 1903 freight engine. Visitors to the site can take a ride through history in a steam-engine train.

Steamtown National Historic Site re-creates the story of railroading in early twentieth century America with historic buildings, steam locomotives, and passenger cars.

Theodore Roosevelt Birthplace

National Historic Site

Where our twenty-sixth President grew up

Theodore Roosevelt, who was nicknamed "Teedie" by his family, was born in 1858 in a typical New York brownstone in Manhattan's most fashionable residential district.

A frail child who suffered from asthma, Roosevelt learned to read at an early age, despite being unable to attend school regularly. He loved books on nature and history, and he dreamed of having an adventuresome life outdoors. He learned taxidermy, starting what he called the "Roosevelt Museum of Natural History" in the house.

Teedie's father built him a gymnasium on the back piazza of the house, and there he exercised his way to strength and health. He became a robust man who lived a very active life as a Rough Rider during the Spanish-American War, a cowboy in North Dakota, a big-game hunter on three continents, and finally the President of the United States.

Roosevelt's birthplace was demolished in 1916 to make way for a commercial building. After his death in 1919, a historical association purchased the site and built an exact replica of the house, furnishing it with original and period pieces. Included is Victorian horsehair furniture, as well as the special chair Roosevelt used as a child because he was allergic to horsehair.

Visitors can tour the rooms of the home, including the parlor, which Roosevelt once described as "a room of much splendor," and the library, a room to which he attributed a "gloomy respectability."

The house where Theodore Roosevelt was born was demolished in 1916. After Roosevelt's death in 1919, a historical association purchased the site and built this replica.

Theodore Roosevelt Inaugural

National Historic Site

When duty called, the Rough Rider was ready

On September 14, 1901, in the library of the Wilcox home, Theodore Roosevelt became the twenty-sixth President of the United States.

On September 6, 1901, President William McKinley was shot twice during a reception at the Pan-American Exposition in Buffalo, New York. Doctors removed one of the bullets, but failed to find the second, and McKinley died from an infection eight days later.

Vice President Theodore Roosevelt, assured by doctors that McKinley would live, was hiking in the Adirondacks on September 13 when he was suddenly summoned to Buffalo. The next day, in the library of the home of his friend Ansley Wilcox, Roosevelt took the oath of office to become the twenty-sixth President. He stood in front of the bay window on the south side of the room, wearing a frock-coat lent him by Wilcox. The coat is now on display at the house, which was designated the Theodore Roosevelt Inaugural National Historic Site in 1966.

The entire surprise ceremony was over within half an hour, but Roosevelt appeared ready for the job: "Here is the task, and I have got to do it to the best of my ability; and that is all there is to it."

Roosevelt, who was re-elected in 1904, passed more reform bills during his tenure than any other administration since the Civil War. He helped secure the construction of the Panama Canal and the peace treaty ending the Russo-Japanese War, for which he won the Nobel Peace Prize.

Theodore Roosevelt, on vacation and unprepared for the death of President McKinley eight days after an assassination attempt, had to borrow the coat of his friend Ansley Wilcox for the impromptu inauguration ceremony.

ore Roosevelt Inaugural ational Historic Site United States Department of the Interior National Park Service

Thomas Stone

National Historic Site

The former estate of a prominent politician

Habre-de-Venture, a 1771 Georgian mansion near Port Tobacco, Maryland, was the home of Thomas Stone, a member of the Continental Congress and a signer of the Declaration of Independence.

Stone was a young lawyer and prominent member of Maryland society when the political unrest between America and Great Britain began in the early 1770s. He soon became active in politics and was eventually elected to serve in the Provincial Conventions that governed Maryland.

In 1775, Stone became a Maryland representative in the Second Continental Congress, which was meeting in Philadelphia. His legal knowledge and writing skills made him a valuable member of the Congressional committee that completed the first draft of the Articles of Confederation in 1776. Though he is a little-known political figure in history today, Stone was important to the development of Maryland and the United States.

Stone's Habre-de-Venture plantation was made a national historic site in 1978, one year after fire swept through the main block of the house. The National Park Service is currently

Fire destroyed the main section of the Georgian-style plantation home, located in southern Maryland, in 1977. The Park Service intends to reconstruct the building.

in the process of restoring the house to its late-nineteenth-century appearance.

Habre-de-Venture was a five-part colonial plantation house; two hyphens connected the central block of the house to its east and west wings. The wings of most five-part houses extend in a straight line; Habre-de-Venture's formed a graceful arc.

77

Touro Synagogue

National Historic Site

A testament to religious freedom in America

The first Jewish synagogue in America stands as a testament to the religious freedom of the colony that became the state of Rhode Island.

The founder of the colony, Roger Williams, who was banned from Puritan Massachusetts, helped shape a new government that had no power over spiritual matters. The news of this new colony spread, and by about 1658, Rhode Island's first Jewish community was founded by a group of Sephardic Jews who came here from Spain and Portugal.

At first, they held services in private homes and rented buildings. In 1677, they bought a cemetery plot, but it wasn't until the next century that they had finally raised enough money to build a permanent synagogue.

Peter Harrison, who designed King's Chapel in Boston and Christ Church in Cambridge, volunteered to design the synagogue. Ground was broken in 1759, and the church was finally finished four years later. The Rev. Isaac Touro, spiritual leader of the Newport Jewish community, dedicated the synagogue.

Often called Harrison's masterpiece, the synagogue has the classic lines of Georgian architecture. Inside, the building is ornate and airy. Twelve Ionic columns, representing the 12 tribes of ancient Israel, support a gallery. Above these, 12 Corinthian columns rise to the domed ceiling, from which hang five massive brass candelabra. Throughout the historic site, established in 1946, are many sacred religious objects, including the Holy Ark, which contains a 500-year-old scroll.

The ornate interior of Touro Synagogue contrasts with its plain brick exterior. In the Orthodox tradition, women sit in the gallery and men sit below.

Vanderbilt Mansion

National Historic Site

An Old World palace on the banks of the Hudson River

*V*anderbilt Mansion is not just a historic house—it's a monument to an amazing era of American history.

In the period between the Civil War and World War II, American financiers and industrialists made personal fortunes as the United States became a leading industrial nation. The new millionaires built elegant homes reminiscent of Old World estates on the banks of the Hudson River. The grandest of all was the baroque palace built by Frederick Vanderbilt.

Fredcrick was the grandson of industrialist Cornelius Vanderbilt and the son of William Henry Vanderbilt, the richest men in America in their times. Frederick Vanderbilt and his wife Louise bought Hyde Park, as the property was known, in 1895, attracted to the area for its scenic charm and nearness to New York City. When the Vanderbilts discovered that their new home was structurally unsound,

The new American millionaires of the late nineteenth century built grand European-style estates and lived as though they were the heirs to centuries of wealth.

SHARING THE FAMILY FORTUNE

Though the Vanderbilts spent lavishly on several grand homes, a private railroad car, yachts, automobiles, and entertaining, they also gave generously to their favorite causes. The Vanderbilt fortune helped support opera houses, art galleries, museums, hospitals, libraries, and educational institutions.

Cornelius Vanderbilt gave a million-dollar gift in 1873 to the Tennessee university that now bears his name, and Frederick, in turn, gave to his alma mater, Yale University. Louise Vanderbilt established a reading room at St. James Chapel in Hyde Park and provided for the higher education of qualified young women. Outside Hyde Park, she supported, among other institutions, St. Anthony's Home for Working Girls.

■ ■ ■

they had it demolished and built a new house on the site.

Vanderbilt hired the best architects, craftsmen, and artists to build the 50-room home, which includes marble columns in the drawing room, antique twisted columns in Frederick's bedroom, and a carved wooden ceiling in the dining room. An 1897 ceiling fresco by Edward E. Simmons was discovered under a layer of paint when the ceiling was cleaned in the Gold Room. The cost of the new house was $660,000.

The house was surrounded by 600 acres of farm, gardens, woods, and lawns designed to look like an English park. The immense estate was originally cared for by more than 60 full-time employees, 13 of which tended the gardens and lawns alone.

Like most Hudson River families, the Vanderbilts only used this home for a few weeks in the spring and fall and an occasional winter weekend. While there, Louise loved to entertain. Visitors arrived by boat or train (the estate had its own dock and station) or by private car. During the day, guests toured the estate or played golf and tennis. After a formal dinner, the party played bridge or danced in the drawing room.

The mansion has many lavish guest rooms, all decorated in eighteenth-century French style. Each room has its own color scheme. In the morning, guests could have breakfast in their rooms, served on special breakfast sets that matched the decor.

After Louise died, Frederick lived the rest of his life here among his beloved trees and gardens. Louise's niece inherited the estate and, in 1938, donated it to the public. It was designated a National Historic Site in 1940.

Frederick Vanderbilt loved the outdoors and was proud of winning prizes for his flowers at the Dutchess County Fair. He always gave the prize money to the 13 gardeners who tended the estate's lawns and gardens.

■ ■ ■

The Vanderbilt's Hudson Valley home was one of several owned by the family. They spent summers at Newport, Rhode Island, and the winter social season at their New York City townhouse.

■ ■ ■

Weir Farm
National Historic Site

Birthplace of the American Impressionism Movement

Weir Farm National Historic Site pays tribute not to a single artist, but to an entire style that developed there. Near the turn of the century, Julian Alden Weir invited fellow artists to his farm near Branchville, Connecticut. The rocky, uneven land of the New England countryside, a bane to farmers, proved to be an inspiration to artists.

The artists who visited the farm, including Albert Pinkham Ryder, John Twachtman, and Childe Hassam, were struggling to find their artistic identity under the growing influence of the French Impressionists. When Weir first saw the works of Monet and Renoir in 1876, while he was studying at the Ecole des Beaux-Arts in Paris, he described the exhibition as "worse than the Chamber of Horrors." Fifteen years later, however, the artists at Weir Farm had devised their own version of French Impressionist techniques, and the American Impressionist Movement was born.

Unlike the earlier Hudson River painters who found their creative drive in spectacular examples of nature, the American Impression-

The Weir Farm National Historic Site contains picturesque barn-red clapboard buildings and the home and studio of the central figure in the American Impressionist Movement.

Weir purchased the Branchville, Connecticut, farm in 1882 and built his painting studio there. For nearly four decades he lived and worked in the New England countryside.

■ ■ ■

Weir's tools and supplies still clutter his studio on the farm, as if the artist might return to work at any moment.

■ ■ ■

ists preferred more intimate views, such as the play of light on a stretch of land or a simple meadow. The peaceful, pastoral settings in Weir's paintings, such as "The Laundry," "Building a Dam," and "The Border of the Farm," still influence the way many Americans think of the New England landscape.

The friendship between the American Impressionists, nurtured at Weir Farm, was important to the development of the movement. Many of the artists came up on the weekends from New York, and they painted each other's families, as well as the barns, ponds, houses, and gardens of the farm.

A great deal of the original Weir Farm remains, including the studios, barns, and houses. In addition, the site, authorized in 1990, includes 60 of the 62 acres of Weir Farm, helping to preserve the open space that inspired a movement of American art.

PRESERVING AN ARTISTIC TRADITION

J. Alden Weir's artistic legend has carried on at Weir Farm through the work of living artists.

In 1931, Weir's daughter Dorothy married the sculptor Mahonri Young, a grandson of Brigham Young. Already recognized for his small studies in bronze of the common working man, Young came to live at the farm and continued his work. He built a studio there to accommodate his monumental public work. Dorothy Weir Young, who trained at her father's side, was also an accomplished artist in both oils and watercolor.

Since Mahonri Young's death in 1957, the cultivation of art continues at Weir Farm with the work of Sperry and Doris Andrews and visiting artists.

■ ■ ■

Washington, D.C.

A Capital Worthy of a Great Nation

Washington, D.C., is one of the few cities in the world planned and built specifically to serve as a seat of government. The man George Washington selected to lay out the city that was to bear his name was Pierre-Charles L'Enfant, a French-born engineer and architect who had served in the American Revolutionary Army.

L'Enfant envisioned a capital he termed "magnificent enough to grace a great nation." He drew a plan with broad, tree-lined avenues radiating from the Capitol Building and the "President's Palace," with generous amounts of open spaces to provide dramatic vistas. The result is a picture-postcard setting of massive marble government buildings, gleaming white monuments, and beautiful parks adorned by flowers and splashing fountains.

The illuminated dome of the Capitol appears behind the Washington Monument, the tallest structure in Washington, D.C.

The White House, begun in 1792, was originally called the President's House and later became known as the Executive Mansion.

Thomas Jefferson Memorial

National Memorial

A shrine to one of our most-admired statesmen

During cherry blossom season each spring, the Thomas Jefferson Memorial upstages almost everything else in the nation's capital. The 19-foot-tall bronze statue of our third President seems to be holding court over the cotton-candy fairyland known as the Tidal Basin.

The memorial, which was not completed until 1943, raised a few concerns among city planners. If Pierre-Charles L'Enfant's initial plan for the layout of the city was to be maintained, there was no place for a Jefferson monument. The memorial was therefore built on land reclaimed from the Potomac River; in retrospect, of course, the site selected is perfect.

Designer John Russell Pope, who died before the memorial was completed, decided to personalize it by incorporating Jefferson's own architectural designs for the rotunda and columns. His elegant design of the open-air circular rotunda with its low, graceful dome and classical-style columns is a worthy tribute to the man whose accomplishments far exceeded simply being President of the United States.

Jefferson was the author of the Declaration of Independence and, among other things, a statesman, architect, inventor, and botanist. At a White House dinner for Nobel Prize winners in 1962, President John F. Kennedy remarked to his guests: "I think this is the most extraordinary collection of talent, of human knowledge, that has ever been gathered together at the White House—with the possible exception of when Thomas Jefferson dined alone."

Rudolph Evans sculpted the memorial's 19-foot-tall bronze statue of the famous American statesman.

The colonnaded Thomas Jefferson Memorial is a grand tribute to the third President of the United States.

The memorial centers on the imposing figure of Jefferson, decked out in fur-collared greatcoat, addressing the Continental Congress. The five-ton statue, sculpted by Rudolph Evans, stands atop a six-foot-high black granite pedestal.

Inscriptions engraved on the interior walls of the memorial further document the scope and brilliance of Jefferson's thinking: From the Declaration of Independence, "These colonies are, and of right ought to be, free and independent states"; from a 1789 letter to James Madison, "I know of but one code of morality for men whether acting singly or collectively"; from his writings on slavery, "Nothing is more certainly written in the book of fate than that these people are to be free"; and from his own personal credo, "I have sworn upon the altar of God eternal hostility against every form of tyranny over the mind of man."

Evening is an ideal time to call on Mr. Jefferson. Visitors will avoid the traffic and the crowds, and the relative solitude promises a more personal connection with the grandeur of the monument and the man it represents.

Kennedy Center for the Performing Arts

National Memorial

The largest cultural facility of its kind

The Kennedy Center for the Performing Arts is the largest cultural facility of its kind; it is also designed to serve as a memorial to President John F. Kennedy. More than 8,000 visitors pass through the complex daily.

Even if one never sees a single performance here, a tour through the building, designed by Edward Durell Stone, is sure to be one of the highlights of any sightseeing itinerary. The courtly rectangular structure, massive in size and surrounded on all sides by a broad colonnade of slender pillars, is covered with Carrara marble from Italy. Many of the materials, decorations, and furnishings throughout the building are donations from more than 40 countries.

Inside, two vast red-carpeted halls—the Hall of States and the Hall of Nations—connect with an even vaster grand foyer. An opening onto the River Terrace provides a resplendent view of the Potomac River.

The Grand Foyer is one of the largest rooms in the world, 75 feet longer than the Washington Monument is high. Occupying center stage is the memorial bust of President John F. Kennedy. The rough-hewn bronze sculpture, created by American sculptor Robert Berks,

Built along the Potomac River, the Kennedy Center for the Performing Arts includes an opera house, a concert hall, theaters, and restaurants.

Some of the city's most prestigious cultural events are held in the Kennedy Center's three-tiered, 2,300-seat Opera House.

is seven feet high, weighs 3,000 pounds, and sits atop a travertine marble pedestal.

The Kennedy Center has five theaters, varying in size, orientation, and audience appeal, as well as the American Film Institute theater. All have been designed to offer exceptionally fine acoustics, sight lines, and technical capacities.

Eisenhower Theater. President Dwight David Eisenhower was the first to initiate plans to develop a national center for the performing arts. The 1,200-seat theater named for him hosts major touring productions, often before they open on Broadway.

The likeness of Eisenhower in the lobby, a bronze bust by Felix de Weldon, was presented by the Texas State Society to commemorate the first native Texan to become President of the United States.

The Terrace Theater. The smallest and most intimate of the major Kennedy Center performing-arts outlets is located on the Roof Terrace level. The 500-seat Terrace Theater is the place to come to hear the finest in chamber music and choral recitals, or opera, dance, and theatrical productions on a smaller scale. It's also the stage for Imagina-

The Grand Foyer, one of the largest rooms in the world, is lighted with 18 Orrefors crystal chandeliers donated by the government of Sweden.

tion Celebration, the center's national youth art festival, and the annual American College Theater Festival, featuring productions of the six finalists in the competition.

Opera House. Designed on a grand scale for grand opera, this three-tiered, 2,300-seat theater showplace plays host to such diverse groups as the Dance Theater of Harlem, the Stuttgart Ballet, and the Grand Kabuki of Japan, as well as the Washington Opera. Many top-notch musical productions are staged here as well. The Opera House is also the setting each year for the nationally televised Kennedy Center Honors Gala, which recognizes the contributions of outstanding performance artists to America's cultural life.

The Concert Hall. This 2,750-seat theater, the largest of the Kennedy Center halls, is home to the National Symphony Orchestra. It is also the setting for appearances by visiting orchestras, the annual Holiday Festival, the Messiah sing-along, and the summer pops series. Acoustics throughout are unsurpassed.

The Theater Lab. Located near the Terrace Theater on the rooftop level, the 250-seat experimental performance center is the smallest of the Kennedy Center entertainment areas. During the day, the Theater Lab presents a full complement of children's shows, improvisational theater, teachers' workshops and other intimate productions and exhibits. At night, the lab turns into a cabaret.

The American Film Institute (AFI). Located in the Hall of States, the Institute, which seats 225, is a grand repository of every kind of film imaginable.

Usually two films are shown daily—one a fairly recent release, one a classic. The AFI also sponsors audience-participation discussions with major directors, film stars, and screenwriters.

The Grand Foyer contains a bronze bust of President John F. Kennedy by sculptor Robert Berks. The artwork is seven feet high and weighs 3,000 pounds.

Lyndon Baines Johnson

Memorial Grove on the Potomac

A living memorial to a master of compromise

The Lyndon Baines Johnson Memorial Grove of 500 white pines forms a living memorial to the thirty-sixth President. Inscriptions carved in pink granite, quarried from the Texas hill country where Johnson was born, detail the former President's views on such issues as education, civil rights, and the environment. The memorial, which is located in the Lady Bird Johnson Park on the George Washington Memorial Parkway, overlooks the Potomac River and offers a sweeping view of the capital. Tulips, daffodils, and other flowers decorate the park.

LBJ, who was a Texas senator and John F. Kennedy's Vice President, took over the presidency when Kennedy was assassinated in 1963, and served until 1969. He had a down-home, comfortable style with people and was considered a master of compromise. He was the youngest Senatorial Minority and Majority Leader ever.

As President, he instituted several important programs, including the Civil Rights Act of 1964; Medicare; the Fair Packaging and Labeling Act; The Water Quality, Clean Water Restoration, Clean Air, and Air Quality acts; the Space Program; and the War on Poverty. Despite his successes, Johnson was eventually brought down by his role in the Vietnam War.

The memorial includes a recorded address by the President's wife, a picnic area, and a mile of walking trails.

A 45-ton block of Texas granite is the centerpiece of the memorial, which is surrounded by a grove of white pine trees.

Lincoln Memorial

National Memorial

A monument as grand as the man it glorifies

Like the man it commemorates—whose vision united the country—the Lincoln Memorial acts as a visual focal point that unifies the city's landmarks. From it, one's gaze can take in the White House, the Capitol dome, and the Jefferson Memorial.

If a monument can ever capture the grandeur and majesty of the man it commemorates, this one does. The classic design of the memorial—borrowed from ancient Greece—is elegantly simple. Architect Henry Bacon masterfully re-created a rectangular Doric temple similar to the Parthenon. It has 36 marble columns representing the 36 states that belonged to the Union when Lincoln died; their names appear on the frieze above the row of columns.

The memorial is as tall as a nine-story building, though it appears shorter. It was completed in 1922. At the time the site was selected, it was a desolate swamp at the edge of the Potomac that had to be drained before construction.

Inside, the seated Mr. Lincoln is a commanding presence. Considered one of the great sculptures of the world, the 19-by-19-foot statue took Daniel Chester French four years and 28 blocks of ivory-white marble to carve. Two 60-foot murals by Jules Guerin allegorically portray the freeing of the slaves and the unity of North and South, Lincoln's greatest achievements.

The statue appears to be gazing at the Reflecting Pool, which stretches 350 feet toward the Washington Monument and, behind it, the Capitol dome. At night, reflections of the illuminated monuments bounce off the shimmering water to create one of Washington's most spectacular vistas.

The 19-foot-high seated figure of Abraham Lincoln, which took sculptor Daniel Chester French four years to complete, looks out over the Mall toward the Capitol.

The Lincoln Memorial, designed by architect Henry Bacon, was commissioned in 1911. In 1968, Martin Luther King, Jr., gave his "I Have a Dream" speech here.

National Mall

Designed to be the focal point of the capital

Included in Pierre-Charles L'Enfant's original design of Washington, the National Mall serves as the focal point of the capital city—and indeed of the nation, as L'Enfant intended. The broad swath of green, as wide as a football field is long, stretches for a mile from the U.S. Capitol to the Lincoln Memorial. Along the way, it is lined by many of the most revered and familiar of American monuments and buildings, including the Washington Monument, the Vietnam War Veterans Memorial, several of the Smithsonian Institution museums, and the National Archives.

L'Enfant, who had attracted the attention of George Washington during the Revolutionary War, was chosen by Washington in the second year of his presidency to survey the site of a capital city for the young country. L'Enfant's plan envisioned a vast grassy mall connecting the Hall of Congress with what he described as "a Presidential Palace."

The mile-long National Mall, lined with museums and monuments, stretches from the Capitol to the Lincoln Memorial.

Springtime is cherry blossom time along the Tidal Basin.

THE AMAZING SMITHSONIAN

With a collection estimated to total more than 137 million items, the Smithsonian Institution has been called "the nation's attic." Even with 13 museums at its disposal—several of which are located along the National Mall—the Institution has room to display only about one percent of its catalogued items at any given time.

The world's largest museum complex had fairly modest beginnings. When he died in 1859, James Smithson, a wealthy English bachelor who had never even visited America, bequeathed $500,000 to the United States "to found at Washington, under the name of the Smithsonian Institution, an establishment for the increase and diffusion of knowledge among men."

Today, the Smithsonian covers several square blocks in the heart of Washington, attracting more than 24 million visitors each year.

■ ■ ■

Though both the White House and Capitol were completed in 1800, finalization of L'Enfant's grand vision took much longer. The area remained an untended pasture and swamp for many years. Gradually, the original plan was implemented. Railroad tracks were removed, a canal was filled in, shacks were demolished. The Washington Monument, centerpiece of the Mall, was completed in 1888. The Lincoln Memorial and the long rectangular Reflecting Pool that mirrors its image in shallow water were added to the setting during the 1920s. The nearby Jefferson Memorial was dedicated in 1943.

The Mall doesn't serve only as a visual delight intended for snapshots taken by visitors to Washington. It's a vibrant urban park that provides enjoyment to Washington residents and visitors alike. Its gravel pathways are packed with joggers from nearby government office buildings. The western end of the green is criss-crossed by playing fields that attract soccer and volleyball players, as well as other sports enthusiasts. The Mall is also the setting for the July Fourth fireworks and the Christmas Pageant of Peace.

The Smithsonian's first building on the Mall, known as the Castle, opened in 1855.

■ ■ ■

Theodore Roosevelt Island

National Memorial

A wildlife haven along the Potomac River

Conservation was a major interest of Theodore Roosevelt. During his presidency, the U.S. Forest Service, five national parks, 150 national forests, and countless other refuges for nature were established. It is therefore fitting that the memorial to the nation's twenty-sixth President should be an island in the Potomac River that provides an urban haven for wildlife.

This 88-acre enclave of forest and marsh is reached by footbridge from the Virginia shoreline; no cars are allowed. The island offers 2½ miles of walking trails that provide good views of a variety of different environments—marshes, swamps, and woods. Visitors can anticipate encounters with cottontail rabbits, muskrats, chipmunks, birds, and other animals.

On the island's northern end, circled by a moat, stands a 17-foot-tall bronze statue of Roosevelt, his hand uplifted as though he were speaking. A 30-foot-tall granite shaft provides a backdrop for this likeness, and four granite tablets are inscribed with words spoken by him that expressed his philosophy about manhood, youth, nature, and the nation.

Markers along the hiking trails provide information about the island and its history. During spring and summer, park rangers lead guided tours.

A bronze statue of Theodore Roosevelt is located on the northern end of the 88-acre island that bears his name.

U.S. Capitol

The most important building in the country

The majesty of the Capitol dome dominates the downtown Mall area, giving one a powerful sense of its significance. Not only is it one of the nation's most beautiful buildings, it is probably the most important. Here, at the seat of Congress, history is created virtually every day.

The Capitol, located at the east end of the Mall, is also the center of the city's architectural design. All major streets, numbered and lettered, extend outward from the Capitol's base.

Visitors can take a tour to learn about the many impressive artistic and architectural accomplishments in the Capitol. Especially noteworthy are the works of Constantino Brumidi, the "Michelangelo of

A fresco by Constantino Brumidi, the "Michelangelo of the Capitol," decorates the dome of the Rotunda.

Major Pierre-Charles L'Enfant chose a flat-topped hill for the site of the U.S. Capitol. The area surrounding it is still known as Capitol Hill.

the Capitol." He devoted 25 years of his life to decorating the building's interior, several of which were spent on his back, painting the famous fresco in the eye of the Rotunda's dome and the frieze that encircles it. His work depicts important events in the life of the young country.

Statuary Hall contains bronze and marble statues honoring native sons from every state, including such heroes as Ethan Allen, Daniel Webster, and Henry Clay. The site once contained the House of Representatives, but a minor acoustical problem led them to look for another location. Guides demonstrate how, in a particular spot in the room, the smallest whisper can be heard clear across the chamber. This must have wreaked havoc during partisan caucuses.

Just as important as the history of Congress is seeing it in action today. A visit to either the House or the Senate while it is in session can provide an insight into the legislative process no history book can match. Even more revealing is a visit to a congressional hearing, where lively debates often take place.

Statues, paintings, and copies of the original Declaration of Independence, the Constitution, and Bill of Rights are on display in the Capitol.

Statues of great Americans decorate the central Rotunda of the Capitol Building, which was finished in 1829.

Vietnam War Veterans Memorial

A painful reminder of our nation's longest war

Almost as much controversy surrounded the creation of this memorial as did the war it commemorates.

Jan Scruggs, a former infantry corporal during the war, spearheaded a movement in 1979 to create a tangible symbol of recognition from American society for the soldiers who fought and died in Vietnam. The design had to meet four criteria: It had to be reflective and contemplative in character, harmonize with its surroundings, contain the names of all who died or were missing in action, and make no political statement about the war. Of the 1,421 submissions, 21-year-old Maya Ying Lin's design was chosen. The memorial was dedicated in 1982.

Dedicated in 1982, the Vietnam War Veterans Memorial was designed by Maya Lin, a Yale architectural student.

Friends and relatives take rubbings of the more than 58,000 names inscribed on the memorial.

A life-size statue of three American servicemen, by Washington sculptor Frederick Hart, was added to the memorial in 1984.

Some protested that the simple severity of the polished wall did not adequately represent the heroism of the war victims. A personal look at the black marble monument usually deflects such criticism. To appease the protesters, however, a life-size statue of three Vietnam soldiers by Washington sculptor Frederick Hart was erected nearby in 1984.

People usually approach this memorial with more emotion than they do other monuments. The evocative testimonial to the men and women who gave their lives or are still missing in the longest war in our nation's history (1959–1975) is fittingly located on the Mall between the Lincoln Memorial and the Washington Monument. For some, it is the main reason they come to Washington.

The 492-foot black granite walls are angled to form a V, one side facing the Washington Monument, the other side facing the Lincoln Memorial. Some find the monument's stark simplicity eloquent; others are put off by it. No one remains unaffected, however, while slowly passing the almost 60,000 names etched upon the stone. Especially moving is the nighttime ritual of searching for the name of a loved one in the light of a flickering match.

Names of casualties are inscribed in chronological order of the date of death. Many mourners leave behind flowers, flags, or other personal remembrances that are in sharp contrast to the public character of the place.

Not only does the mirrorlike marble reflect the surrounding trees and monuments; the shiny surface seems to echo the sentiments and emotions of those who pass by as well. Every seasonal nuance—cloud formations, sunlight, falling snow, or mist—plays upon the luminous ebony exterior to create ever-changing images.

HONORING VETERANS OF KOREA

Across the Reflecting Pool from the Vietnam War Veterans Memorial is another, equally significant, tribute to our armed forces.

Dedicated on July 27, 1995, the Korean War Veterans Memorial gives long-overdue recognition to the soldiers who fought in the Korean War (1950–53), a bloody conflict in which 54,000 Americans perished—almost as many as died in Vietnam during our ten-year involvement there.

Occupying a 7½-acre site in a grove near the Lincoln Memorial, the memorial consists of a Pool of Remembrance and a triangular field dominated by stainless-steel statues of 19 battle-weary infantrymen on patrol. Off to the side is a granite wall with hundreds of faces etched on it, all of them reproduced from actual photos of American soldiers and support troops taken during the war.

Washington Monument

National Memorial

Washington's most famous landmark

As much a monument to the city as it is to the man it immortalizes, the 555-foot-tall marble obelisk has become the visual symbol most people associate with the Washington area.

Although a monument to George Washington was first conceived in 1783—16 years before his death—it was not until 65 years later that construction was begun. Six years after that, in 1854, work on the monument stopped because of lack of funds and the impending Civil War—and because of an unpleasant incident involving the Pope. Pius IX sent a block of African marble from a Roman temple to be included in the monument. Its subsequent theft set off such political turmoil that already meager public contributions to the construction effort dwindled to nothing, and the project ran out of funds.

Work wasn't resumed until the federal government took it over in 1876. The original design of architect Robert Mills had been modified to create the sleeker, more contemporary feel of the monument as it exists today. The time gap, however, left a visible mark on the structure itself. Looking upward 150 feet from the base of the monument, it is apparent that the marble stones are a darker color than those below. The stone came from the same Maryland quarry, but by the time work resumed, the marble was coming from a different stratum. The monument was opened to the public in 1888.

Incomparable panoramas of the Washington landscape can be witnessed from the top of the monument. The views of the Lincoln and Jefferson memorials, the Capitol, and the White House are unmatched from any other perspective. At night, the views are even more spectacular.

Like a giant sundial, the daggerlike shadow of the Washington Monument stretches across the Mall.

The 555-foot Washington Monument is the tallest masonry structure in the world.

The White House

The official home of our First Family

One of the most famous addresses in the world is 1600 Pennsylvania Avenue. It's the oldest public building in Washington, home to every President except George Washington. Of its 132 rooms, only five are open to the public, and visitors won't find the President in any of them. Still, it's exciting to get even this close. This is the only residence of a head of state that is regularly open to the public.

Construction of the "President's Palace" began in 1792, and since then it has seen much refurbishing. It was first painted white after the British burned it during the War of 1812. In the 1940s, White House construction was considered so unsound that President Truman worried his bathtub might sink through the floor during a state reception. He moved across the street to Blair House for the next four years while his "home" was totally reconstructed.

Washington's most famous address is 1600 Pennsylvania Avenue. George Washington selected the site and approved the design for the White House.

Once used primarily by First Ladies to receive their guests, the Red Room is filled with paintings and priceless antiques.

Its most recent makeover occurred in 1961, when Jacqueline Kennedy brought back to the White House many of the historically accurate and original furnishings that had been removed over the years. She created for the White House a resident museum of American history, complete with many original portraits of Presidents and First Ladies, exquisite antiques in authentic settings, and historically significant memorabilia.

In addition to the five-room tour, visitors catch glimpses of other rooms—but only glimpses; the tour moves pretty quickly. Some of the other rooms visitors may see include the Vermeil Room; the Library, from which the President often makes his televised fireside appearances; the China Room, with an impressive ceramics display; the Diplomatic Reception Room, with state flag emblems of the 50 states woven into its carpet; and the Jacqueline Kennedy Garden. Neither the Oval Office nor the First Family's living quarters are included on the tour. The tour focuses on five rooms:

The Green Room, which President Monroe used as a card room, features one of the three marble mantels ordered by him during his tenure.

The East Room. Every kind of social event, from gala receptions and wedding festivities to bill-signing ceremonies and press conferences, has been held here. The well-known Gilbert Stuart portrait of George Washington, which was painted in 1796 and is the oldest original possession in the White House, hangs on the east wall.

The Green Room. Although traditionally the setting for small teas and receptions, President Thomas Jefferson chose to use it as his personal dining room.

Most of the furnishings date from 1800 to 1815 and are outstanding examples of the Sheraton style. The famous Scottish cabinetmaker of that time, Duncan Phyfe, provided several pieces that continue to adorn the room today.

The Blue Room. The most formal of the three parlors, it is used regularly to receive guests and heads of state and is the setting each year for the White House Christmas tree.

The French Empire furnishings, which are the mainstay of the room's interior design, still include many pieces that graced the room during the administration of James Monroe (1817–1825). The portraits of several Presidents are displayed along the walls—John Tyler, by George Healy; John Adams, by John Trumbull; Andrew Jackson, by John Wesley Jarvis; and Thomas Jefferson, by Rembrandt Peale.

The Red Room. This room is sometimes used by the First Lady to receive guests. Its vibrant decor is rivaled only by its priceless antiques. The furnishings, which date from 1810 to 1830, contain one of the White House's finest pieces of American Empire furniture, a small round table of mahogany and fruitwoods, which stands near the fireplace. It's one of several intriguing pieces attributed to Charles-Honore Lannuier, whose New York workshop was one of the artistic centers of the period.

State Dining Room. This room, decked out in white with gold highlights, is stately and somber compared with the colorful rooms preceding it. As many as 140 guests can be accommodated here. The only picture in the room is the portrait of Abraham Lincoln by George Healy, painted in 1869. It hangs above the marble buffalo-head mantel, which is the focal point of the room.

The Oval Office, the private office of the President of the United States, is the true seat of power in the White House.

THE HOME OF OUR PRESIDENT

Built between 1792 and 1800, the original home of our President and First Family was designed by James Hoban, an Irish-born architect who is said to have based his design on the palace of the duke of Leinster in Dublin, Ireland.

During the War of 1812, British troops set fire to the building, completely destroying the interior. To hide smoke stains on the outside walls, the structure was painted white, and only then became known as the White House.

The west wing of the White House was built in 1902. The building's colonnaded north portico and semicircular south portico were added in the 1920s, and an east wing was added in 1942. Today, the White House contains 54 rooms, including a doctor's and dentist's office, a television studio, solarium, indoor swimming pool, and a nuclear bomb shelter.

The South

National Monuments and Historic Sites

People settled this area of North America thousands of years ago, so it is not surprising that much of the region's history is told by its architecture. One prehistoric culture left behind huge earthen mounds—perhaps the first human mark on the landscape. The remains of the massive forts of the first Europeans to set foot in North America still remind us that the United States began as little more than an outpost on the way to the Indies. The Spanish settlement of St. Augustine, Florida, still survives today, though little remains of Britain's first settlement at Jamestown, Virginia.

The history of the South is also preserved in the sites that honor Americans' struggle for equality, from the Civil War to the civil rights movement.

Nomadic bands of Indians began using Alabama's Russell Cave for shelter as far back as 9,000 years ago, as evidenced by the pottery, weapons, and tools unearthed at the site.

Rows of tombstones at Andersonville, a Georgia prison camp where 13,000 Union soldiers died during the Civil War, are a stark reminder of a bleak period in American history.

111

Alibates Flint Quarries
National Monument

Where native peoples made their tools and weapons

On the harsh, dry, high plains of the Texas Panhandle, in a region known as Llano Estacado, humans carved out a living for more than 12,000 years.

At the Alibates Flint Quarries, in the red bluffs above the Canadian River, pre-Columbian Indians quarried agatized dolomite, chipping and flaking it to make spear points, knives, scrapers, and other tools. Archaeologists theorize that people of the Ice Age Clovis Culture hunted with spears tipped with colorful Alibates flint points. They dug by hand or used sticks or bone tools to reach the flint layer, which could be up to six feet thick. Later Indians continued to use the rainbow-hued flint to make tools, but they also traded it for Pacific Coast seashells, Minnesota pipestone, painted pottery from Pueblo Indians of the Southwest, and other goods.

Alibates Flint Quarries National Monument, authorized in 1965, offers guided tours of the quarries. The monument also contains the ruins of several Plains Village Indian dwellings.

Between A.D. 1150 and 1500, these ancestors of the Pawnee and Wichita Indians built villages of rock-slab houses containing up to 100 rooms. On a bluff near the dwellings they carved turtles, bison, and other images into the rock. Historians believe that a long, severe drought, combined with raids from aggressive tribes nearby, caused the Plains Village Indians to abandon this area.

Native Americans carved this turtle and other images into a bluff near where they quarried Alibates flint for knives, arrowheads, and other tools.

Booker T. Washington

National Monument

The former home of a famous black educator

Booker T. Washington—educator, philosopher, and civil rights leader—was born a slave on a farm in Virginia in 1856. His mother, a cook, was owned by the Burroughs family. Many years later, in his autobiography, *Up From Slavery,* Washington remembered his childhood: "The early years of my life, which were spent in the little cabin, were not very different from those of thousands of other slaves."

Booker T. Washington National Monument contains a replica of the little kitchen cabin in which Washington was born. "The cabin was without glass windows," he wrote. "It had only openings in the side which let in the light and also the cold, chilly air of winter." Washington and his sisters slept on the dirt floor bundled in rags. The interior has been re-created to appear as Washington described it in his book.

Other buildings on the reconstructed 207-acre farm include the smokehouse, blacksmith shed, tobacco barn, and horse barn. The site of the Burroughs' house is outlined in stone. As a boy, Washington learned about news of the outside world by listening in on Burroughs family conversations as he fanned flies from their dinner table.

Washington longed to attend school, but it was illegal to educate slaves. "I had the feeling that to get into a schoolhouse and study would be about the same as getting into paradise," he wrote.

When he was nine, the Emancipation Proclamation freed the slaves, and his family moved to West Virginia. At 16, he walked 400 miles back to Virginia to enroll in a new black school where students could pay their way by working. He went on to found the Tuskegee Institute in 1881 and became the country's leading black educator.

Booker T. Washington, an educator and civil rights leader, founded Tuskegee Institute in 1881.

Booker T. Washington National Monument includes the reconstructed one-room log cabin where Washington was born a slave in 1856.

113

Castillo de San Marcos

National Monument

A remnant of Spain in northeast Florida

Castillo de San Marcos National Monument preserves the oldest stone fort in the United States. The impressive structure was built to guard the nation's oldest city, St. Augustine, Florida, from British invasion. For many years it was the northernmost outpost of Spain's empire in the New World, which was founded just after Columbus landed on the continent and decades before the English settled Jamestown.

Begun in 1672, the fort has 12-foot-thick stone walls that are 32 feet high. The structure survived the salt, wind, and other elements that destroyed its nine wooden predecessors. One of the earlier wooden forts was set on fire by the troops of Sir Francis Drake in 1586. Even though the raiders burned down the entire town, residents remained safe inside the fort.

Castillo de San Marcos, begun in 1672 and finished a quarter of a century later, withstood every attack, thanks to its massive walls made of a locally quarried stone known as coquina.

During the Revolutionary War, the British government imprisoned three signers of the Declaration of Independence here.

Castillo de San Marcos National Monument

A watchtower perched atop a bastion provided the sentry stationed there with an unobstructed view of the sea.

■ ■ ■

The fort also survived major sieges by the British in 1702 and 1740. British troops took over Castillo de San Marcos only after Spain ceded Florida to Great Britain in 1763.

During its long history, the Castillo has had many different tenants. The British used the fort as a staging base for attacks during the Revolutionary War. It was also used as a prison for captured Indians during the Seminole War of 1835–42 and for Yankee soldiers during the Civil War. It was last used as a military prison during the Spanish-American War. Renamed Fort Marion in 1825, the fort was proclaimed a national monument in 1924, and its original name was later restored.

A trip to Castillo de San Marcos is an opportunity to explore more than 300 years of history. The fortress, which sits on a 20-acre park in downtown St. Augustine, is essentially a hollow square, but with diamond-shaped bastions at each corner that held cannons to protect the fort.

A moat surrounds the fortress. The drawbridge in the ravelin, which shielded the fort's only entrance, and the main drawbridge are working reconstructions. On weekends, visitors encounter actors dressed in Spanish colonial costumes, including gunners who re-create battle drills and fire cannons.

Soldiers, who normally lived in town, slept and prepared meals in the guard rooms when they were on 24-hour guard duty. The bombproof storage rooms around the central courtyard, which originally held gunpowder, tools, lumber, and food, now house museums detailing the fort's history. Artillery, cannonballs, and three Spanish silver coins—a soldier's daily pay—are on display.

The simple but attractive design of the fortress, credited to Spanish engineer Ignacio Daza, is a hollow square with diamond-shaped bastions at each of the corners.

■ ■ ■

116

AN ORDERLY SPANISH COMMUNITY

St. Augustine, established in 1565 by Don Pedro Menendez de Aviles, is the oldest European settlement in the continental United States. It is also perhaps the earliest example of community planning in the nation.

The city was laid out with regular streets, a pleasant central plaza, and many open spaces, including beautiful patios and gardens. Impressive government and religious buildings and comfortable homes suggest that the goal of the city's planners was to create an orderly, healthy, and pleasant environment.

Congaree Swamp

National Monument

A very old forest of bottomland hardwoods

South Carolina's Congaree Swamp National Monument protects the region's last significant old-growth forest of bottomland hardwoods, along with a rich variety of plants and animals.

Southern swamps once extended from the Chesapeake Bay to east Texas, but most were cut down or flooded behind dams. In 1976, Congaree Swamp gained permanent protection as a national monument and has been designated part of the international Man and the Biosphere program due to its great genetic diversity. The swamp has some 90 species of trees, and many hold the state record for size.

The Congaree River, a small link in a river system that drains much of South Carolina, is formed at the confluence of the Saluda and Broad rivers. It floods an average of ten times a year, depositing rich nutrients to support the plant life that has adapted to survive in the floodplain.

Sycamores, whose roots can tolerate periodic inundation, dominate the stream banks. Bald cypress trees grow in low areas of standing water, their "knees," or wood projections, sticking out of the

Congaree Swamp National Monument protects the last significant stand of southern bottomland forest in the United States.

Raised boardwalks allow visitors the opportunity to experience this unique swamp, which floods an average of ten times a year, without getting their feet wet.

■ ■ ■

PRECIOUS PINE TREES

Towering above the dense canopy of trees at Congaree Swamp are the loblolly pines, which stand 100 feet tall or higher and are up to 300 years old. One of the largest in the monument is 15 feet around and 145 feet tall. Congaree is an unusual swamp because loblolly pines and hardwoods are rarely found growing together in a floodplain.

■ ■ ■

water. Cherry-bark oak, sweetgum, and holly need higher, drier soils, and they, along with the great loblolly pines, are found on slightly higher ground.

Many Congaree Swamp trees have shallow, disk-shaped root systems that make them susceptible to toppling. When a big tree falls, it opens up a gap in the thick forest canopy as big as a half-acre, allowing sunlight to reach the forest floor and initiate new plant growth.

Animals survive the frequent floods by running for higher ground, swimming to the bluffs on either side of the river, or by climbing trees to wait out the flood.

Twenty miles of hiking trails, two raised boardwalks that are wheel-chair accessible, and a marked canoe trail cover the monument's 22,200 acres of river, floodplain, and forest. Congaree Swamp is a great place to walk, birdwatch, fish, camp, and canoe.

Fort Frederica

National Monument

England's southernmost New World stronghold

England tried establishing Utopia in the American wilderness in 1732, when a city for the "worthy poor" of Britain was established on Saint Simons Island in the unoccupied territory below the Carolinas.

In this new town called Frederica, slavery and rum were forbidden, and people of all different religions and nationalities were accepted. Everyone was given an equal-sized plot to farm. Soon an orderly town sprang up, complete with Georgian-style homes and a major thoroughfare, Broad Street, shaded by orange trees.

By the 1740s, about 500 farmers, tradesmen, and craftsmen prospered in Frederica. The town wasn't founded purely for humanitarian reasons, though. Frederica was England's southernmost stronghold in its struggle to wrest control of land in the New World from Spain. One of the settlers' first jobs, in fact, was to build a fort.

In 1845, a visitor remarked that Frederica was defended "by a pretty strong Fort of Tappy, which has several 18 Pounders mounted on a Ravelin in its Front, and commands the River both upwards and downwards...."

In 1739, war broke out between Britain and Spain. Three years later, at the Battle of Bloody Marsh near Fort Frederica, Spain was defeated. By 1758, no longer needed for military purposes, Frederica fell to ruin. Fort Frederica National Monument preserves the once-flourishing town and the Bloody Marsh Battle Site.

Built by the British to protect southern Georgia from the Spanish, the fort contained an entire town within its walls.

Fort Matanzas
National Monument

A Spanish outpost that protected St. Augustine

Visitors to Florida's Fort Matanzas National Monument arrive by boat, just as Spanish soldiers did in the eighteenth century. The island outpost was built in the 1740s to protect the city of St. Augustine.

Though St. Augustine was well-positioned with water on three sides, if an enemy ship crossed into the Matanzas River, it could attack the city's rear. The fort on Matanzas Island prevented ships from entering the inlet to the river. A stairway now leads to the fort, but originally it was a wooden ladder that was drawn up each night.

Two of the five original cannons that guarded the inlet remain on the gun deck, left behind when the Spanish departed in 1821. At the rear of the gun deck, under the stairs, is a cistern that caught rainwater, the only source of fresh water on the island.

Below the gun deck were the enlisted men's quarters, where seven to ten soldiers cooked, ate, and slept while on duty here. The officer's quarters housed just one officer, usually a corporal or sergeant. A narrow ladder leads to the top of the tower, which provides good views of the inlet to the south and the waterway leading to St. Augustine to the north.

Self-guided nature walks reveal the monument's various habitats: a tidal salt marsh, a coastal dune hammock, and an open area of dunes and scrub. Free ferry service is available from adjacent Anastasia Island.

Fort Matanzas was built on Rattlesnake Island in 1742 as an outpost of St. Augustine's Castillo de San Marcos.

Fort Pulaski
National Monument

Site of a landmark Civil War battle

Fifteen miles east of Savannah, Georgia, in the mouth of the Savannah River, stands Fort Pulaski, one of the best surviving examples of nineteenth-century brick and masonry coastal fortifications.

Designed by French military engineer General Simon Bernard, with a dike designed by future Confederate leader Robert E. Lee, the five-sided fort features superb architecture with arched casements, iron doors, and drawbridges spanning a moat.

Part of a system of coastal forts built between 1820 and 1850, Fort Pulaski, with its 7½-foot-thick walls made of 25 million bricks, represented the state of the art when it was completed in 1847 at a cost of $1 million.

The officers' quarters at Fort Pulaski have been restored to illustrate what life was like in the nineteenth-century garrison.

In 1862, Union forces breached the walls of Fort Pulaski after 30 hours of bombardment by rifled cannons, making masonry forts obsolete.

Fort Pulaski National Monument

A drawbridge spans the moat surrounding Fort Pulaski National Monument. Local alligators sometimes use the waterway.

Ironically, it was only 15 years later that the obsolescence of masonry forts was revealed when Fort Pulaski's fabled walls were breached by an experimental new weapon: the rifled cannon. Using a spiral-grooved barrel to put a spin on its projectile, the rifled cannon produced dramatic increases in both range and accuracy.

The new artillery was first used in battle on April 10 and 11, 1862, against Confederate troops occupying the fort. Firing from more than a mile away, the guns breached the walls in at least two places, forcing the Confederates to surrender the fort after a siege of only 30 hours. The bullet-pocked walls stand today as a reminder of this landmark battle.

Completed in 1847 as part of a series of forts that protected major seaports from foreign attack, Fort Pulaski was the ultimate defense system of its day.

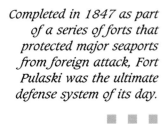

A French military engineer designed the brick-and-masonry Fort Pulaski, built between 1829 and 1847. Southerner Robert E. Lee designed the fort's dike.

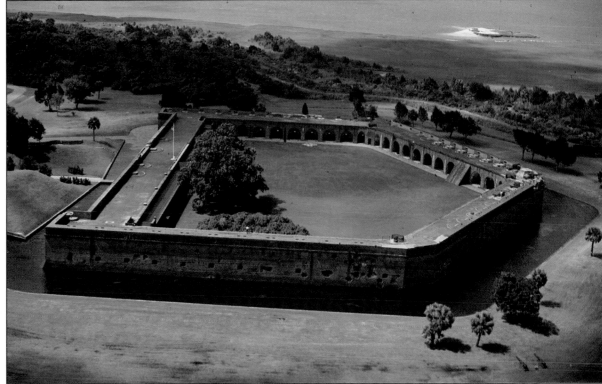

Fort Sumter
National Monument

The place where the Civil War began

*A*t the mouth of Charleston Harbor are the desolate remains of the once-grand Fort Sumter, where the sparks flew that ignited the Civil War.

In late 1860 and early 1861, South Carolina, prompted by the election of Abraham Lincoln to the presidency, voted to secede from the United States rather than give up slavery. By March of 1861, six other states had joined the rebellion, electing a provisional government and taking over nearly all of the federal forts and navy yards within their boundaries.

Fort Sumter was one of the few exceptions. After blockading the fort for four months and repeatedly demanding the surrender of the fort, Confederate troops stationed at nearby forts Moultrie and John-

Union gunfire reduced Fort Sumter to rubble, but the South didn't surrender the stronghold until 1865.

■ ■ ■

Fort Sumter was one of a series of coastal fortifications built by the United States after the War of 1812. It was named after South Carolina Revolutionary War patriot Thomas Sumter.

■ ■ ■

On April 12, 1861, the first shot of the Civil War was directed at Fort Sumter. Sumter's lower casement guns fired back during the 34-hour bombardment.

■ ■ ■

Tour boats operating from Charleston City Marina and nearby Patriot's Point bring visitors to Fort Sumter.

■ ■ ■

son fired the first rounds of the Civil War on Sumter, forcing a surrender of the starving troops in less than two days.

Northern forces were never able to retake the fort, although they eventually reduced the five-foot-thick brick walls to rubble during 17 months of increasingly heavy shelling. The heaped remains of the shattered walls, it turned out, were better able to take the shelling than were the original brick walls.

After a final unsuccessful two-month bombardment, the majority of Union troops involved in the siege were diverted to the campaign on Richmond. When the fort was finally abandoned by the Confederates, who were fleeing the advance of General William T. Sherman, it had absorbed seven million tons of ordnance without falling to the Union forces.

Following the end of the war, the fort was partially refurbished, though not to its original specifications. It was used again during the Spanish-American War, when a new battery was installed in the central court. The guns were never fired in battle, though, and the war ended quickly.

Small garrisons manned the guns again during World War I and World War II. In 1948, Fort Sumter was declared a national monument by act of Congress.

SYMBOL OF SOUTHERN DEFIANCE

Fort Sumter shared Charleston Harbor with eight other military installations, all under Confederate control from the onset of the Civil War.

Although it may seem that Union forces went to absurd lengths to try to recapture it, Fort Sumter was greatly valuable to the Confederacy. It was important as a strategic stronghold that enabled commerce of weapons and raw goods—despite the near-complete Union blockade of the South—and, perhaps equally important, it had value as a symbol of the South's courage and defiance.

■ ■ ■

George Washington Birthplace

National Monument

Where the leader spent much of his childhood

Fields of tobacco and wheat, farm buildings, groves of trees, and colorful country gardens were the scenes of George Washington's early childhood.

Our country's first President was born on February 22, 1732, in a modest plantation manor house along the banks of Popes Creek, Virginia. He lived there until he was almost four and spent long periods there as a boy. Having grown up watching his father's slaves working the farm—and later helping his brother run it—Washington always claimed to be first a farmer, and second a public servant.

Today, the Popes Creek farm operates much as it did in Washington's day. Costumed interpreters demonstrate eighteenth-century farming techniques, and the farm animals and crops are species that were common in colonial times. Many of the herbs and flowers commonly found on eighteenth-century Virginia plantations grow in the garden.

The original home burned down on Christmas Day, 1779, while Washington was far to the north with the Continental Army. Now a memorial home typical of the upper classes of the time stands in its place, filled with period colonial furnishings. An oyster shell outline marks the location and dimensions of the original house.

Popes Creek Plantation is part of the George Washington Birthplace National Monument, which includes the working farm, family cemetery, a picnic area, and more than 500 acres of grounds crossed by hiking trails.

George Washington, commander in chief of the Continental Army and first President of the United States, began his career as a frontier surveyor of Virginia's Shenandoah Valley.

■ ■ ■

A 1930 reconstruction of a typical plantation house replaces the building in which the first President was born, which burned down in 1779.

■ ■ ■

Ocmulgee
National Monument

The ancient home of the Mound Builders

The Ocmulgee National Monument, located east of Macon, Georgia, contains traces of more than 10,000 years of continuous human occupation, from Ice Age hunters to the Creeks of historic times. The most significant period of occupation, however, was between A.D. 900 and 1100, when the Mississippians built their massive temple mounds here.

Around A.D. 700, a new civilization in the Mississippi Valley expanded on the developments made by an earlier culture called the Hopewell and brought a more complex way of life to the region. The Mississippians, or Temple Mound Builders, built towns housing thousands of people, turned small-scale farming into an industry that produced enough food for everyone, and built earthen mounds on an enormous scale.

At the Ocmulgee site, the Mississippians built a compact city of thatched huts on a bluff overlooking the Ocmulgee River and planted crops of corn, beans, squash, pumpkin, and tobacco in the bottom-lands. Along the river, the two or three thousand residents built a series of temple mounds for their religious and political ceremonies. The monument contains nine mounds, including the largest, Great Temple Mound, which rises more than 40 feet from a base that is 300 feet by 270 feet. A half-mile walk leads visitors to this impressive mound. These flat-topped pyramidal mounds were bases for their temples, which were constructed of poles and thatch.

Between A.D. 900 and 1100, a farming culture known as the Mississippians built earthlodges and huge, flat-topped mounds of earth.

IMPRESSIVE EARTHWORKS

The Mississippians disappeared long before settlers began to arrive in the Mississippi Valley, leaving behind only these mysterious mounds.

American settlers arriving in the 1700s and early 1800s were reminded of the great Egyptian pyramids and gave their new towns names like Memphis, Alexandria, and Cairo. Few believed that the local Indians, whom they considered to be uncivilized savages, were responsible for the mounds. Instead, they credited the mounds to ancient Babylonians, the Vikings, and even space aliens.

Some settlers did recognize the contributions of Native American cultures. When naturalist William Bartram visited Ocmulgee in the 1770s, he spoke with respect of "the wonderful remains of the power and grandeur of the ancients."

The 700-acre site also includes an ancient burial mound on the west side. Like the temple mounds, the Funeral Mound was flat-topped and had steps leading up the side. Excavations have revealed more than 100 burials here and an unusual number of fine pottery pieces, effigy figures, shell and copper jewelry, and copper sun disks. These items are on display at the visitor center, along with arrowheads and farming implements excavated at this ceremonial city.

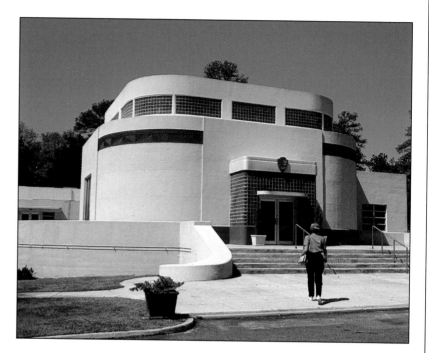

Nearly all the Mississippian buildings have disappeared, but part of an earthlodge survived and has been reconstructed. It was built 1,000 years ago and was probably used as a council house. The building seats about 50 people on an eagle-shaped platform and on a low bench along the wall.

The visitor center, an interesting art deco building that blends well with the surroundings, contains exhibits and a major archaeological museum. A short film detailing the life of the "People of the Macon Plateau" plays throughout the day.

Other features of the monument include prehistoric trenches, which may have been used for defense purposes, and the remains of a trading post built by English traders about 1690. Excavations have revealed the variety of goods traded here, including axes, clay pipes, beads, bullets, flints, and muskets. More than five miles of walking trails wind through the monument.

The visitor center at Ocmulgee National Monument contains an archaeological museum displaying artifacts unearthed from the mounds.

Poverty Point

National Monument

Homeland of an ancient Indian culture

Three thousand years ago, Poverty Point was the center of the most advanced civilization north of the Rio Grande. Prehistoric people built a town of massive earthen mounds here; archaeologists estimate it took some five-million labor hours to haul the dirt in basket by basket.

The central part consists of six rows of concentric arcs, forming an enormous semicircle. Each arc of raised earth was originally 10 to 15 feet high. It is believed that these ridges served as foundations for dwellings.

Connected to the outermost arc is Poverty Point Mound, a huge mound shaped like a bird with outstretched wings. It measures approximately 700 by 800 feet at its base and rises 70 feet into the air. The Poverty Point inhabitants established an extensive trade network here; then, between 1400 and 1350 B.C., they abandoned the site.

The visitor center has many artifacts on display, including beads and small stone tools unique to this culture. The center's Lookout Point, which has a scale model of the entire facility at its base, offers an excellent perspective of the enormity of the site's mounds. The monument also offers self-guided interpretive trails, special guided tours, and the opportunity to observe archaeologists at work.

Poverty Point was designated a national monument in 1988, but it is owned and operated by the Office of State Parks, State of Louisiana.

Poverty Point National Monument contains some of the largest prehistoric earthworks in North America. The ridges and depressions were originally thought to be natural, but aerial photos in 1952 revealed that the ridges formed a giant symmetrical pattern.

Russell Cave
National Monument

Revealing clues about the earliest Americans

Russell Cave National Monument in the hill country of northern Alabama contains one of the richest archaeological deposits in the United States, representing more than 9,000 years of continuous use.

The first nomadic bands of Native Americans arrived at Russell Cave long before the rise of the first true civilizations in Egypt and the Near East. They brought with them chipped flint points for their hunting spears, which were later found 12 feet below the present floor of the cave. This ready-made dwelling allowed them to concentrate on finding food rather than shelter.

For thousands of years, charcoal from their fires, animal bones, tools, weapons, and broken pottery piled up in the entrance of the cave. The layers of artifacts were first discovered in the 1950s, and the site was declared a national monument in 1961. A slide program on the fascinating history of the cave and its various excavations is shown at the cave entrance.

The visitor center museum has a sampling of the treasure-trove of artifacts unearthed at Russell Cave, including spearheads, fishhooks, pottery, and shell jewelry. Rangers use atlatls (sticks used for launching spears), grind corn, crack walnuts, make stone tools, and cut leather thongs, demonstrating the daily life and work of the prehistoric people of Russell Cave.

Nature and hiking trails let visitors explore the more than 300-acre monument on the side of Montague Mountain.

Russell Cave National Monument preserves 310 acres of limestone bluffs and woods on the side of Montague Mountain.

Native Americans inhabited Russell Cave for about 8,000 years, leaving behind tools, pottery, and other artifacts.

Andersonville

National Historic Site

A memorial
to American
prisoners
of war

Andersonville National Historic Site preserves the remains of the most notorious Confederate-operated prisoner-of-war camp, at the same time serving as a memorial to all Americans who have been held as prisoners of war.

Camp Sumter, as Andersonville was officially known, was built in Georgia in early 1864 to accommodate large numbers of Union prisoners who were to be moved out of the Richmond (Virginia) area. The largest of the Confederate prisons, the camp originally covered more than 16 acres of land enclosed by a 15-foot-high stockade of pine logs. It was later enlarged to 1,620 feet by 779 feet.

Weathered tombstones are a sad reminder of the nearly 13,000 Union prisoners who died here of disease, exposure, and malnutrition.

A stockade wall of 20-foot pine logs surrounded the prison. Along the wall are the remains of tunnels dug by prisoners—some an attempt to escape, others an attempt to reach fresh drinking water.

■ ■ ■

The historic site is a memorial to those who died here, but it also pays tribute to the prisoners who survived—and to all American prisoners of war.

■ ■ ■

Sentry boxes, which prisoners called "pigeon roosts," stood at 30-yard intervals along the top of the stockade. Inside, approximately 19 feet from the wall, was the "deadline," which prisoners were forbidden to cross.

The camp was initially designed to hold no more than 10,000 prisoners, but during its 14 months of existence, more than 45,000 soldiers were confined here. An estimated 13,000 died—from disease, malnutrition, poor sanitation, overcrowding, and exposure to the elements.

As one prisoner wrote in his diary, "There is so much filth about the camp that it is terrible trying to live here." After the

Andersonville National Historic Site

Still an active cemetery, Andersonville continues to accept American war veterans for burial, even as more construction is being planned to restore the historical site.

■ ■ ■

war, Captain Henry Wirz, the prison's commander, was found guilty of war crimes and hanged, and Andersonville prison ceased to exist.

The visitor center contains exhibits on Andersonville and other Civil War prisons, the cemetery, and the systems of exchange and parole used during the war, as well as a database listing prisoners and guards at Andersonville. The 12,912 prisoners who died here are buried in the cemetery under rows of white marble headstones. The cemetery continues to accept deceased veterans.

Relatively few grave markers at Andersonville read "Unknown Soldier" thanks to the work of Clara Barton and a 19-year-old Union prisoner of war.

■ ■ ■

A statue of three forlorn prisoners bears an inscription from an Old Testament prophet: "Turn you to the stronghold, ye prisoners of hope."

■ ■ ■

Several structures from the original camp survive, including the Dead House, a small structure built of tree branches outside the stockade where the dead were brought before they were carried by wagon to the cemetery for burial. Other remnants include earthworks, stockades, and holes dug by prisoners in an attempt to escape or to reach fresh drinking water.

Congress authorized the historic site in 1970 "to provide an understanding of the overall prisoner-of-war story of the Civil War, to interpret the role of prisoner-of-war camps in history, to commemorate the sacrifice of Americans who lost their lives in such camps, and to preserve the monuments" within the site.

A MEASURE OF DECENCY

Most of the headstones at the Camp Sumter cemetery would read "Unknown Soldier" if it weren't for the work of Dorence Atwater and Clara Barton.

Atwater was a 19-year-old Union POW at Andersonville who tended the books in which prisoners' deaths were listed. In the hopes of someday notifying the relatives of the dead interred at Andersonville, Atwater made his own copy of the register, which he smuggled to Washington, D.C. In July of 1865, Atwater and nurse Clara Barton used this list to identify and mark the graves of the dead at Andersonville.

■ ■ ■

Andrew Johnson

National Historic Site

A memorial to a tailor who became President

Andrew Johnson was born in 1808 and apprenticed to a tailor as a child. At age 16, he ran away and traveled throughout the South. When he settled down in Greeneville, Tennessee, he began work as a tailor and eventually accumulated enough wealth that he owned eight slaves, as well as several properties and industrial buildings.

Johnson married Eliza McCardle, the daughter of a shoemaker, in 1827, and she taught him writing and mathematics. He joined debate clubs, and, despite never attending a day of school, became an educated man with a commanding speaking style. He launched his political career in his tailor shop, giving fiery speeches.

The future President was first elected to local and state offices, then to the United States Congress. A supporter of the agrarian lifestyle, he introduced the Homestead Act, which opened public lands to anyone who would farm a 160-acre parcel.

When the Civil War broke out, Johnson was the only senator from a seceding state to remain in Congress. In the North he was a hero, but his fellow Southerners felt betrayed. Johnson's sons and sons-in-law were harassed, and his property confiscated. Eliza escaped through enemy lines to join Johnson in the North.

In 1864, Abraham Lincoln chose Johnson to be his running mate. "Andy Johnson, I think, is a good man," Lincoln said. On April 15, 1865, when Lincoln was assassinated, the former tailor became President.

The Andrew Johnson National Historic Site, designated in 1963, contains the rough-hewn tailor shop Johnson bought in 1831, two of his houses, and the national cemetery where Eliza and Andrew Johnson are buried.

The home of the nation's seventeenth President is preserved at the Andrew Johnson National Historic Site in Greeneville, Tennessee.

Carl Sandburg Home

National Historic Site

A chance to sample the writer's idyllic life

A trip to Carl Sandburg's home in North Carolina is a chance to sample the idyllic life led by this poet, author, lecturer, minstrel, political activist, and social thinker.

Visitors can stroll about the farm, as Sandburg did to refresh himself while writing. In the barn area one finds a small herd of goats and, in the summer, park rangers demonstrating cheese-making. Sandburg's wife and daughters made cheese, yogurt, and ice cream from their herd of goats.

Rangers also lead poetry and music programs, reminiscent of evenings on the farm when Sandburg would read to or sing with his family after dinner, before heading upstairs to his office where he often worked until morning.

Carl Sandburg spent the last 22 years of his long and productive life at Connemara, his North Carolina farm and home.

A FAMILY OPERATION

While Carl Sandburg was tucked away in his study writing, the other members of the Sandburg family kept Connemara running smoothly.

His daughter Margaret tended the library, painted, and worked in the flower garden. Another daughter, Janet, helped care for the farm—which included at one time a large vegetable garden, an orchard, cows, chickens, and hogs—and performed plenty of routine chores such as cheese- and butter-making. Mrs. Sandburg ran the farm business, and she bred and cared for her large, prize-winning goat herd, which numbered up to 200 animals.

Sandburg was a newspaperman before turning full-time in 1932 to other forms of writing, including poetry, biography, autobiography, history, children's literature, books on American folk music, and a novel. He won the Pulitzer Prize in 1940 for the four-volume set, *Abraham Lincoln: The War Years.* Five years later, he bought this farm and home in North Carolina, which he called Connemara. He lived there for 22 productive years.

Much of Sandburg's writing was influenced by his early experiences. He grew up in a small prairie town in the Midwest and left school after the eighth grade to work and travel. He traveled across the country as a hobo, served as a soldier in the Spanish-American War, and worked as a political reformer. He returned home in 1898 to study at Lombard College, where he began writing seriously.

His first success came in 1914 when nine poems, including "Chicago," still his most famous work, were published. Known as the "poet laureate of the people," he gave voice to common people, outcasts, and immigrants, as revealed in the famous closing lines of the aforementioned classic:

"Laughing the stormy, husky, brawling laughter of Youth, half-naked, sweating, proud to be Hog Butcher, Tool Maker, Stacker of Wheat, Player with Railroads and Freight Handler to the Nation."

While Carl Sandburg wrote, his wife and daughters raised goats and made cheese, yogurt, and ice cream on their farm.

Charles Pinckney
National Historic Site

Tribute to a man who shaped our Constitution

Charles Pinckney National Historic Site in the South Carolina low country is dedicated to a man who fought in the Revolutionary War and helped shape the Constitution of the United States.

Pinckney was born in 1757 to a prominent family and grew up on Snee Farm, a coastal plantation. The 715-acre farm was a working plantation for almost 250 years. Rice was the main crop, though indigo and cotton were also grown, and slaves made up the labor force. In 1817, Pinckney sold the farm to settle his debts.

Pinckney began his public career at age 22 and went on to become one of South Carolina's most distinguished political leaders. The successful statesman served as one of four South Carolina delegates at the Constitutional Convention, and he was a four-term governor of the state. His four decades of public service also included terms as a state legislator, U.S. congressman and senator, and ambassador to Spain.

Congress authorized Snee Farm as a historical site in 1988 to preserve what was deemed a landmark of national value. Two years later, part of the original farm, including the house Pinckney grew up in (built by his father in 1754), were acquired by the Park Service.

Only 28 acres of the Snee Farm remain. The rest has been absorbed by surrounding communities. The story-and-a-half gabled house on the site was built in the 1820s, after Pinckney sold the property. It is typical of the simple but refined coastal cottages once common throughout the region. The site tells the story of Charles Pinckney, Snee Farm, and the United States as a young, emerging nation.

Although born to a life of wealth and privilege, Charles Pinckney fought in the Revolutionary War and was one of the principal framers of the Constitution.

Fort Davis
National Historic Site

A key post in the defense of West Texas

New brick and woodwork reveal the painstaking effort to preserve one of the fort's original officers' quarters.

◼ ◼ ◼

Fort Davis National Historic Site contains the most impressive remains of any Indian Wars frontier fort. The installation has also earned a significant spot in history as the first military fort in western Texas and one of the first such posts where African-American soldiers served.

On the eve of the Mexican War, Texas joined the Union. In this new state, nearly 600 miles of wilderness stretched between San Antonio and El Paso, where wagon trains, gold seekers, and mail coaches were prey to Indian attacks.

In 1854, a pine fort, named for Secretary of War Jefferson Davis, was built in a canyon near Limpia Creek to protect travelers on the San Antonio-El Paso road. By 1856, six stone barracks were added to house enlisted men, who spent much of their time escorting mail and freight trains through West Texas.

Texas seceded from the Union early in 1861, and Fort Davis was abandoned. Apaches wrecked the deserted fort, and by 1867, when federal troops returned to Fort Davis, little of value remained. Substantial rock and adobe buildings were eventually constructed to house up to 12 companies of cavalry and infantry, including black soldiers.

Of the fort's original 50 buildings, more than 20 have been restored, including officers' quarters, a small kitchen, a furnished commissary, and a hospital. Foundations outline the buildings that did not survive.

Half of the more than 50 original buildings at Fort Davis survive, making it the most outstanding example of an Indian Wars frontier fort.

◼ ◼ ◼

BUFFALO SOLDIERS

From 1867 to 1885, black regiments stationed at Fort Davis participated in the Indian Wars. The soldiers, most of whom were former slaves from southern plantations, worked long, hard hours for little pay and marginal living conditions, yet they had excellent morale.

The black regiments had fewer problems with alcoholism and desertion than the army did overall. They took part in most of the major military expeditions on the Texas frontier and earned a reputation as good soldiers among whites and Native Americans. The Apaches and Comanches called them "Buffalo Soldiers" because of their skin color.

Despite their notable military accomplishments on the Texas frontier, black soldiers didn't serve alongside white soldiers again until the Second World War.

Fort Raleigh
National Historic Site

At the site of England's mysterious "Lost Colony"

Many people mistakenly believe that Jamestown was the first English colony in what is now the United States, but the real site of the first colony was Roanoke Island, a place shrouded in mystery.

In the late 1500s, England tried settling North America. The first colony, at Roanoke Island, off the coast of what is now North Carolina, failed. In 1587, more than one hundred men, women, and children tried to start another colony on the island, under the leadership of John White.

Later that year, Virginia Dare, White's granddaughter and the first English child born in the New World, arrived. The colonists had settled in and planted crops, but White was afraid they would soon run out of provisions, so he returned to England. By the time he got back to Roanoke, in 1590, nothing was left of the colony. The only clue to the colonists' fate was a single word carved on a tree—Croatoan—the Indian name for the nearby island of Hatteras.

Before White sailed for England, the colonists had agreed that if they had to leave the fort, they would carve a Maltese cross above

In a quiet wooded area at the northern tip of Roanoke Island is the site of the first English colony in what is now the United States.

Extensive excavations in the 1930s and '40s revealed the original site of Fort Raleigh, which was reconstructed in 1950. Digs continue to reveal artifacts illuminating the lives of the first English colonists.

■ ■ ■

the name of their destination. No cross was carved on the tree. White returned to England in 1591 without discovering the whereabouts of his family and the other colonists. Archaeologists began excavating the site in the 1940s, but no graves, signs of a massacre, or other clues have surfaced to solve the mystery of the Lost Colony.

Today, Fort Raleigh's landscape is similar to what the colonists found when they landed here more than 400 years ago. The quiet, wooded site includes cedar, oak, holly, and other trees that may have been used by the colonists to build boats, houses, or furniture.

A nature trail winds through the 150-acre site, and a small earthen fort has been constructed the same way the original one was—by digging a moat and throwing the earth inward to form its walls. The fort is square with two pointed bastions on two sides and an octagonal bastion on the third. Historians think houses would have been built near the road leading from the fort entrance.

In addition to the original moat, excavations have turned up many artifacts, including a wrought-iron sickle, an Indian pipe, and metal counters used in accounting. A recent dig revealed what appears to be the remains of America's first scientific laboratory: pieces of smelted lead, pottery, crucible, charcoal, and distilling apparatus used in metallurgy.

Artifacts are displayed at the visitor center, which also includes exhibits on the colonists and Elizabethan life, plus copies of John White's watercolors. The Lost Colony presents the story of the Roanoke each summer through a combination of drama, music, and dance.

ELIZABETHAN GARDENS

Near Fort Raleigh, the Garden Club of North Carolina created the Elizabethan Gardens as a memorial to the first colonists.

The sixteenth-century formal gardens resemble those that graced the English estates of the wealthy backers of the colony. The gardens cover more than ten acres and include an antique statuary and other garden ornaments dating to the sixteenth century, a replica Tudor gate house, and a beautiful display of native and imported plants.

■ ■ ■

Jamestown
National Historic Site

The first English settlement in America

In the Age of Exploration, Europe was pushing westward toward the riches of the East when North America got in its way. Near the turn of the sixteenth century, England decided to colonize the new continent, not so much for the riches the New World might offer, but as a springboard to the Indies. In 1607, 13 years before the Pilgrims landed at Plymouth Rock, English settlers set foot in Virginia after more than four months at sea and settled Jamestown, the first permanent English settlement in America.

On a small, low island they built a stockaded, triangular fort and planted crops. Captain John Smith soon became the colony's leader, but he was badly injured in 1609 and returned to England. The colonists, now numbering 500, tried to stock up for the winter, but the Powhatan Indians prevented them from reaching their livestock, which was corralled outside the fortress. That winter was called the "Starving Time," and only 60 people remained alive by spring.

Despite these hardships, colonists continued to arrive at Jamestown. In 1619, the first Africans reached America as indentured servants. This was before the slave laws, which explains why they were allowed to buy their freedom and some land of their own. The colonists thought they could make a good living with a glassworks factory, but they hoped to find gold, too. The gold they eventually discovered was tobacco.

Nathaniel Bacon led the first American rebellion against royal

The foundations of many houses and buildings in America's first permanent settlement have been excavated and covered by a protective layer of brick.

The only original remains at Jamestown National Historic Site are those of the settlement's church.

Jamestown National Historic Site

Captain John Smith, leader of the first permanent settlement in America, kept Jamestown going despite hunger and hardship.

■ ■ ■

Opposite page (left): Nearby Jamestown Settlement, administered by the Jamestown-Yorktown Foundation, includes a re-creation of the settlers' first homes.

■ ■ ■

The only original remains at Jamestown National Historic Site are those of the settlement's church.

■ ■ ■

authority in Virginia in 1676, burning Jamestown in the process. Jamestown languished after that, and in 1699 a new capital was established at Williamsburg, marking the end of America's first permanent colonial town.

Little remains of the original settlement, preserved as Jamestown National Historic Site since 1940 and owned and administered by the Association for the Preservation of Virginia Antiquities. Two roads with markers loop through the 1,500 forested acres of Jamestown Island, which is little changed from the days of the colonists. The National Park Service maintains a visitor center containing a theater, museum, and exhibits at the edge of the original townsite. Paths lead from here to the remains of the city.

The only original seventeenth-century structure that remains is the Old Church Tower, now in ruins. Lines of bricks mark the foundations of the settlement's other buildings. In a reconstructed glasshouse, the first industry of Jamestown lives on as craftsmen demonstrate the art of glassblowing.

Near the Park Service site, but not part of it, is Jamestown Settlement, run by the Jamestown-Yorktown Foundation. Here, visitors can see re-creations of a Powhatan village, the palisaded settlement, and the three ships that brought the first English settlers to Jamestown.

AN INDIAN PRINCESS

America's first legend is the story of Captain John Smith and the Indian princess Pocahontas. Smith was on a surveying expedition in a remote area of Virginia when he was taken prisoner by a Powhatan hunting party. He delayed his execution by demonstrating the "magic" of his compass, and his captors brought him to their chief, also called Powhatan. According to Smith, the chief's daughter, nicknamed Pocahontas, or "playful one," saved his life by begging her father to let Smith go.

Captivated by the English settlement, Pocahontas visited it several times, and she saved all the colonists by warning them of a Powhatan plan to attack the fort. Later, she married a colonist named John Rolfe, resulting in several years of peaceful relations between the Powhatans and the colonists.

■ ■ ■

Jimmy Carter
National Historic Site

A small town that helped shape a President

The Jimmy Carter National Historic Site is dedicated as much to the thirty-ninth President as it is to the rural southern community that he was born and raised in and still calls home.

The residents of Carter's hometown were a bit surprised that one of their own would seek the presidency: "It was a little shocking that someone we knew wanted to be President, but if Jimmy wanted to be President, why not?" said Mrs. Maxine Reese, campaign manager at the headquarters in town.

Carter was born in Plains, Georgia, on October 1, 1924. He went to school and began his political career here. The historic site, established in 1988, includes some of the town sites associated with the former President, including the hospital where the President was born, brother Billy's gas station, and the Plains High School, a combined elementary and secondary school that Carter attended for 11 years.

The Plains Railroad Depot, formerly Carter's presidential campaign headquarters, serves as the visitor center. It contains photographs and a video on Carter's life and presidency. The Carter Boyhood Home and Farm, where Carter lived from age four until about 18, is three miles outside of Plains. Carter and his three younger siblings were brought up here with an appreciation for nature and a sense of responsibility cultivated by completing various assigned chores.

Jimmy Carter, who served as President from 1976 to 1980, continues to work for peace and human rights around the world.

The Plains railroad depot, which served as Carter's campaign headquarters, is now the visitor center at the Jimmy Carter National Historic Site.

Maggie L. Walker

National Historic Site

Honoring a black woman who rose to prominence

Maggie Lena Walker, daughter of a former slave, rose to prominence as a businesswoman, newspaper editor, and bank president, all at a time when women were denied the vote and married women couldn't own property.

Walker, born Maggie Mitchell in post-Civil War Richmond, Virginia, lost her father when she was young. Maggie had to help her mother do laundry to support the family, but she also was able to complete school and worked as a schoolteacher for three years until she married Armstead Walker, Jr.

When Maggie was 14, she joined a humanitarian organization called the Independent Order of St. Luke; 18 years later, she had worked her way up to the organization's top leadership position. In 1901, she established the *St. Luke Herald,* a newspaper for the black community of Richmond. Two years later, she established the St. Luke Penny Savings Bank and became the nation's first woman to serve as a bank president. The bank still thrives, having survived the Great Depression and the collapse of many savings and loans. Walker was an advocate of civil rights and helped organize the National Association for the Advancement of Colored People (NAACP).

Maggie Walker's home from 1904 until her death in 1934 has been preserved as the Maggie L. Walker National Historic Site since 1978. The 25-room house is furnished with original family pieces.

Maggie L. Walker, daughter of a former slave and the first female bank president in the United States, lived in this house from 1904 until her death in 1934.

153

Martin Luther King, Jr.

National Historic Site

The Atlanta neighborhood where the civil rights leader lived

When Martin Luther King, Jr., was a young man of 25 in 1954, he accepted a pastoral position in Montgomery, Alabama. A year later, an event took place that changed his life—and the lives of many other Americans—forever.

Rosa Parks was arrested for refusing to give up her bus seat to a white man, and King led the group that was organized to defend her. From that day on, he committed himself to the nonviolent struggle for civil rights. A religious man who practiced what he preached, he earned a doctorate in theology, studied Gandhi's teachings of nonviolence in India, and was eventually awarded a Nobel Peace Prize for his efforts on behalf of racial justice.

Dr. Martin Luther King, Jr., galvanized the struggle for civil rights while advocating social change through nonviolent action.

Made of Georgia white marble, the crypt of Dr. King sits on a concrete base in the reflecting pool of the Martin Luther King, Jr., Center for Non-Violent Social Change in Atlanta.

Located in a plaza across the street from the King Center is the "Behold" Monument, by Patrick Morelli. The statue is dedicated to Dr. King "for his moral courage and nobility of spirit."

■ ■ ■

As a child, King was shaped by the close-knit Atlanta neighborhood he grew up in. Auburn Avenue, where King lived, was the main thoroughfare of a prosperous black neighborhood. A ten-block stretch of that street is now preserved as the Martin Luther King, Jr., National Historic Site and includes several homes and businesses significant in King's life.

King was associate pastor of the Ebenezer Baptist Church, which is open to the public. The church offered spiritual guidance, but it also was dedicated "to the advancement of black people and support of every righteous and social movement." In 1957, King organized chapters of the Southern Christian Leadership Conference here. And it was here that King's body lay in state after he was assassinated in 1968. Thousands of mourners followed the mule-drawn wagon that carried his coffin from Ebenezer Church through the streets of the city. In 1974, King's mother was assassinated as she sat at the organ in the church.

King's boyhood home, which is also open to the public, is just down the street from the church. He was born in a back bedroom on the second floor of the handsome house at 501 Auburn Avenue. The residence has been carefully restored with 1930s furnishings to look as it did when King grew up here, attending a nearby all-black grade school.

A plaque by the door reads, "The successes, failures and injustices he witnessed as a young boy remained with him as he transcended this neighborhood to awaken the social conscience of a nation."

A DREAM FOR ALL HUMANITY

"I have a dream that one day on the red hills of Georgia, sons of former slaves and the sons of former slave owners will be able to sit down together at the table of brotherhood...."

On August 28, 1963, more than 200,000 people participated in a "March on Washington" to dramatize the sorry state of race relations in the United States.

It was there, at the Lincoln Memorial, that Martin Luther King, Jr., uplifted the crowd with his now famous "I Have A Dream" speech.

The rising tide of the civil rights movement, which enjoyed one of its shining moments that day, had a strong effect on national opinion, eventually resulting in the Civil Rights Act of 1964.

■ ■ ■

Ninety Six

National Historic Site

A British stronghold destroyed by patriots

The village of Ninety Six in South Carolina is said to have gotten its name from the distance it lay from the Cherokee town of Keowee. The trail between the two villages was a busy trade route, and by the beginning of the Revolutionary War, Ninety Six was a thriving trading post.

On November 18, 1775, 1,800 loyalists attacked a force of less than 600 patriots gathered there in the first major land battle in the South. The two sides fought to a standoff and declared a truce, but the next six years were marked by fierce factional fighting.

The most famous confrontation was a siege that took place in the spring of 1781. Ninety Six had become an important British stronghold, garrisoned by 550 seasoned loyalists and protected by a stockade fort on one side and an earthen "star" fort on the other. Patriot General Nathanael Greene arrived with more than 1,000 men and began to lay siege to the town. Word came shortly that a large relief force of British soldiers was on its way to aid the besieged loyalists, and Greene decided to storm the post before he was trapped by the approaching army.

The general divided his forces between the stockade fort on the west and the star fort on the east, attacking both simultaneously. The west contingent fought their way into the stockade fort, but the troops attacking the star fort met fierce resistance and were repelled after heavy casualties on both sides. With time running out, Greene removed his troops under darkness. Though technically they had failed in their mission, Greene and his men had so damaged the fort that it was abandoned by the British a few weeks later.

In the early months of the Revolutionary War, the village of Ninety Six was the scene of several confrontations between loyalists and patriots. Historical reenactments keep the war alive today.

Palo Alto Battlefield

National Historic Site

Where our war with Mexico was launched

Palo Alto Battlefield National Historic Site in Texas, the only site in the entire National Park System dedicated to the Mexican-American War, presents both nations' perspectives on the battle over a boundary.

In 1845, when Texas entered the Union, it brought with it a boundary dispute with Mexico. On May 13, 1846, President James K. Polk declared war, and the first battle of the Mexican-American War was fought on the plains of Palo Alto. General Zachary Taylor's troops met about 4,000 Mexican soldiers armed with dated cannons and ammunition. The cannonballs fired at the American troops traveled so slowly that U.S. soldiers simply side-stepped the incoming rounds. With the help of newly manufactured cannons that fired farther and faster than the Mexican arms, the United States Army pushed back the Mexican troops.

This victory and others paved the way for U.S. invasion and occupation of the northeastern portion of Mexico, south of the Rio Grande. The war ended on February 2, 1848, with the Treaty of Guadalupe Hidalgo, which expanded the United States by more than half a million square miles. Surrender of California and New Mexico territories in addition to the disputed border cost Mexico half of its territory.

All land within the 3,400-acre park, authorized in 1978, is under private ownership, and the site is not yet open to the public.

The first battle of the 1846-48 Mexican War took place on the plains of Palo Alto, now preserved as the Palo Alto Battlefield National Historic Site.

Tuskegee Institute

National Historic Site

Famous black university founded by an ex-slave

Tuskegee Institute in Alabama is among the nation's most prestigious institutions of higher education. It is also a national historic site honoring the ambition and dedication of the school's founder, Booker T. Washington.

In 1881, Washington, a former slave, founded the first secondary and teacher-training school for African Americans with an enrollment of just 30 students. A year later, students literally built the school, bricks and all, and students who couldn't afford tuition worked their way through school. Washington believed in learning by doing.

Though not all black leaders agreed with the philosophy, the Tuskegee Institute was designed to teach blacks practical skills like agriculture, building, and basket weaving. Still, it attracted young scholars like George Washington Carver, another former slave, who

Tuskegee Institute was founded in 1881 to teach black students practical skills, such as agriculture and construction. Many of the buildings on campus today were actually built by students.

Carver's home, The Oaks, was built by students in 1899. The house was designed by R. R. Taylor, the first African-American graduate of MIT and a Tuskegee professor.

■ ■ ■

In 1938 the school honored George Washington Carver, head of the agriculture department, by establishing this museum. On exhibit are Carver's plant collections, as well as his paintings and needlework.

■ ■ ■

carried out his well-known agricultural research there. The school was especially successful at training teachers, many of whom returned to the plantation areas of the South to educate other blacks. The institute evolved into a degree-granting college in 1927.

The functioning campus comprises some 160 buildings, including several of the original structures built with student-made bricks. The George Washington Carver Museum, which also houses the visitor orientation center, features exhibits relating to Carver's varied talents, including plant collections, art, and needlework. Washington's campus home, The Oaks, which was built by students in 1809, is open for tours.

Buck Island Reef
National Monument

One of the nation's few underwater parks

Buck Island Reef National Monument, one of the nation's few underwater parks, combines a barrier island and one of the Caribbean's most beautiful barrier reefs. Part of the Virgin Islands, the 880-acre monument, which lies just north of St. Croix, includes 176 acres of land and 704 acres of water, offering visitors an opportunity to explore two fascinating worlds.

An underwater snorkeling trail, complete with easy-to-read interpretive signs, meanders through a vibrant coral forest of trees, branches, and spires. Elkhorn coral-patch reefs rise like haystacks as high as 40 feet. Purple sea fans sway lazily in the current, and multicolored sponges cling to the corals.

Visitors can swim through this underwater fantasyland accompanied by schools of electric blue and yellow fish and other weird sea creatures. Parrot fish munch on live coral, sea snails creep along the reef, and spiny lobsters hide among the coral, waiting for night to come out to feed.

Many other marine animals thrive in the warm waters of the Caribbean Islands, including three endangered sea turtles: hawksbill, leatherback, and green. The turtles return to Buck Island every two to three years to nest in shoreline forests and on beaches.

Buck Island Reef National Monument, one of the nation's few underwater marine parks, can only be reached by boat.

Buck Island Reef provides some of the most spectacular snorkeling in the Caribbean. A snorkel trail with underwater interpretive signs leads divers through coral reefs.

The coral barrier reef nearly surrounds Buck Island, a tropical dry forest that is 6,000 feet long and half a mile wide. The island has an impressive variety of plant life, nicely complementing the water's dazzling display of animal life. The 228 species of plants and trees include giant tamarind trees, thorny acacias, and guinea grass.

A nature trail loops along the island's crest, then continues south through frangipani trees, organ-pipe cactus, Ginger Thomas, and bromeliads. A side trail takes visitors to an observation point with splendid views of the coral reef and nearby St. Croix. The island, like the sea, supports a variety of animal life, including endangered brown pelicans, threatened least terns, hummingbirds, and lizards.

A DIVERSE ECOSYSTEM

Living coral reefs are the world's most diverse marine ecosystems. Though they may look like geological formations, the reefs are actually complex colonies of individual animals called polyps.

Like underwater construction workers, these tiny animals build the reefs by attaching themselves to the hard skeletons of their predecessors, then producing their own limestone skeletons. The fragile coral structure expands as new polyps constantly grow on the old, their skeletons cemented together by blue-green algae.

Coral reefs, which have existed for millions of years, only grow in tropical waters where sea temperatures are more than 70 degrees year-round. Unfortunately, pollution, overfishing, warming of the seas, boat damage, and other factors are causing coral reefs around the world to disappear.

Christiansted

National Historic Site

Recalling Danish rule of St. Croix Island

The elegant buildings and eighteenth-century fort along the waterfront on St. Croix Island provide a link to the days when sugar was king and the Danes ruled the area we now call the Virgin Islands.

Nearly 250 years after Columbus came upon an island in the New World and named it Santa Cruz, the Danish West India & Guinea Company bought St. Croix from the French and began planting sugar. Dozens of sugar factories sprang up, and the settlement of Christiansted was established in honor of King Christian VI. The population soon reached 10,000, of which nearly 9,000 were slaves imported from West Africa.

The Christiansted National Historic Site preserves seven historic buildings, including the Danish West India & Guinea Company Warehouse, built in 1749. That same year, a fort was completed to protect the new town from pirates, privateers, and slave uprisings.

The island's first governor, Frederick Moth, envisioned a town with boulevards, promenades, and handsome buildings, like the beautiful city Christiania (now Oslo, Norway). The graceful archi-

Opposite page: *Fort Christiansvaern, completed in 1749 with additions in 1835–41, is the best-preserved of the Virgin Island fortifications.*

The Danish West India & Guinea Company bought St. Croix from France in 1733. For their first settlement on the island, the Danes chose a protected harbor on the northeast coast.

CLASH OF CULTURES

The first skirmish between Europeans and native people of the New World took place in the water just off St. Croix.

Columbus reached the island on his second voyage in 1493 and named it Santa Cruz (Holy Cross). He saw that the island was inhabited, so he sent some crew members to shore to "have speech with the natives."

A canoe of Caribs met the boat, but attempts at communication failed, and a fight soon broke out. The Spaniards, two of whom were wounded, killed one Carib and took the rest captive.

tecture, spacious interiors, and arcaded sidewalks in Christiansted reflect Moth's vision and the growing wealth of the citizenry.

Between 1760 and 1820 the economy boomed. St. Croix became the capital of the "Danish Islands in America" and home to royal governors. The Government House, completed in the 1830s for governors to conduct business and hold receptions, has been restored to its 1840s appearance. At the 1830 Customs House, the government collected duties on imports and exports after they were inspected and weighed in the Scale House.

Two churches, the Lutheran Church built in 1744 and the Steeple Building from 1753, still grace the waterfront. The Steeple Building now houses a museum, which contains one of the largest archaeological collections in the Caribbean.

By 1848, the island's golden years were coming to an end. Natural disasters, competition from beet sugar, and the abolishment of slavery all contributed to the economic collapse of St. Croix.

Christiansted National Historic Site preserves the picturesque architecture from the turn of the nineteenth century when St. Croix was a colony of Denmark.

San Juan
National Historic Site

Spain's formidable New World fortresses

San Juan National Historic Site traces its history back to the days just after Columbus sailed into the Caribbean and claimed the land for Spain.

Shortly thereafter, in about 1508, Ponce de Leon built the first settlement on Puerto Rico near what is now known as San Juan Harbor. Spain built a rich empire in the New World, and the harbor became a trading center for gold, silver, pearls, and other riches.

No ship or settlement in the Caribbean was safe from attack, so Spain built massive forts at San Juan Harbor to protect the whole island. The Park Service site contains three forts and the city walls of Old San Juan. These are some of the oldest European structures in the Americas.

The first and most formidable of these fortresses is the 350-year-old El Morro Castle, begun in 1539 to protect the harbor entrance with

The bright stonework of the San Juan cemetery and chapel contrasts sharply with the ancient walls of Old San Juan.

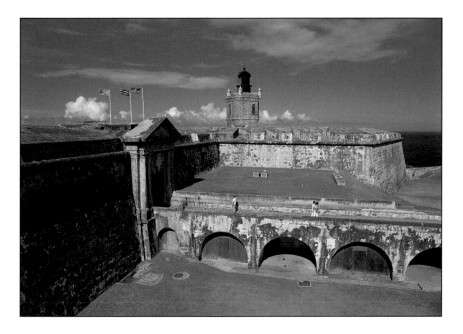

The oldest fort on United States soil, El Morro once represented Spain's might in the New World. Indian slaves laid the first stone blocks of the fort around 1539.

■ ■ ■

Opposite page: The scarred walls and turrets of El Morro Castle have guarded San Juan for more than 450 years, surviving cannon fire, earthquakes, and hurricanes.

■ ■ ■

firepower. Its tiered walls are 20 feet thick and rise 140 feet above the sea. Inside the bombproof walls are barracks, cisterns, supply and storage rooms, dungeons, a chapel, an armory, and offices.

A second fort, San Cristobal, was begun about 1634. It was designed to defend the city from attacks coming from inland and the north coast, following a surprise English land attack in 1598 and the burning of the city by the Dutch in 1625. The fort was completed between 1766 and 1783, and a century later one of its guns fired the first shot of the Spanish-American War in Puerto Rico. It covers 27 acres and has five structures connected by tunnels. Today it houses the site's visitor center and exhibits.

The third and smallest fort is El Canuelo on Cabras Island, opposite El Morro. Its role was to prevent attacks on the western side of the harbor. The original wood fort, built in 1610 on the site, burned during the Dutch attack of 1625. It was replaced by the present stone fortress in the 1660s.

The ancient walls of Old San Juan, constructed of 40-foot-high blocks of solid sandstone, hug the coastline in both directions from El Morro, part of the strong ring of battlements and walls that protected the ancient city. Founded in 1521, the city now is a mixture of modern buildings and historic houses, making it a New World city with Old World charm.

THE END OF SPANISH RULE

Spain's four-century rule of San Juan Island ended when it turned over its forts to the United States on October 18, 1898.

Earlier that century, the Spanish colonies in the New World had gained independence, leaving only Cuba and Puerto Rico as remnants of Spain's once mighty empire.

The Spanish-American War followed a revolution in Cuba. San Juan's forts were bombarded on May 12, 1898, but the defenses survived with no serious damage. Two months later the U.S. forces landed on the southern coast of Puerto Rico, but by that time an armistice had been negotiated, and San Juan changed hands peacefully.

■ ■ ■

The Middle West
National Monuments and Historic Sites

*I*n the mid-1800s, the Midwest was the gateway to the vast, unknown frontier. In the land west of St. Louis, where woodlands and prairies gave way to the seemingly unending plains, a great clash of cultures took place as white settlers pushed ever farther westward.

The historical drama of this region is preserved in the artifacts and earthen dwellings of American Indians, the outposts of the fur trade, the weathered homesteads and rutted wagon trails, and the battlefields of the Indian wars. It is also the scene of another kind of battle—a legal and moral one—played out at a grammar school in Kansas. Though the Midwest is often overlooked by tourists who expect more action on the coasts, its history is anything but dull.

Rising 800 feet above Nebraska's North Platte Valley, Scotts Bluff was an important landmark for travelers on the Oregon Trail.

Abraham Lincoln raised his family in this Greek Revival House, located in Springfield, Illinois. It was the only house the Lincolns ever owned.

Agate Fossil Beds

National Monument

An amazing concentration of ancient skeletons

Under the grass-covered hills along the Niobrara River in western Nebraska, sedimentary beds contain a rich concentration of 19-million-year-old fossils. Captain James Cook discovered the fossil beds in 1878 and acquired the site, called Agate Springs Ranch. Since then, fossil bones from the site have been exhibited around the world, and in 1965 the ranch was made a national monument.

At the beginning of this century, the ranch became a headquarters for two noted paleontologists. In 1904, O. A. Peterson from the Carnegie Museum began the first scientific excavations on a hill overlooking the site. The next year, Professor E. H. Barbour from the University of Nebraska excavated an adjacent hill. Their respective domains became known as Carnegie and University hills.

The paleontologists found dozens of skeletons in their excavations, including a small type of rhinoceros that was new to science. The site is probably an ancient waterhole where thousands of these drought-stricken animals, and various other species, died. Perhaps the strangest-looking creature was the Moropus, a heavily built mammal with the head of a horse, neck of a giraffe, torso of a tapir, front legs of a rhinoceros, and hind legs of a bear. The ferocious Dinohyus, or "Terrible Pig," was a monstrous beast more than seven feet tall and ten feet long.

A paved interpretive trail leads to quarry sites on

The frozen Niobrara River lies 200 feet below the summits of Carnegie and University Hills, both of which contain a rich concentration of 19-million-year-old fossils.

The monument's first fossils were extracted from University Hill in 1905. Paved interpretive trails connect quarry sites today.

Carnegie and University hills where the fossil layer is partially exposed, allowing visitors to see the fossil bones of ancient mammals in their natural state. Another trail leads to two sites that contain "devil's corkscrews," fossils that initially confounded paleontologists. The corkscrews turned out to be fossilized burrows built by palaeocastors, ancient beavers who were more like prairie dogs than modern-day beavers.

Except for livestock grazing the hills, the surrounding landscape is relatively wild, inhabited by mule deer, pronghorns, coyotes, and other animals. Cottonwoods and willows follow the river through the flat, open valley, which is carpeted with grasses and wildflowers.

Effigy Mounds

National Monument

Prehistoric burial sites of Woodland Indians

High above the Mississippi, earthen mounds in the shape of birds, bears, and simple cones mark the once-flourishing Woodland Culture of the Upper Mississippi River Valley.

From 500 B.C. to A.D. 1300, Woodland Culture Indians, who were hunters and gatherers, lived in this area. They collected wild rice, nuts, fruits, berries, and freshwater mussels, and their prey included deer, bear, and bison. Like other Indians of their age, these prehistoric people also built distinctive burial mounds.

While many of the mounds have been lost, northeastern Iowa's Effigy Mounds National Monument, proclaimed in 1949, preserves

Woodland Indians lived along the bluffs of the Mississippi River in northeast Iowa from around 500 B.C. until the fourteenth century.

Along Pleasant Ridge are ten effigy bear mounds, each about three feet high and 80 to 100 feet long.

LOST AND FOUND

The first written mention of the Effigy Mounds area appeared in Jonathan Carver's *Travels Through the Interior Parts of North America in the Years 1766, 1767, 1768*. For nearly a century after that, the mounds on the bluff tops and in the valley received little attention.

In 1881, however, Theodore H. Lewis and Alfred J. Hill began an ambitious survey of the mound groups of the Mississippi River Valley. Their surveys produced excellent maps of the mounds, several of which, such as the Marching Bear Group, are now part of the monument.

■ ■ ■

Though prehistoric Americans built burial mounds in various places, they only built them in the shapes of birds and other animals in southern Wisconsin and adjacent areas in Illinois, Minnesota, and Iowa.

■ ■ ■

The upper Mississippi River Valley as seen from Eagle Rock. A self-guided tour of the major mounds leads visitors past several scenic overlooks.

■ ■ ■

191 known prehistoric mounds. A self-guiding walk leads visitors past major features within the monument, including Little Bear Mound and scenic overlooks of the Mississippi River. Great Bear Mound, the most monumental of the animal forms here, is 70 feet across the shoulders, 137 feet long, and 3½ feet high. The Marching Bear Group consists of ten bears, along with several bird mounds, high atop 300-foot-high bluffs.

The mounds do contain burials, as well as artifacts, including copper beads, chipped blades, and stone and shell ornaments, indicating that the Woodland Culture was part of an extensive trade network.

George Washington Carver

National Monument

The farm where the educator grew up

George Washington Carver National Monument was one of the first national park sites to highlight the life and work of a black American. The site preserves the farm where Carver grew up and includes a museum with displays and films about Carver's boyhood.

A successful educator, botanist, agronomist, and artist, Carver was born a slave on the Moses Carver farm in southwest Missouri in the early 1860s. The log cabin in which he was born was destroyed by a storm, but a log outline marks its location. As a baby, Carver and his mother were kidnapped by a band of Confederate soldiers. Carver was eventually found in Arkansas and returned to the farm, but he never saw his mother again.

Carver and his brother Jim were raised by Moses and Susan Carver as members of the family. Carver was a frail child who was often excused from doing the daily chores. With time on his hands, he would wander "day after day...in the woods alone in order to collect my floral beauties and put them in my little garden I had hidden in brush...." Because of his skill with flowers, neighbors began call-

George Washington Carver became interested in gardening and native plants as a boy. Carver went on to become the director of agricultural studies at Tuskegee Institute in Alabama.

The George Washington Carver National Monument includes a partially reconstructed log cabin marking the probable location of the cabin where the famous scientist and educator was born.

175

HELPING POOR FARMERS

In the South, many poor, one-horse farmers were bound to land that was exhausted from cotton production. George Washington Carver wanted to help these farmers by teaching them about soil-enhancing, protein-rich crops like soybeans and peanuts.

To do so, he passed out free, easy-to-read bulletins with information on crops and cultivation techniques, as well as recipes for nutritious meals.

Carver's work helped boost the regional economy and the future of black farmers.

ing him "the Plant Doctor." Today, a self-guided nature trail winds through the woods where Carver developed his love for plants.

Carver's 20-year struggle for formal education began when he was a boy. He was not allowed to attend the local church school, so at the age of 12 he moved to a nearby town to go to a school for blacks. The struggle paid off, and Carver eventually became a research botanist at Iowa Agricultural College (now Iowa State).

He left that promising career to work with Booker T. Washington at Tuskegee Institute in Alabama, a somewhat risky move since it was not considered a very prestigious university at the time. There he taught botany and agriculture to the children of ex-slaves while developing practical new farming techniques.

Moses and Susan Carver, who lived in this Missouri farmhouse, raised George Washington Carver after his mother was kidnapped during the Civil War.

Grand Portage
National Monument

Where the voyageurs met to trade and brawl

Centuries ago, hardy French-Canadian fur traders paddled 16 hours a day and carried their canoes and hundred of pounds of goods across land trails, often while singing nostalgic French songs.

Each July, hundreds of these voyageurs converged on the North West Company's headquarters on the western shore of Lake Superior to trade, eat, brawl, and party. The wooden buildings of the post, built in the late 1700s, have been reconstructed by the National Park Service as part of Grand Portage National Monument.

A water highway linked Montreal, capital city of the Great Lakes fur trade, with fur-rich northwestern Canada. Where streams were unnavigable, voyageurs carried their canoes and cargo over a "portage" or trail. Grand Portage, the "Great Carrying Place," by-

Each July, more than a thousand voyageurs met at the British Northwest Company stockade to trade, drink, and party in the Great Hall.

VOYAGEUR RENDEZVOUS

In 1793, a North West Company trader named John Macdonell wrote one of the few known descriptions of the busy Grand Portage post during its heyday, offering a glimpse into life at the annual rendezvous.

He wrote that the "North Men [those who spent winters west of Lake Superior] . . . while here live in tents of different sizes pitched at random, the people of each post having a camp by themselves, and through their camp passes the road of the portage." The more frugal "Pork-eaters" (the Montreal men) slept under their canoes.

As for the stockade, "the Gates are shut always after sunset, and the Bourgeois and clerks Lodge in houses within the pallisades, where there are two Sentries keeping a look out all night, chiefly for fear of accident by fire."

passed rapids on the lower Pigeon River and was an ideal spot for the company's headquarters.

From 1784 to 1803, Grand Portage was the largest and most profitable fur-trading post on the Great Lakes. After a harsh, lonely winter in the wilderness, fur traders greatly enjoyed the headquarters' plentiful food and free-flowing liquor, often spending what they had just received for the past year's work. They feasted and danced each day until daybreak before taking up their paddles and heading out for another season of travel and trapping.

The Great Hall, furnished in 1797 style, is where the traders talked business by day and celebrated all night. Food was prepared in the kitchen to the rear of the hall. The stockade, constructed from cedar pickets, was the business office of the company. At the fur press, bulky beaver pelts were compacted and tied into neat 90-bound bales. Outside the stockade is a warehouse that now exhibits historic items, including two authentic birchbark canoes.

The nine-mile portage past the rapids is open to hikers and cross-country skiers. The scenery along the trail, shaded by spruce, maple, aspen, and other trees, is little changed from the days when voyageurs passed through carrying their heavy loads.

Today, visitors can hike or ski along the trails that voyageurs walked, carrying canoes and hundreds of pounds of trade goods.

Homestead
National Monument of America

A tribute to those who settled the Great Plains

Tucked away in a grassy corner of southeastern Nebraska is Homestead National Monument of America, site of one of the first claims staked under the Homestead Act of 1862. The quiet, 160-acre site preserves a small remnant of the streamside woods and tall-grass prairie that pioneers encountered on the Great Plains.

Daniel and Agnes Freeman claimed the quarter-section and began to "improve" the land, as the Act directed. They busted sod, cultivated the land, and built a brick schoolhouse. After five years of hard work, the land was theirs.

The one-room schoolhouse, built in 1871, still stands. It was used until 1967 and also served as a church and polling place. In 1899, Daniel Freeman took the school board to court because the teacher was giving Bible lessons at school. The case went all the way to the Nebraska Supreme Court, which ruled in Freeman's favor, upholding the principle of separation of church and state.

The site also contains the Palmer-Epard cabin, relocated to the monument from a nearby homestead. Built in 1867, it is typical of frontier houses in the region, erected when timber was available. When it wasn't, homesteaders cut blocks of densely packed sod to construct homes called "soddies," or they lived in hillside dugouts.

A 2½-mile trail winds through the restored prairie and past the Freeman family cemetery.

Log homes like the Palmer-Epard Cabin were typical of those in eastern Nebraska during the homesteading era. The cabin was built in 1867 of mixed hardwoods and homemade bricks set in lime mortar.

Jewel Cave
National Monument

A hidden world of fascinating formations

Hidden beneath the Black Hills of South Dakota is the subterranean world of Jewel Cave, where countless crystal formations sparkle with the brilliance of gems. When Jewel Cave National Monument was proclaimed in 1908, less than half a mile of cave had been discovered. Explorations in the past 30 years have revealed more than 100 miles of twisting and turning passages, making it the fourth-longest known cave in the world.

The cave began forming millions of years ago as the Black Hills were being created. The forces that uplifted mountains also created faults in the earth. Beginning 30 to 50 million years ago, slightly acidic water seeping into these cracks and crevices dissolved the surrounding limestone and hollowed out the passages of Jewel Cave. When the water table lowered, caverns lined with a variety of formations remained. The process continues today, as water seeping into the cave alters its delicate formations.

Many of Jewel Cave's formations were formed as water trickling into the cave left behind tiny deposits of minerals. Formations called stalactites hang like icicles from the ceilings, while stalagmites reach up from the floors. Where they meet, columns and pillars divide the chambers. Water trickling down slanted ceilings created formations that look like draperies, some 30 feet long. Other formations are more mysterious. Hydromagnesite balloons—tiny silver bubbles that are found in few other caves—have yet to be explained.

Jewel Cave's spectacular formations—including this one, known as Thunderhead Dome—were formed over a period of millions of years as water gradually seeped through faults in the earth's crust.

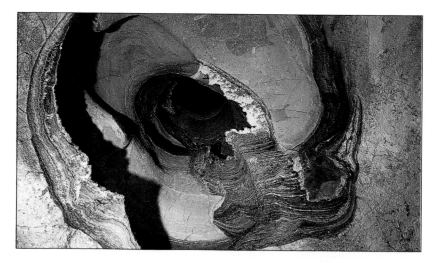

The same geological forces that created the rugged Black Hills of South Dakota left faults in the earth that eventually formed Jewel Cave.

The most abundant formations, and the ones for which Jewel Cave is named, are the jewellike crystals of calcite known as dogtooth spar and nailhead spar. Jewel Cave has the most extensive collection of calcite crystals known, coating nearly every chamber wall with layers six inches thick. Some are translucent, formed only of pure calcite. Others contain additional minerals and appear yellow, red, or opaque white. Individual crystals can be as tiny as a grain of rice or as large as a goose egg.

Though much of the cave is closed to the public because of its scientific value, several trails allow visitors to see the formations up close. The scenic tour leads through much-decorated rooms featuring sparkling calcite crystals and colorful stalactites, stalagmites, and draperies. The historic trail follows the paths of early cave explorers, and the formations are illuminated by old-style candle lanterns. A spelunking tour provides the chance to explore the wild, undeveloped portions of Jewel Cave.

Above ground is a ponderosa pine forest, home to whitetail deer, elk, marmots, golden eagles, and many other species. Hiking trails through the monument's two square miles allow visitors to sample the rugged hills, canyons, and prairies of the Black Hills.

NATURAL CAVE ART

Jewel Cave contains some of the world's most rare and unusual formations. Helictites, small formations made of calcite, twist and turn as though they were formed in a chamber without gravity. Another calcite formation, called popcorn, grows in small knobby clusters. Veins of calcite deposited in a crisscross pattern are called boxwork. Frostwork, needle-like formations of calcite or aragonite, are as delicate as blown glass.

Flowers, needles, spiders, and cottony beards of the mineral gypsum also decorate the cave. Underground sparklers called scintillites are composed of the reddish rock called chert coated with sparkling clear quartz crystals. These formations were unknown until discovered in Jewel Cave.

Pipestone
National Monument

The sacred quarries of the Plains Indians

O n the western slope of the Coteau des Prairie in south-western Minnesota are quarries of a unique soft stone, ranging in color from mottled pink to brick red, that is considered sacred to the Plains Indians.

According to Indian legend, the people of the Plains were made from the stone. Sioux, Crow, Blackfoot, and Pawnee people carved ceremonial pipes from the substance to communicate with the spiritual world. But they also used the pipes to connect with other tribes—and whites—through trade.

Plains Indians probably began digging at this quarry in the seventeenth century, when they acquired metal tools from European traders. The durable yet soft stone was perfect for carving, and this location was apparently the best source for pipestone. The quarries were used by tribes across the prairie, though by about 1700 the Dakota Sioux controlled the quarries, and other tribes had to trade for the pipestone. Archaeologists have discovered pipestone pipes thousands of miles from this area.

Plains Indians smoked tobacco in these red clay pipes to mark important activities, such as preparing for war, trading goods and hostages, and ritual dancing. The pipes and tobacco were stored in animal-skin pouches with

A trail past the quarries at Pipestone National Monument leads to Pipestone Creek and Winnewissa Falls.

Native Americans continue to quarry pipestone to make crafts for ceremonial use and for sale. The Sioux traditionally leave an offering of tobacco and food as thanks for the sacred stone.

other sacred objects, and even the ashes were disposed of in special places. Pipes were valued possessions and were often buried with the dead.

Pipestone pipes were carved in a variety of shapes, and their evolution parallels the Plains Indian culture in transition. The simple tube shape of earlier carvers developed into elbow and disk forms and more elaborate animal and human effigies. The T-shaped calumets, a popular form, were widely known as "peace pipes" because they were the pipes white Americans usually saw at peace ceremonies. Effigies in the shape of white politicians and explorers, some far from flattering, attest to the Plains Indians' increasing contact with whites.

The Sioux lost control of the pipestone quarries in 1928. Pipestone National Monument was created in 1937 and opened to the public, though only Indians are allowed to mine the sacred stone. Fall is the best time to see this ancient tradition taking place.

The Upper Midwest Indian Cultural Center in the visitor center sponsors demonstrations of pipemaking using stone from this quarry. It also sells pipes, beadwork and quillwork, and pottery. A three-quarter-mile self-guiding trail loops past the exposed red rock of the quarries and through the tall grasses of the virgin prairie, still used by Indians for cultural and religious activities.

Scotts Bluff
National Monument

A prominent landmark for early travelers

Rising 800 feet above the plains in the Nebraska panhandle, Scotts Bluff served as a prominent landmark for early travelers. The massive promontory is a cross-section of high plains that formed in the continent's interior after the uplifting of the Rocky Mountains.

Four or five million years ago, the land began to erode at a relatively fast rate, but certain concretions, in isolated patches near the surface, were more durable than the surrounding materials. This protective top, known as caprock, has kept Scotts Bluff from eroding away. Fossils of huge turtles, rhinoceri, camels, and mammoths imbedded in the bluff attest to the rich diversity of animal life once found here.

Plains hunters camped in the vicinity as far back as 5,000 to 10,000 years ago. Indians called the craggy bluff *Me-a-pa-te,* meaning "hill that is hard to go around."

In the early 1800s, fur traders began to pass by the monument. The bluff is named after a fur trader named Hiram Scott, whose skeleton was discovered nearby in 1828. The first wagons took the overland route that would become known as the Oregon Trail in 1843. Thousands made their way past Scotts Bluff, some pausing to carve their names into the soft sandstone.

The 2,998-acre monument includes a visitor center, museum complex, and a short segment of the actual Oregon Trail.

Scotts Bluff was a prominent landmark for generations of travelers. When pioneers reached the bluff, they knew that at least one third of the trail to the West Coast lay behind them.

Scotts Bluff is just one of a series of curious landforms south of the North Platte River in western Nebraska.

Abraham Lincoln Birthplace

National Historic Site

A grand memorial to a great President

Fifty-six steps, one for each year in Lincoln's life, lead to the entrance of a granite temple at the Abraham Lincoln Birthplace National Historic Site, established in 1916. Enshrined in the temple is a one-room log cabin.

Around the turn of the century, a group of famous benefactors, including Mark Twain and William Jennings Bryan, raised money to buy the farm where Lincoln was born, as well as a log cabin that had been part of a traveling exhibit, and built the memorial to house it. Though it appears now that this was not the cabin Lincoln was born in, it is representative of the sixteenth President's humble beginnings.

Abraham Lincoln was born in 1809 in a log cabin near Sinking Spring on the family's farm. The spring provided reliable water, but the red clay and stony ground of the farm were not very fertile. The Lincolns' cabin was probably a typical frontier home of the time—approximately 18 by 16 feet with a dirt floor, one window and one door, a small fireplace, and a shingled roof. Greased paper, animal skin, or an old quilt may have hung over the window to keep out insects and cold wind.

The visitor center has a museum about Lincoln, which includes a copy of the family Bible. Several hiking trails in the 116-acre park lead through the fields and woods of Lincoln's birthplace.

Located in Hodgenville, Kentucky, the stately granite memorial contains a nineteenth-century log cabin once thought to be Abraham Lincoln's birthplace.

Brown v. Board of Education

National Historic Site

A milestone in the fight for equality

*I*n September of 1950, Linda Brown was denied admission to Sumner Elementary, an all-white school near her home in Topeka, Kansas. Instead, she was forced to travel nearly three miles to attend Monroe Elementary, one of three all-black schools in the Midwestern city.

A year later, her father, Oliver Brown, and 12 other plaintiffs went before the U.S. District Court of Kansas to challenge an 1879 Kansas law that permitted segregated elementary schools. They lost the case, but Thurgood Marshall, an attorney for the National Association for the Advancement of Colored People (NAACP), argued their appeal before the U.S. Supreme Court in December of 1952. Two years later, the Supreme Court ruled unanimously that "separate but equal" had no place in the American public education system.

The National Park Service preserves Monroe Elementary and other sites that were central to the Supreme Court's landmark decision in Brown v. Board of Education.

■ ■ ■

That decision, which many point to as the beginning of the civil rights movement, is honored at the Brown v. Board of Education National Historic Site. The focal point of the site is Monroe Elementary at 1515 Monroe Street. Declining enrollment forced the school to close in 1975, but since then, it has undergone renovations. Most of the original wooden doors, floors, and paneling in the school have survived. Sumner School is still an operating elementary school. The site was designated in 1992, nearly 40 years after the landmark ruling. It is not open to the public, although visits may be arranged with advance notice.

THE COURT'S OPINION

When the U.S. Supreme Court issued its historic ruling on the Brown v. Board of Education case, Chief Justice Earl Warren stated that, in the Court's opinion, education is the very foundation of good citizenship:

"Today it is a principal instrument in awakening the child to cultural values, in preparing him for later professional training, and in helping him to adjust normally to his environment. In these days, it is doubtful that any child may reasonably be expected to succeed in this life if he is denied the opportunity of an education. Such an opportunity...is a right (that) must be made available to all on equal terms."

■ ■ ■

Chicago Portage
National Historic Site

A key water route found by French explorers

In 1673, Indian guides showed French explorers Louis Joliet and Jacques Marquette a short land route, or portage, that connected the Great Lakes with the Mississippi River System, revealing one of the key water routes across the continent and ultimately establishing Chicago as a major trade center.

A memorial to that important discovery, the Chicago Portage National Historic Site, established in 1952, preserves that vital link as part of the I & M Canal National Heritage Corridor.

Marquette and Joliet paddled their canoes up the Illinois and Des Plaines Rivers to Portage Creek, where they carried their goods and canoes about a mile and a half to the Chicago River and continued to Lake Michigan. Joliet immediately envisioned a canal connecting the two waterways to bypass the portage.

It wasn't until 1848 that the Illinois and Michigan Canal was completed, linking the Chicago River at Bridgeport to the Illinois River at La Salle. Despite competition from railroads, the canal was a successful commercial route and helped spur the growth of Fort Dearborn into the metropolis that Chicago is today.

The Forest Preserve District of Cook County is developing the site. At present, a marker and 20-foot statue commemorate Marquette and Joliet and their Indian guides. Visitors can follow the portage trail used by the explorers along a sandy ridge in Ottawa Trail Woods to the site of Laughton's Trading Post, where Indians and traders bartered their goods.

A monument at the Chicago Portage National Historic Site honors the French explorers Marquette and Joliet and their Indian guides, who discovered the portage connecting the Great Lakes with the Mississippi River system in 1673.

Chimney Rock

National Historic Site

A famous landmark on the Oregon Trail

An estimated 300,000 pioneers followed the Oregon Trail west to start new lives. The route, which typically took several months to travel, became the single greatest path for western expansion.

Along the way, travelers could see a tall spire of rock rising out of the vast prairie in what is now southwestern Nebraska. Five-hundred-foot-tall Chimney Rock, which could be seen for miles, became the most famous landmark on the trail. Chimney Rock signaled that the first leg of the journey was over, and that the second phase, with its difficult mountain passage, was about to begin.

Chimney Rock was more than a landmark, however. Because it was situated next to an inviting spring of cool, clear water, it provided travel-weary pioneers with an ideal setting to rest. Many of the travelers, intrigued by this natural curiosity, took the time to carve their names on the massive stone spire.

The elegant spire of Chimney Rock rose like a beacon on the plains for settlers traveling the Oregon Trail.

Chimney Rock National Historic Site

Oregon Trail pioneers weren't the first whites to use Chimney Rock as a landmark. The spire guided early mountain men—trappers and traders—as they traveled between the Rocky Mountains and the Missouri River on their seasonal trading trips. A small group of traders on their way back from Astoria in Oregon Country in 1813 were probably the first white people to see the rock. In 1827, Joshua Pilcher first used the name Chimney Rock in a written report of his journey up the Platte Valley for a fur trapper rendezvous at Salt Lake. The landmark was declared a national historic site in 1956.

Today, Chimney Rock is some 50 to 100 feet shorter than it was in the days of covered wagons, and the thousands of pioneer inscriptions that were carved into the rock are lost in the rubble at the base. The rock column is composed of Brule clay, combined with volcanic ash and Arickaree sandstone, which has kept the spire from eroding completely. Though weathering has slowly robbed Chimney Rock of some of its height, it will likely continue to attract visitors for a good many more centuries to come.

Chimney Rock towers 450 feet above the North Platte River in the Sand Hills of Nebraska. A reliable spring at the formation's base made it a popular resting spot for wagon trains.

Fort Larned
National Historic Site

Protecting travelers on the Santa Fe Trail

Nine of the fort's original buildings remain, including these officers' quarters. The middle building, home to the fort's highest-ranking officer, was the only single-family residence at the fort.

Fort Larned in Kansas, established in 1859 to protect travelers and the U.S. Mail on the Santa Fe Trail, is one of the country's best-preserved frontier posts of that era.

Seven adobe buildings were constructed in the fort's first year, and in the winter of 1864–65 a stone blockhouse was added for protection. More buildings were added the following year. The U.S. Army used the fort as a base during the Indian War of 1867–68. Fort Larned hosted Kit Carson, Buffalo Bill Cody, General George Armstrong Custer, and other famous Indian fighters, as well as the 10th

Fort Larned National Historic Site

U.S. Cavalry, an African-American regiment stationed across the West during the Indian wars.

In the early 1870s, the fort's role was to protect construction workers on the Santa Fe Railroad. By 1878, organized Indian resistance was broken and the rail line finished. Fort Larned, its old adobe buildings already crumbled, was abandoned.

Today, nine original stone buildings still outline the five-acre parade ground in what is now the Fort Larned National Historic Site. In 1988, the National Park Service reconstructed the hexagonal stone block house. The fort has many furnished rooms that show how the soldiers lived, and the surrounding prairie has been restored with a mixture of native grasses and colorful wildflowers.

The earth along the Santa Fe Trail is still cut with deep-worn ruts from the thousands of ox- and mule-drawn wagons that traveled the route. A portion of the trail has been preserved as part of the site.

Fort Scott
National Historic Site

Keeping the peace between settlers and Indians

Fort Scott was established on the rolling prairie in 1842 and named for General Winfield Scott, who was insulted to discover he was the namesake of such a little outpost.

Colorful dragoons, members of an elite mounted regiment trained to fight on foot or on horseback, were employed here to keep peace between the Indians and white settlers, but the fort saw so little action that it was abandoned in 1853. During the Civil War, the post was reactivated as a supply base, and later it protected workers building a railroad from Texas to Kansas.

The Park Service has restored several of the original frame-and-brick structures and reconstructed others. One of the original buildings is the 1843 hospital, which now contains the visitor center and a refurnished ward. The reconstructed infantry barracks contain a museum featuring fort history, information on Indians of the area, and archaeological discoveries from the fort. The dragoon barracks, also reconstructed, house exhibits of uniforms and other items related to the lives of soldiers at the fort in the 1840s.

Throughout the fort are fully furnished rooms, such as Captain Sword's parlor in the restored officers' quarters. Military life at the fort is re-created by interpreters in period costume, and the original plant life surrounding the fort is preserved within two restored plots of tall-grass prairie.

During summer weekends, Park Service personnel conduct one-hour tours of the 16-acre site, which includes 18 original and reconstructed buildings.

Fort Smith

National Historic Site

A military outpost on the rolling prairie

ort Smith National Historic Site on the Arkansas-Oklahoma border contains the remnants of two forts that helped keep the peace on the rough and lawless frontier.

The first Fort Smith was built in 1817 to maintain peace between the local Osage Indians and the newly arriving Cherokees, who were being pushed into Osage territory from their homelands in the Southeast. The only remains of this fort are the foundations, which were discovered in 1963.

The fort was abandoned in 1824 and a second Fort Smith built in 1838 to protect white settlers and as a base for possible military operations against Indian uprisings. The enlisted men's barracks and

The wing containing the barracks, courthouse, and jail at Fort Smith was known as "Hell on the Border" for its terrible conditions.

"Hanging Judge" Parker sentenced at least 79 men to death in an attempt to keep peace on the lawless frontier. The gallows could accommodate a dozen men at once.

the stone commissary are still standing, but the two officers' quarters and the wall that surrounded the fort are gone.

The fear of Indian uprisings was replaced by fear of general lawlessness, so the Federal Court for the Western District of Arkansas moved into the fort. Judge Isaac C. Parker presided over the court at Fort Smith from 1875 to 1896. During this time, the "Hanging Judge" tried 13,000 cases and had 79 men hanged.

The courthouse where Judge Parker heard trials still stands. The basement became a primitive jail, which was referred to as "Hell on the Border." The reproduction of the 1886 gallows, which could hang up to 12 men at a time, is a powerful reminder of those turbulent times.

Fort Smith contains the remnants of two frontier military forts and a federal court on the Arkansas-Oklahoma border.

Fort Union Trading Post

National Historic Site

A center of commerce for the Plains Indians

*I*t may be hard to imagine that a lonely outpost perched on the windswept prairie was once a bustling center of trade, but for nearly 40 years Fort Union Trading Post was the "vastest and finest" of a string of such compounds crossing the prairie west of the Mississippi.

The American Fur Company built the fort in 1828 near the junction of the Missouri and Yellowstone rivers in what is now North Dakota. It quickly became a headquarters for trading beaver furs, buffalo hides, guns, and other goods with Plains Indians, including the Assiniboin, Crow, Blackfeet, and Sioux. During its heyday, Fort Union Trading Post employed up to 100 people, including many men who were married to Indian women and had families.

The cosmopolitan crowd included Americans (black and white), Englishmen, Germans, Frenchmen, Russians, Spaniards, and Italians. At trading time, hundreds of Plains Indians camped outside the fort's walls.

The end of the Plains Indians' traditional way of life doomed the fort. Buffalo herds were diminishing

During the trading season, Plains Indians pitched their tipis on the grassy lands surrounding Fort Union.

Established by the American Fur Company near the confluence of the Missouri and Yellowstone rivers, Fort Union was the major trading post on the northern plains in 1829.

The Bourgeois House, Fort Union's most impressive structure, has been reconstructed after excavations uncovered its original foundations. Artifacts recovered from the fort's lively days include beer bottles, eating utensils, china, and pottery.

■ ■ ■

in the mid-1800s, and smallpox epidemics kept many of the Plains tribes away from the fort. By the Civil War, trade had declined and the post was falling to pieces. Eventually it was dismantled and used to complete nearby Fort Buford.

When the National Park Service acquired the property in 1966, the entire site was covered by grass, and only mounds marking building foundations remained. Since then, the Park Service has excavated the stone foundations and reconstructed portions of the post, including the walls, stone bastions, Indian trade house, and the Bourgeois House, which originally housed the chief trader and today serves as the visitor center. Excavations have recovered artifacts relating to life at the fort, including beer bottles, buttons, trapping gear, and china. The surrounding lands maintain the look of an authentic mid-1800s trading post.

Rangers give tours of the fort, and each summer thousands attend the annual Mountain Men Rendezvous, re-creating the lives of frontier fur traders.

Harry S Truman

National Historic Site

The simple home of a plain-speaking President

The site includes the Trumans' simple home in Independence, Missouri, where the couple retired after Harry left public service in 1953.

Harry S Truman lived in the house at 219 North Delaware Street from 1919, when he married Bess, until 1945, when he became President. In 1953, the Trumans took up their old life at the house in Independence, Missouri, and lived there the rest of their days.

The large frame home, with its lumpy sofas and linoleum, is what one might expect of a President who was known for his "plain speaking." The Trumans' favorite room for reading, talking, and relaxing was the library, which displays Truman's impressive book collection. Neighbors and visiting dignitaries alike were entertained in the living room, which the Trumans furnished with a combination of family heirlooms and new items.

The family ate dinner each night in the formal dining room, though Harry and Bess had breakfast and lunch at the simple kitchen table. The house also contains family portraits, memorabilia, and Margaret Truman's baby grand piano, which she took with her to the White House.

Truman began his political career in Independence as an administrative judge. When he took over the presidency from Franklin Roosevelt in 1945, he had his work cut out for him. Not only was he succeeding perhaps the most popular President since Washington, but the country was in the midst of World War II. His decision to end the war with Japan by using the atomic bomb changed the world forever.

The nation's thirty-third President, Truman had his work cut out for him when he took office after the sudden death of Franklin Roosevelt in 1945.

Herbert Hoover

National Historic Site

A look at the life of our Quaker President

erbert Hoover National Historic Site presents the two phases of Hoover's life—his Quaker upbringing and his long public career—in the setting of a late-nineteenth-century Iowa farm community.

The site includes the small cottage built by Herbert's father Jesse in 1871. Herbert was born here in 1874, and the two-room dwelling, with its rope bed and feather tick, looks much as it did then. Some of the Hoovers' original furniture, including Herbert's childhood cradle, are on display.

Farther south on Downey Street is the larger home that the family moved into in 1879. Nearby is a blacksmith shop similar to the one operated by Hoover's father.

Hoover and his family worshipped at the Friends Meetinghouse. The building, completed in 1857, now sits about two blocks from its original site. Hoover's mother, Hulda, was a well-educated woman who often spoke before services. The Quaker principles of honesty, hard work, simplicity, and generosity that Hoover learned here helped guide him through the difficult years of his presidency.

Also included in the historic site is the one-story schoolhouse that the Friends, or Quakers, who settled the area built in 1853. Hoover's brother Theodore attended school here.

Hoover's father died when he was only six years old. Three years later, Hulda died of pneumonia, and Hoover eventually went to live with relatives in Oregon. As a young man, he traveled around the world as a mining engineer. He later headed a variety of relief efforts that helped feed millions of hungry people in more than 33 nations, earning him a reputation as a great humanitarian.

West Branch, Iowa, where Herbert Hoover was born in 1874, is an excellent example of a mid-American town in the 1880s.

HOOVER'S LEGACY

erbert Hoover may be remembered by many as the President who couldn't raise the country out of the Great Depression, but his humanitarian efforts paved the way for the successful anti-Depression measures of the New Deal.

His administration is noted for many accomplishments, including reforms in criminal procedure in Federal courts, the creation of the Federal Power Commission, improvement of waterways, and the conservation of oil and other natural resources.

Lincoln Home

National Historic Site

The only house the President ever owned

Abraham Lincoln's frame house in Springfield, Illinois, is the only residence our sixteenth President ever owned.

Lincoln moved to Springfield when he was a 28-year-old state representative. About a year-and-a-half later, he met 21-year-old Mary Todd, who came from a prominent family. Three years later, they decided to marry, but Mary's socially conscious family didn't think Lincoln measured up. The family reluctantly blessed the union, and the couple were married in 1842.

Two years later, they purchased the modest home at Eighth and Jackson streets. The couple lived on a tight budget, so Lincoln did all the chores around the house, including chopping wood, carrying water, and milking the cows. As the family grew, they renovated and expanded the home until it was a distinguished two-story house befitting a lawyer and rising politician.

In 1846, Lincoln was elected to the House of Representatives, and the family moved to Washington. His unpopular stance against the Mexican War, however, cost him politically, and in 1849 Lincoln moved back to Springfield, feeling he had no future in politics. But in 1856, the issue of slavery brought Lincoln back to Washington. In the Senate race he ran against Senator Stephen Douglas as a member of the newly formed Republican Party.

The Lincolns lived on a tight budget their first years in the Springfield house. Lincoln himself chopped the wood to keep the stove burning.

The frame house where Abraham and Mary Todd Lincoln lived for 16 years is now the Lincoln Home National Historic Site.

Lincoln lost the election, but the eloquent speeches he gave in a series of debates with Douglas won him national acclaim. Four years later, Lincoln was elected President of the United States.

In January 1861, the Lincolns packed up the house in Springfield. They sold some of the furniture and household goods and put the rest in trunks labeled "A. Lincoln, White House, Washington, D.C." In 1887, more than two decades after Lincoln's assassination, the house was donated to the State of Illinois.

In 1971, the National Park Service acquired the President's home as part of the Lincoln Home National Historic Site, which today encompasses a four-block historic district of perhaps a dozen mid-nineteenth-century homes.

James A. Garfield
National Historic Site

The home of a short-lived but dynamic President

In 1880, more than 17,000 people from around the country traveled by train to Mentor, Ohio, to hear James A. Garfield campaign for the presidency from the front porch of his home. The 30-room mansion, known as Lawnfield, is now preserved as the James A. Garfield National Historic Site.

Garfield bought the home in 1876 for his large family, which included five children and his mother. The home has been restored to its 1870–1890 appearance. Original furniture and memorabilia are featured throughout, including Garfield's Civil War equipment, his Congressional desk, the Garfield Presidential China, and a waxed funeral wreath sent by Queen Victoria.

The twentieth President was shot at the train station in Washington, D.C., on July 2, 1881, just four months after his inauguration. Because his tenure as President was so short, he is perhaps better known as a Civil War hero and U.S. congressman. Garfield, like Lincoln, was born in a log cabin and worked his way up to the highest office in the country.

Four years after his assassination, Garfield's wife Lucretia added a wing to the house to accommodate the Memorial Library, the first presidential library. Rather than the usual display of presidential documents, the library contains Garfield's extensive book collection, and in the study is the chair where he would spend nights reading, his leg slung over the arm.

Visitors are allowed to explore the Garfield home on their own, although representatives from the Western Reserve Historical Society, who help oversee the site, are prepared to present a 15-minute lecture about Garfield on request.

James A. Garfield, who conducted a "front porch" presidential campaign from his home in Ohio in 1880, was assassinated shortly after taking office.

Knife River Indian Villages

National Historic Site

Remnants of Northern Plains culture

Located in central North Dakota, where the Knife River joins the flow of the Missouri, are the remains of one of the oldest inhabited sites in North America. At least 11,000 years ago, nomadic hunters came to this area, attracted by the strong yet beautiful Knife River flint. The Hidatsa and Mandan people traded the flint for goods with other tribes and built a flourishing and stable community of villages.

Knife River Indian Villages National Historic Site, established in 1974, includes three village sites, making it the best-preserved complex of Northern Plains culture. Exhibits at the visitor center and a full-scale earthlodge will further visitors' understanding of the lives of the first inhabitants of this place.

The Knife River area was primarily the home of the Hidatsa. To the south were their Mandan neighbors, who lived similar lives of hunting, tending crops, and trading.

Women were responsible for most of the day-to-day work, including gathering wild plants, preparing food, making tools, tanning hides, and, until horses came to the plains, hauling supplies.

The Mandan, Hidatsa, and Arikara Indians built villages and gardens along the Missouri River in what is now North Dakota.

The men spent their time seeking spiritual knowledge, hunting buffalo and other big game, and making war. Their lives were not easy, but the Mandan and Hidatsa had time for games and storytelling. An open area in the center of each Mandan village was for dancing and rituals.

Women also built, maintained, and owned the earthlodges. These well-insulated homes were actually made of earth and wooden posts, and some of them were spacious enough to house as many as 30 people.

THREE TOWNS

Big Hidatsa was the farthest north of the Knife River villages. It was established by the Hidatsa sometime around the year 1600 and inhabited until 1845. By far the largest of the villages, Big Hidatsa had 100 earthlodges housing more than 1,000 people.

Sakakawea was south of Big Hidatsa. A group of Hidatsa Indians established this village in the late-eighteenth century and lived there until 1834, when Sioux raiders burned the town. Sakakawea at one time probably had 47 lodges and a population of approximately 500 people.

Lower Hidatsa is one of the longest continually lived-in villages on the Upper Missouri. It was home to Hidatsa Indians from 1525 until about 1780–85, when the population was decimated by smallpox. The site has 51 house structures, indicating a population of 500.

Ulysses S. Grant
National Historic Site

The estate of the Union general and President

On March 1, 1872, President Ulysses S. Grant established Yellowstone National Park—America's first national park. It has been called the best idea the country ever had, and it was the landmark of Grant's administration. More than 115 years later, in 1989, Congress established the Ulysses S. Grant National Historic Site, adding Grant's Missouri estate, White Haven, to the list of Park Service holdings.

The historic site preserves the nearly ten-acre estate near St. Louis where Grant and his family lived from 1854 to 1860. The property includes the main house and lands, as well as slave quarters and outbuildings. The years Grant spent farming at White Haven were difficult ones, but historians believe that these experiences helped him develop the skills and character necessary to lead the Union Army and the nation during the Civil War.

During those years, when Grant was constantly in the public spotlight, he returned to the big white house in Missouri to relax and spend time with his wife Julia. He lost the house in a failed Wall Street deal in 1885, shortly before his death.

Grant's role as Union general during the Civil War is commemorated at Civil War sites and at the Park Service's General Grant National Memorial. The White Haven site is the first to focus primarily on Grant's life and presidency.

As President, Ulysses S. Grant signed the act that preserved the Yellowstone Valley as the nation's first national park on March 1, 1872.

White Haven, the childhood home of Grant's wife Julia, is preserved today as the Ulysses S. Grant National Historic Site.

William Howard Taft

National Historic Site

The elegant home of an influential statesman

The stately home where William Howard Taft was born in 1857 sits high atop one of Cincinnati's most prominent hilltops.

■ ■ ■

On a prominent hilltop overlooking the city of Cincinnati stands the large Greek revival-style house where William Howard Taft was born in 1857. The house is a reminder of an elegant era when Mount Auburn was known as the city's "Fifth Avenue," and it is restored to look as it did when the twenty-seventh President and tenth Chief Justice lived here as a child and young adult.

Taft lived in the home continuously until he went to Yale College in 1874. After college, his career skyrocketed. When he became President in 1909, it was only the second time he had been elected to office. As President, Taft introduced the income tax and the federal budget, and he inaugurated the presidential tradition of throwing out the first baseball of the season.

The house was almost demolished in 1938, eight years after Taft's death. In 1969, it was designated a national historic site. Letters from Taft's mother Louise, describing the home to her family in Massachusetts, guided the restoration efforts. All the family portraits and many of the books in the house belonged to the Tafts while they lived there, and it is furnished with a combination of original and period pieces.

In addition, the site has exhibits detailing the life and career of the only man to serve the nation as both President and Chief Justice of the Supreme Court.

William Howard Taft was the only man to serve as President of the United States and Chief Justice of the Supreme Court.

■ ■ ■

Jefferson National Expansion
National Memorial

A tribute to the people who settled the West

The great arc of silver rising above St. Louis is a tribute to the soaring mind of Thomas Jefferson, the courage of the people who settled the West, and the simple beauty of architecture.

In 1803, Thomas Jefferson completed the Louisiana Purchase, which more than doubled the size of the United States. Lewis and Clark set off from St. Louis on their cross-country expedition, and the city soon became a jumping-off point for explorers, traders, and settlers heading west in the 1800s.

In 1947, American architect Eero Saarinen won a national contest to design a memorial to honor America's westward expansion. The Jefferson National Expansion Memorial, better known as the Gateway Arch, was finished in 1965. At 630 feet high, it is the nation's tallest monument, besting the Washington Monument by 75 feet. The structure is made out of stainless steel, and its simple curved design is able to withstand extreme temperatures, heavy winds, earthquakes, and other environmental stresses without an inner frame or skeleton to hold it up.

At the base of the Arch is the Museum of Westward Expansion, which displays 100 years of history using maps, paintings, historic photos, and Indian and pioneer artifacts, including such objects as a Spanish carreta, a bull boat, and a Plains Indian tipi. An adjacent auditorium shows a film on the construction of the arch.

The Jefferson Expansion National Memorial, a 630-foot stainless steel arch, commemorates the westward expansion of the United States.

The Gateway Arch soars above St. Louis, once the staging area for explorers, traders, and settlers headed west.

THE OLD COURTHOUSE

The memorial also preserves a little piece of Civil War history at the Old Courthouse, where the famous Dred Scott trials of 1847 and 1850 were held.

Scott was a slave who traveled with his owners from Missouri to live in the free state of Illinois. He sued for his freedom, claiming that living four years in a free state entitled him to freedom. The local court ruled for Scott, but the U.S. Supreme Court later ruled that blacks were not "persons" and therefore had no right to sue in court.

Many believe that this ruling helped bring about the Civil War.

Mount Rushmore
National Memorial

A granite shrine to democracy

Pointing to a 5,725-foot granite outcrop in the Black Hills of South Dakota more than 75 years ago, sculptor Gutzon Borglum declared: "There's the place to carve a great national memorial. American history shall march along that skyline." Today, the 60-foot faces of Presidents George Washington, Thomas Jefferson, Theodore Roosevelt, and Abraham Lincoln gaze out from Mount Rushmore in a shrine to democracy.

The memorial started as an idea to draw sightseers to the Black Hills. In 1927, President Calvin Coolidge dedicated the site, and Borglum began 14 years of work designing, blasting, and carving the face of the mountain.

The four Presidents chosen for the memorial led the country from colonial times into the twentieth century: Washington commanded the Revolutionary Army and was the first U.S. President, Jefferson authored the Declaration of Independence and advocated westward expansion, Lincoln restored the Union and ended slavery in America, and Roosevelt promoted conservationism and other progressive causes. Borglum died in 1941, and his son, Lincoln Borglum, supervised the completion of his father's masterpiece.

Mount Rushmore can be viewed 24 hours a day, year-round, but it is best photographed in the morning light from the Main View Terrace. Easy trails lead to a visitor center, which has exhibits and a short film, and to the Sculptor's Studio, containing original carving tools and scale models of the memorial.

Sculptor Gutzon Borglum carved the faces of Presidents George Washington, Thomas Jefferson, Theodore Roosevelt, and Abraham Lincoln into South Dakota's Mount Rushmore.

The hard granite of Mount Rushmore was blasted away with dynamite, then carefully sculpted to create the 60-foot-tall faces.

The Southwest

National Monuments and Historic Sites

*I*n 1906, outraged at the plundering of historic sites in the Southwest, President Theodore Roosevelt signed the Antiquities Act into law. The legislation gave the President the power to protect historic treasures by designating them national monuments (and, later, national historic sites). Since then, many places in the region have been recognized as significant to the history of the evolving frontier, from the prehistoric ruins of Indian settlements to early Spanish missions to U.S. military outposts.

National monuments in the Southwest also preserve natural areas of special significance. The list includes fantastic caves and deserts, forests of ancient redwoods and giant sequoias, and spectacular canyons and rock formations.

Located on Navajo land in northeastern Arizona, Canyon de Chelly is treasured both for its scenic beauty and for its prehistoric Indian ruins.

The California home of Eugene O'Neill, considered by many to be America's greatest playwright, is preserved as a memorial to his life and work.

Aztec Ruins
National Monument

A pueblo settlement abandoned long ago

The Great Kiva, once the center of ceremonial life in the village, was reconstructed on partially standing walls in the 1930s and is the only restored kiva of its kind in the Southwest.

When the first white settlers reached the Animas Valley, they were intrigued by the great stone ruins there. Believing them to be the work of a long-vanished culture from the south, they named the ruins, and their town, Aztec.

The pueblo ruins were actually built and abandoned by an ancient people of the Colorado Plateau long before the Aztecs were established in the Valley of Mexico. Nevertheless, they were proclaimed the Aztec Ruins National Monument in 1923.

Ancestors of today's Pueblo Indians, the Anasazi were among the earliest farmers in this area, raising crops in the valley's fertile bottomlands. They also were skilled masons, and in the early 1100s, they built a huge sandstone "apartment building" on a rise overlooking the river. They constructed the pueblo by alternating large rectangular blocks of sandstone with bands of smaller stones in an attractive pattern.

Known as the West Ruin, the structure had somewhere between 350 and 400 rooms and stood three stories high. The pueblo was built in an E-shape around a central plaza containing a great kiva, a circular building used for ceremonies. There are several other kivas in the monument, but only this one has been reconstructed and opened to the public.

The monument also preserves the Hubbard Site, a rare, tri-wall structure with a kiva inside. At one time, up

The village at Aztec Ruins prospered for many years, then was abandoned around A.D. 1200. Around 1225, people of the Mesa Verde culture moved into the abandoned pueblo and remodeled it.

to 300 people may have lived here, grinding corn on the rooftops, making baskets and pots, tending crops along the river, and hunting animals nearby. Some of the tools, baskets, and pottery excavated from the ruins are on display at the visitor center.

Sometime around A.D. 1200, the Anasazi abandoned the pueblo, perhaps fleeing drought or some other catastrophe. About 25 years later, another group of Anasazi took over the deserted pueblo, remodeling the main structure and erecting new dwellings. They flourished for approximately 50 years, then abandoned the site, now known as the East Ruin.

EXPLORING THE RUINS

Geologist John S. Newberry was among the first to investigate the ruins in 1859. He found the pueblo well-preserved, with many rooms untouched since the inhabitants left.

Less than 20 years later, when anthropologist Lewis H. Morgan explored the ruins, he found that a quarter of the pueblo's stones had been carted away by settlers to build their homes.

A few years later, a group of boys and their teacher decided to explore the site. According to one of the boys, Sherman S. Howe:

"We struck the second floor... and broke a hole through about two-and-a-half feet in diameter, but could see nothing but a black dungeon below.... Some thought it might be full of rats, skunks, bats, or rattlesnakes. We could imagine a hundred things. I believe the dread of ghosts was the worst."

Bandelier
National Monument

Prehistoric ruins and spectacular canyons

Bandelier National Monument on the Pajarito Plateau of New Mexico combines prehistoric pueblo ruins with nearly 50 square miles of virtually undisturbed canyon country.

A network of well-maintained trails, some following ancient Indian footpaths, connect the monument's ancient ruins and spectacular natural features. One popular hike is to Frijoles Canyon, an oasis in this dry country. A perennial stream winds through cottonwoods between steep canyon walls.

Located in a broad clearing are the Anasazi ruins of Tyuonyi. A graceful semicircle of stone and mud buildings nearly encloses a broad central courtyard with three kivas—subterranean chambers used for ceremonial purposes. The ruins once stood three stories high and had 400 rooms. Anasazi lived here from about 1200 to 1550, growing corn, beans, and squash.

The base of the northern wall of Frijoles Canyon, which means "bean" canyon, is honeycombed for two miles with cave dwellings gouged out of the solid cliff. The ceilings of these dwellings are still black from cooking fires, and ancient rock drawings, some very faint, decorate the walls.

In a separate section of the monument, 11 miles north of the Canyon, the Tsankawi Interpretive Trail leads to cultural sites, volcanic formations, and panoramic views of the landscape. Some sections of the trail are deeply rutted from

Bandelier National Monument, in the canyons of the Jemez Mountains, contains a rich collection of thirteenth-century Pueblo Indian cliff dwellings.

Makeshift stairs lead into one of the cliff dwellings. Some of the rooms contain original rock paintings and traces of cooking fires.

214

Bandelier National Monument

The large circular pueblo known as Tyuonyi once stood three stories high and had 400 rooms.

The bulk of Bandelier National Monument is undisturbed wilderness, with dramatic rock walls and a rich plant life.

centuries of use by Indians. Tsankawi is a large, unexcavated ruin high on a mesa, providing sweeping views of mountains and valleys. Along the trail are ancient images carved into rocks, called petroglyphs. The visitor center has slide programs to orient visitors to the archaeological significance of Bandelier.

The monument, established in 1916, is also significant for its geology. The Pajarito Plateau consists largely of compacted volcanic ash and basaltic lava ejected thousands of years ago during a great volcanic eruption. The caldera, or saucer-shaped depression created when the summit of the volcano collapsed, is one of the world's largest. The rugged Jemez Mountains, in fact, are the rim of this caldera.

Black Canyon of the Gunnison

National Monument

A 2,000-foot chasm cut through solid granite

Black Canyon of the Gunnison National Monument in Colorado preserves a 2,000-foot chasm cut through granite by the Gunnison River. According to geologist Wallace Hansen, who mapped the region almost 50 years ago, "Several western canyons exceed the Black Canyon in overall size. Some are longer, some are deeper, some are narrower, and a few have walls as steep. But no other canyon in North America combines the depth, narrowness, sheerness, and somber countenance of the Black Canyon of the Gunnison."

The gash through the canyon was formed by the unrelenting power of the Gunnison River cutting through the rock for two million years. One of the nation's few unspoiled wild rivers, it is still working away at the canyon, though some of its power has been tamed behind three dams.

The Gunnison River runs for 53 miles through Black Canyon, though only the most spectacular 12 miles of the gorge lie within the monument. Steep, dark canyon walls of schist and gneiss block out much of the sun, filling the canyon with heavy shadows, hence its name. At its most narrow point, the north and south rims are only 1,300 feet apart and the canyon floor only 40 feet wide.

Black Canyon of the Gunnison National Monument contains a 12-mile stretch of the deepest and darkest section of the gorge. The sheer cliff walls plunge as deep as 2,000 feet.

The floor of Black Canyon is home to much wildlife, but humans have rarely attempted to negotiate the canyon's steep walls. It appears that prehistoric people, and later the Utes, used the rims but never actually lived in the gorge.

Hiking trails are available at both rims, but climbers headed for the bottom of the canyon have to make their own paths. The rims also have roads leading to the very edge of the canyon, complete with overlooks and interpretive signs.

Dragon Point on the south rim offers a good look at Painted Wall, a dark outcropping of rock laced with pink intrusions that resemble Chinese dragons. The wall was formed when molten material was forced under great pressure into the cracks and joints of the base rock. Peregrine falcons nest on these sheer walls.

Other wildlife at home in the canyon and on the rims include squirrels, badgers, weasels, marmots, black bears, and cougars. At night, visitors are likely to hear the call of coyotes echoing through the canyon.

FORBIDDING CHASM

The steep, rugged walls of Black Canyon have proved a mighty barrier to humans for centuries, helping to preserve its wild state.

Ute Indians and early settlers were afraid that anyone entering the inner gorge would not come out alive. Members of the Hayden Expedition in 1873–74 were the first white men to explore the canyon.

John W. Gunnison, for whom the river is named, led a party to the upper reaches of the canyon in 1853, but gave up before reaching the bottom of the gorge. Four years later, Lieutenant Joseph Christmas Ives navigated the Colorado River in a prefabricated steamboat as far as the Black Canyon, but no farther.

These explorers, as well as later surveyors for the Denver & Rio Grande Railroad, all proclaimed the Black Canyon to be "inaccessible."

Cabrillo
National Monument

A memorial honoring the "Columbus of California"

In 1542, Juan Rodriguez Cabrillo, the "Columbus of California," set out in search of the island of California, which he heard was inhabited by lusty Amazon women who carried swords of gold. He probably also dreamed of finding the Strait of Anian, a mythical water route from the Pacific through North America to the Atlantic.

Cabrillo's ships poked along the coast as far north as Oregon, but he didn't find the strait. He did, however, land in California, becoming the first European to do so, and he took possession of the entire coast for the King of Spain.

Cabrillo National Monument commemorates the Portuguese explorer near where he arrived on Point Loma. The visitor center, with a larger-than-life statue of Cabrillo nearby, has displays about the explorer and his expedition.

Juan Rodriguez Cabrillo landed at Point Loma on San Diego Bay in 1542. He promptly claimed the entire coast for Spain.

A larger-than-life statue of Juan Rodriguez Cabrillo in battle-dress stands guard near the visitor center.

■ ■ ■

Before Cabrillo arrived, Digueno Indians lived on Point Loma. A walk along the Bayside Trail introduces visitors to some of the plants (yucca and sage) and animals (rabbits, squirrels, and others) that they used for food, clothing, and shelter.

The monument also includes the Old Point Loma Lighthouse, built between 1851 and 1855. Workers used sandstone from the hillside for the walls and old floor tiles from the ruins of an abandoned Spanish fort. An elaborate iron and brass structure held the light, which had been imported from France and used state-of-the-art technology. The lighthouse guided sailors into the harbor until 1891, when it was closed because fog and low clouds too often obscured its light. It has been refurbished and is open to the public.

One thing that has remained constant here is the rich sea life. On the western side of Point Loma, tidepools are alive with sea anemones, limpets, starfish, crabs, and hundreds more species of plants and animals.

Each year, from late December to the end of February, thousands of California Gray Whales migrate past the site of the monument, as they have for countless centuries.

A lightkeeper lit the oil lamp in the Old Point Loma Lighthouse for the first time at dusk on November 15, 1855. The light was extinguished for the last time on March 23, 1891.

■ ■ ■

Canyon de Chelly

National Monument

Home to the Navajo for more than 2,000 years

History is still being made at Canyon de Chelly National Monument. In the shadow of prehistoric pueblo ruins, perched high on sandstone walls, stand modern Navajo log dwellings called hogans, representing nearly 2,000 years of human settlement.

Despite being named a national monument in 1931, Canyon de Chelly, located on the Navajo Reservation, is home to a viable community of Navajo people. It is unclear exactly when the canyon was settled, but by about 2,000 years ago, people of the Basketmaker culture were living here year-round.

The Basketmakers were attracted by the dependable water source that makes Canyon de Chelly (from the Navajo expression for "where the water comes out of the rock") an oasis in this parched land. The

Canyon de Chelly extends from the highlands of the Defiance Plateau and Chuska Mountains in the east to the arid Chinle Valley far to the west.

The dramatic red rocks of Canyon de Chelly contain many reminders that an ancient civilization once lived here.

Canyon de Chelly National Monument

canyon has three main branches: Canyon de Chelly down the center, Canyon del Muerto veering to the northeast, and Monument Canyon heading to the southeast.

The Basketmakers wove baskets and planted crops on the canyon floor, as Navajo do today. They scooped storage areas out of the sandstone beneath overhanging cliffs to store surplus food, and as the population grew, they began to build apartmentlike cliff houses called pueblos into the red rock canyon walls. By the thirteenth century, more than 800 pueblo-dwellers, which we call the Anasazi, lived in the canyon.

Wind and water carved Defiance Plateau into a labyrinth of canyons and natural stone statues, including Spider Rock, an 800-foot sandstone spire.

No one knows what the Anasazi, Navajo for "Ancient Ones," called themselves, or what language they spoke, because they lived before written language. They did, however, leave a record of their presence on the soaring walls of the canyon in the form of painted images.

Several ancient Anasazi dwellings are contained within the 84,000-acre monument. The only one that visitors can reach via a self-guided trail is White House Ruin, once home to several Anasazi families. The scenic trail descends 600 feet to the canyon floor.

All other trips to the canyon floor require a permit and must be led by a park ranger or authorized Navajo guide. Two roadways following the rims of the canyon provide good views of other pueblo ruins, such as Standing Cow Ruin, one of the largest in the monument. This pueblo had 60 rooms and three underground kivas used for ceremonies.

All along the cliff walls are rock paintings—of handprints, geometric designs, Mexican soldiers, and a large standing cow, chronicling the changing way of life of the people who made their home here.

The road along the north rim of Canyon del Muerto leads to Mummy Cave Ruin, a pueblo that was occupied from about A.D. 350 to 1300, when the Anasazi mysteriously abandoned Canyon de Chelly. In the mid-1700s, the Navajo resettled the canyon and, for the next 100 years, battled Spanish and American troops, eventually securing the right to live in Canyon de Chelly.

White House Ruins, once home to several Anasazi families, is the only pueblo site open to visitors without a guide.

MASSACRE CANYON

One of the finest rock paintings in the monument features a procession of Spanish horsemen marching across a high ledge of dark red sandstone. The soldiers, painted white, are wearing long cloaks and tall, broad-brimmed hats and carrying long rifles.

The painting is believed to be a record of an attack on the Navajo led by Mexican Army Lieutenant Antonio Narbona in 1805. His soldiers drove Navajo warriors and their families deep into a branch of the canyon where all were slaughtered, children as well as adults. From then on, the canyon was known as Canyon del Muerto, or Massacre Canyon.

Capulin Volcano
National Monument

A volcano that hardy hikers can walk into

Capulin Volcano National Monument in northeastern New Mexico is one of the few places in the world where people can walk into a volcano.

A road spirals up the inactive volcano to the summit, where two self-guiding trails begin. One trail leads to a vent at the bottom of the crater; the other, longer trail follows the crater rim. From the highest point on the rim trail, more than 8,000 feet above sea level, one can see three states, as well as stunning views of the Sangre de Cristo Mountains to the west and the Cimarron Cut-Off of the Santa Fe Trail to the southeast.

During the late 1800s, wagon trains heading for Fort Union passed by the volcano. About ten miles from Capulin Volcano is the Folsom Man site, where human remains and projectile points were first found in association with extinct animals.

Capulin Volcano is part of a field of volcanism that began about eight million years ago. Recent studies indicate that Capulin Volcano is approximately 59,000 years old.

During its last eruption, cinders, ash, and other rock debris spewed out and fell back upon the vent, piling up to form a cone-shaped mound rising more than 1,000 feet high—one of the largest and most symmetrically shaped cinder cones in the United States.

Sunrise lights Capulin Volcano, which glowed with the fire of ash and molten lava thousands of years ago.

Casa Grande Ruins

National Monument

A village once occupied by Hohokam Indians

Casa Grande Ruins National Monument in the Gila River Valley of southern Arizona preserves the remains of a village once occupied by the Hohokam Indians. The highly developed Hohokam culture was superbly adapted to survive in this hot land of little rain. Archaeologist Emil Haury, who studied the Hohokam for many years, called them the "First Masters of the American Desert."

The Sonoran Desert receives only seven to ten inches of rain per year, so the Hohokam constructed a miles-long system of dams, headgates, and canals that brought water from all over the surrounding desert to irrigate their crops. They also built large walled arenas that may have been used for ball games like those the Aztec played or as gathering places for other purposes.

The monument preserves an ancient building 60 feet long and four stories high, the largest structure known to exist in Hohokam times. Coming upon this mysterious building, which rose in solitude above the desert, the Spaniards called it Casa Grande, or Great House.

Built before 1350 using a concretelike substance called caliche, the building's walls face the four cardinal points of the compass. Portholes in the walls are struck by the sun's rays as it sets during the summer solstice.

Visitors to Casa Grande can see ancient pottery and tools at the visitor center, or they can wander the mysterious ruins, contemplating why the Hohokam studied the heavens so carefully here.

Casa Grande, a four-story structure built by Hohokam farmers around 600 years ago, was given its Spanish name, which means "Great House," by the Jesuit priest Father Kino when he discovered it in 1694.

Cedar Breaks
National Monument

A natural amphitheater of colorful spires and columns

The Paiutes called the natural amphitheater of Cedar Breaks National Monument in Utah *un-cap-I-cun-ump,* or "circle of painted cliffs," for the colorful spires and columns of rock carved into the mountain.

Shaped like a huge coliseum, the amphitheater plunges more than 2,000 feet, scooping away green alpine meadows. Millions of years of uplift and weathering carved this huge bowl into the western edge of the 10,400-foot-high Markagunt Plateau. Various shades of red, purple, and yellow are ribboned through the limestone, the result of iron and manganese in the rock.

When the first Utah settlers saw the amphitheater, they named it Cedar Breaks— "breaks" to describe the badlands, and "cedar" for the trees, which were actually junipers.

The main route to the monument's scenic attractions is a five-mile road through the high country of Cedar Breaks. The road offers panoramic views of fantastic stone formations, fir and alpine forests, and rolling meadows. In the spring, the meadows rival the colorful rocks, as larkspur, lupine, penstemon, columbine, Indian paintbrush, and other wildflowers bloom.

Gnarled and weather-beaten bristlecone pines grow in the most forsaken spots, where the wind is fierce, the soil thin, and water scarce. Bristlecone pines are some of the oldest living things on earth; one Cedar Breaks specimen has survived for 1,600 years.

The stone spires, columns, and canyons of the Cedar Breaks amphitheater are subtly colored with shades of red, yellow, and purple by iron manganese contained in the rock.

Chiricahua

National Monument

A wonderland of rocks in the land of the Apaches

*I*n the northwest corner of the Chiricahua Mountains, massive boulders weighing hundreds of tons balance easily on a forest of stone pedestals. Called the "Land of the Standing-Up Rocks" by the local Chiricahua Apaches and the "Wonderland of Rocks" by later pioneers, the area has been preserved as Chiricahua National Monument since 1924.

Geologists aren't exactly sure how this land of massive stone spires and columns came to be, but it is believed to be the work of volcanic eruptions and natural erosion. It appears that about 25 million years ago, the nearby Turkey Creek caldera erupted violently, covering the land with white-hot ash. As the ash cooled, it fused into dark volcanic rock known as rhyolite today.

The uplift that created the mountains exposed the rhyolite, then wind, rain, and ice went to work sculpting the rock. The erosive forces carved away at the cracks that had formed in the volcanic rock as the ash cooled, creating natural rock sculptures.

An eight-mile paved road leads up Bonita Canyon to Masai Point, which has panoramic views of the entire park, as well as the desert valleys and mountains beyond. Along the scenic Echo Canyon Trail is a rock grotto created by wind and water.

More than 20 miles of foot trails wind through the 12,000-acre monument, taking hikers past some very unusual rock formations, including Duck on a Rock, Totem Pole, and Big Balanced Rock. The trails allow

As light and shadows move across the landscape, Chiricahua's unusual rock formations take on all kinds of fanciful shapes.

The same forces of nature that sculpted rock formations in some areas carved out beautiful grottos in others.

■ ■ ■

Opposite page: The area preserved as Chiricahua National Monument was known as the "Land of the Standing-Up Rocks" by the Chiricahua Apaches and the "Wonderland of Rocks" by pioneers.

■ ■ ■

visitors to see the formations up close, as well as experience the beautiful landscape more fully.

The cool, lush Chiricahua Mountains contrast greatly with the arid desert below. These "sky islands" contain a unique combination of Southwestern and Mexican species, such as the Chihuahua pine, Apache fox squirrel, alligator juniper, and Arizona cypress.

The visitor center has slide presentations and exhibits on the monument's geological, natural, and cultural history, including information on the Chiricahua Apaches and their famous leaders, Cochise and Geronimo.

FARAWAY RANCH

Chiricahua National Monument also includes Faraway Ranch, a farm and guest ranch in Bonita Canyon started by a Swedish immigrant couple in 1888.

Neil and Emma Erickson were among the first pioneers to settle in this area, and their only neighbors were the Stafford family, who lived in a log cabin nearby. In the 1920s, one of the Ericksons' daughters and her husband turned the homestead into a successful guest ranch. Lillian and Ed Riggs built trails and took guests on horseback trips through the "Wonderland of Rocks." In 1922, they began to promote the idea of a national park here, and two years later Chiricahua National Monument was established.

■ ■ ■

Colorado
National Monument

One man's perseverance made a dream come true

Colorado National Monument, located in the western part of the state, is a tribute to both the land and the man who recognized its value. "I came here last year and found these canyons, and they felt like the heart of the world to me," John Otto wrote in 1907.

Otto lived alone in the wild, desolate canyon country, and he spearheaded a letter-writing campaign urging Congress to declare the area a national park. His dream came true in 1911, when the monument was established and Otto was named caretaker.

Several hiking trails traverse the 32-square-mile monument, including one named in Otto's honor. The Rim Rock Drive and high-country trails provide stunning views of steep canyons, fascinating natural rock sculptures, purple-gray Book Cliffs, and the bold, flat-topped mountain called Grand Mesa.

Down in the backcountry canyons, colorful cliffs and natural rock formations tower overhead. A highlight of backcountry exploration is 450-foot-high Independence Monument, the largest free-standing rock formation in the monument. Like the site's numerous rock spires, domes, arches, windows, and sheer-walled canyons, Independence Monument was carved by millions of years of erosion.

Equally beautiful is the area's wildlife. Mountain lions, desert bighorns, and rattlesnakes blend in with the landscape, while colorful birds and flowering cacti stand out boldly against the scenery.

It has taken millions of years for water, wind, and frost to sculpt the sheer-walled canyons and massive stone formations.

Colorado National Monument preserves 32 square miles of towering natural rock sculptures along the greater Colorado Plateau.

Devils Postpile
National Monument

Cooling lava that formed a fantastic landmark

Sixty-foot columns of basalt rise like organ pipes above pine forests on the western slopes of the Sierra Nevada Mountains in California. Devils Postpile National Monument was established in 1911 to preserve these volcanic remains, as well as 101-foot-high Rainbow Falls.

Some 100,000 years ago, basalt lava flowed from a volcanic vent in the valley of the Middle Fork of the San Joaquin River, filling the valley near the postpile to a depth of 400 feet. As the lava cooled, it shrank and cracked, forming a vertical pattern on the surfaces of the flow. The cracks deepened to form long post-like columns two to three feet in diameter with three to seven sides.

Perhaps 10,000 years ago, a glacier moved down the Middle Fork and over the cracked lava flows, exposing one side of the postpile and polishing its top. Visitors can hike to the top of the postpile to see the cross-section of columns, which looks somewhat like a tiled floor. Though Devils Postpile is not the only example of columnar-jointed basalt, it is one of the finest.

Many hiking trails cross the monument's nearly 800 miles of lodgepole pine and red fir forests, which are home to wildlife ranging from bears to ground squirrels. Loop trails lead to and from the postpile and Rainbow Falls, where the San Joaquin River drops more than 100 feet over a sheer cliff of ancient lava flows.

A stairway and short trail lead to the bottom of the falls. Longer trails lead south of the falls and west on King Creek Trail. At the northern tip of the monument, the John Muir and Pacific Crest trails join and continue through the site. The 211-mile John Muir Trail, named for the famous conservationist and champion of Yosemite, connects Yosemite National Park to Kings Canyon and Sequoia national parks.

A collection of 60-foot-high columns found in a pine forest in the Sierras, Devils Postpile is considered to be among the world's best examples of what geologists call columnar-jointed basalt.

As basalt lava cools, it shrinks and cracks, sometimes forming vertical columns. At Devils Postpile, the columns have from three to seven sides.

234

SODA SPRINGS

The Devils Postpile region is still a volcanically active area, as the nearby Soda Springs attest. The mineral springs, which lie on a gravel bar along the San Joaquin River north of the postpile, were created when pressure inside the earth drove hot gases upward, where they mixed with ground water. The gravel around the springs is stained red from iron in the water, which oxidizes when exposed to air.

Dinosaur
National Monument

Countless fossil bones embedded in stone

Dinosaur National Monument in Colorado and Utah is not a typical dinosaur museum. Instead of the usual exhibit of entire, assembled dinosaur skeletons, the site contains a cliff face of jumbled fossil bones. The quarry site, which was designated a national monument in 1915, is one of the largest known deposits of dinosaur fossil bones in the world.

At first, the cliffs were excavated and loads of fossils shipped to museums around the country, where they were carefully reconstructed into complete skeletons. The fossil bones that remain on-site have been left embedded in the stone, with only their surfaces exposed. What is visible are the bones as they have been randomly collected by the forces of nature.

Around 145 million years ago, this area, where the Yampa and Green rivers now meet, was excellent dinosaur habitat. Several large rivers and many streams crossed the low-lying plain. Ferns, cycads, club mosses, and clumps of tall conifers covered the land, providing forage for large vegetarians. Apatosaurus (better known as Brontosaurus), Diplodocus, Stegosaurus, and other plant eaters thrived, as did Allosaurus and other sharp-toothed carnivores.

As dinosaurs died in or near an ancient river, their bodies were carried downstream, where sometimes they were deposited near the inside of a river bend. Over time, the remains of the dinosaurs mixed with those of turtles, crocodiles, and other river dwellers, and all the fossils were preserved in the sand. Flexible body parts, such as long tails and necks, trail downstream in the river bed, indicating the direction of flow of the ancient river.

Opposite page: *Steamboat Rock stands at the confluence of the Green and Yampa rivers. The canyons carved by these rivers were added to Dinosaur National Monument in 1938.*

A square-shouldered warrior holding a shield, as well as various humanlike creatures, were carved by Fremont Indians into a rock wall at Dinosaur National Monument.

Dinosaur National Monument

Ancient rivers carried the bones of dinosaurs and other animals onto a sandbar where dissolved silica, percolating through layers of sand, gradually mineralized them.

Tons of sand and volcanic ash up to one mile thick eventually covered and compressed the bones. As the Rocky Mountains began to rise to the east, the upheaval and erosion over millions of years exposed the ancient river bed and its bounty of fossils.

Intriguing exhibits, a short film, and ranger programs introduce visitors to the thousands of fossils caught in the sandstone face that makes up one wall of the Dinosaur Quarry Visitor Center. In the summer, paleontologists can be seen working at the site.

In addition to the quarry, the monument encompasses more than 210,000 acres of canyon country. A number of hiking trails cross the basin-and-plateau land. Sagebrush, greasewood, and saltbush survive in the dry, lower elevations, and "pygmy forests" of pinyon pine and juniper, along with stands of Douglas fir, grow higher up, providing habit for a number of animals, including Canada geese, deer, elk, mountain lions, and bighorn sheep.

Fascinating petroglyphs carved by the prehistoric Fremont people decorate cliff walls, while green oases of cottonwoods and box elders trail through the park, following the rivers and their canyons.

The first dinosaur bones were dug from the monument's quarry in 1909. Archaeologists continue to work at the site, exposing the surfaces of dinosaur bones but not removing them.

DINOSAUR QUARRY

Dinosaur Quarry was discovered in 1909 by a paleontologist named Earl Douglass from the Carnegie Museum in Pittsburgh.

Though fur trader William H. Ashley and explorer-scientist John Wesley Powell had each floated down the Green River near the ridge years earlier without noticing the fossils, Douglass knew what to look for. He was aware that similar rocks in Colorado and Wyoming had contained great collections of dinosaur bones, so he began to search this area in 1908.

On August 17, 1909, he wrote in his diary: "At last, in the top of the ledge . . . I saw eight of the tail bones of a Brontosaurus in exact position. It was a beautiful sight."

El Malpais

National Monument

Volcanic badlands with a lively past

El Malpais—"badlands" in Spanish—is rich in spectacular volcanic scenery, beautiful natural features, and traces of long-vanished human settlements.

The 115,000 acres of New Mexico's El Malpais National Monument contain many reminders of its eruptive past: jagged spatter cones, fragile ice caves, and the longest lava tube cave system in North America, extending at least 17 miles. Some tubes contain ice year-round, despite seasonal rises in temperature.

The park has several major lava flows, some of which are interrupted by islands of native plant and animal communities called kipukas. These are undisturbed areas that were encircled but not covered by lava flows.

People have lived in the El Malpais region for more than 10,000 years. Between A.D. 950 and 1350, it was a community of the great Chaco Culture, centered 80 miles to the north. The Anasazi people lived along the edges of these lava flows until the mid-1300s. The monument preserves ruins of the Anasazi, as well as reminders of white homesteaders who struggled to make a living here.

Hiking trails and roads lead to other highlights of the monument, including the Cebolla Wilderness, a forested rimrock area that features prehistoric rock art and historic homesteads; the Zuni-Acoma Trail, an ancient Pueblo trade route; and La Ventana Natural Arch, a large sandstone formation dating from the dinosaur age.

Millions of years of volcanic activity created the sinister-looking landscape, which still bears the scars of five major lava flows.

El Morro
National Monument

A timeless record of long-gone travelers

El Morro National Monument preserves a timeless record of the people who have lived and passed through this region.

A sandstone bluff rises 200 feet from the desert floor. At its base is a pool of cool, clear water, surrounded by cattails, sunflowers, and native grasses. For thousands of years, people crossing the hot, dry desert of what is now New Mexico rested in the shadow of the bluff and refreshed themselves at the pool. For thousands of years, too, they have been compelled to leave their marks on the rock.

The Zuni Indians, descendants of the ancient Anasazi, called this place A'ts'ina, or "place of writings on the rock." The Zuni and their Anasazi ancestors carved images here, including mountain sheep, humanlike creatures, and bear claws. A'ts'ina is still considered a sacred place by modern Zuni.

El Morro rises above a major east-west trail, which has been used since antiquity. The pool of cool, clear water at its base has lured many weary travelers to linger here.

241

HIGHRISE PUEBLOS

Atop El Morro are the remains of two Anasazi pueblos; A'ts'ina, the larger of the two, was built around 1275.

Anasazi builders cut rock into slabs and piled one on top of the other, using clay and pebbles to cement the slabs in place. The pueblo, which once stood about 300 feet high, housed between 1,000 and 1,500 people in at least 875 connected rooms around a central courtyard.

Down on the plain, the Anasazi of A'ts'ina pueblo grew corn and other crops in irrigated fields. Granaries in the pueblo held the surplus for times of need. Rainwater was collected in cisterns on the mesa top, but the Anasazi also used "steps" in the rock to reach the pool at the base of El Morro.

■ ■ ■

Spaniards who passed by called the bluff El Morro, "the headland." Don Juan de Onate, who officially colonized New Mexico in 1598, carved his name on El Morro on April 16, 1605. This is the first known European inscription on the rock. After that, hundreds of Spanish governors, soldiers, and priests left brief notes in stone at El Morro. Pioneers and railroad survey parties also added their stories to the rock.

U.S. soldiers, arriving in the mid-1800s, called the bluff Inscription Rock. In 1849, army engineer James H. Simpson and artist Richard Kern were intrigued by the inscriptions and spent two days copying them. Simpson's written descriptions and Kern's drawings were the first records of Inscription Rock.

Self-guiding trails with wayside exhibits lead from the visitor center to Inscription Rock and the ancient pueblo ruins above. From here, visitors get a great view of the surrounding land, which once rose as high as El Morro. Pinyon and ponderosa pine forests grow nearby, and wildflowers bloom all summer.

The ruins of two Anasazi pueblos top the mesa at El Morro. A'ts'ina pueblo was unearthed by archaeologists in the 1950s.

■ ■ ■

Florissant Fossil Beds

National Monument

A storehouse of petrified insects and plants

According to Western legend, an early fur trapper visiting the Florissant area in the mountains of central Colorado talked of a "petrified forest of petrified trees, full of petrified birds singing petrified songs."

Today, Florissant Fossil Beds National Monument is internationally known for its collection of petrified insects. Even such delicate creatures as butterflies, trapped in rock for millions of years, are almost perfectly preserved, complete with antennae, legs, hairs, and wing patterns. The area also features petrified trees and plant fossils, revealing in stone a picture of life long ago.

Some 35 million years ago, the land was covered by a lake stretching 15 miles. Giant redwoods and other trees bordered the lake, while ferns and shrubs grew thick under the canopy of trees. In this warm, humid environment, many thousands of insects thrived.

A nearby volcano erupted periodically, showering the area with tons of ash, which trapped plants, animals, and insects at the bottom of the lake. As the ash compacted, it transformed into shale and eventually turned the buried plant and animal life into fossils.

Since the area was discovered in the late 1800s, more than 1,100 species of dragonflies, beetles, ants, and other insects have been identified here, including all of the known New World butterflies. The fossils indicate that insects 35 million years ago were much like those today. Fossils of some of the insects and plants found at the monument are on display inside the visitor center.

A highlight of the nearly 6,000-acre monument is the Petrified Forest Loop Trail, which leads to "Big Stump," the remains of a giant sequoia 74 feet in circumference. If the tree were alive today, it would be nearly 300 feet tall.

The petrified stumps of massive sequoias and other trees stand today where they were buried by volcanic mudflows millions of years ago.

243

Fort Union
National Monument

An outdoor museum of life on the frontier

Once the largest military outpost west of the Mississippi River, Fort Union is now a collection of crumbled adobe walls and a few chimneys that rise above the ground. Fort Union National Monument preserves these unreconstructed buildings as an outdoor museum of life on the frontier.

The first Fort Union, which is not open to the public, was a group of shabby log buildings established in 1851 to protect travelers on the Santa Fe Trail and local residents from Indian attacks. A second fort was built in 1861, but the massive earthwork was damp, unventilated, and unhealthy. Most of the troops chose to camp in tents outside the fort.

At its peak, Fort Union was an impressive military fort and major supply depot of more than 50 buildings. It is preserved today as an outdoor museum.

244

Built in 1851 to protect mail coaches and traders headed west on the Santa Fe Trail, Fort Union was once the largest of a hundred frontier posts west of the Mississippi.

Two years later, the largest and final fort, the ruins of which visitors see at the monument, was begun. The fort took six years to build and included a military post, as well as a separate quartermaster depot with warehouses, corrals, shops, offices, and quarters. As a result, there were more civilians than military at the post.

A self-guiding trail identifies the ruins, including the Post Commander's home, an eight-room house with a wide center hall perfect for dancing, and the military prison, where soldiers and civilians alike were confined. The hospital was one of the finest in the West at the time, and civilians could use it for 50 cents a day.

The visitor center displays an interesting collection of artifacts from life at the fort.

Gila Cliff Dwellings

National Monument

Abandoned home of the Mogollon people

At the edge of the Gila Wilderness, the nation's first designated wilderness area, is the small but intriguing Gila Cliff Dwellings National Monument. Established in 1907, this 533-acre site is jointly run by the National Park Service and the Forest Service.

The 44-mile drive from the town of Silver City to the monument winds through the mountains of southern New Mexico, providing breathtaking views of rugged canyons and wild lands that look much as they did when the ancient Mogollon people built their homes in the cliffs of the Gila River Valley.

Visitors can hike throughout the high desert and pine forest of the monument and up to the ruins perched 180 feet above the canyon floor. The dwellings, built in the late 1200s in natural caves, contain about 40 rooms. The Mogollon quarried local stone to build the walls.

The Mogollon were farmers who cultivated squash, corn, beans, and other crops on the mesa tops and along the river. They are known for the distinctive white pottery they made and decorated with black designs of stylized fish and animals.

The Mogollon grew and hunted food, traded with other tribes, and fashioned jewelry and art here. Then, in the early 1300s, they abandoned their homes and left for places unknown.

Gila Cliff Dwellings National Monument preserves the ruined cliffside homes of the Mogollon Indians, who lived here from the late 1270s through the early 1300s.

Great Sand Dunes

National Monument

Mountains of sand sculpted by the wind

The tallest sand dunes in the world rise some 700 feet from the base of Colorado's Sangre de Cristo Mountains. Proclaimed a national monument in 1932, the dunes are a place to explore, watch wildlife, and see geological processes in action.

The building blocks of the Great Sand Dunes, which cover approximately 39 square miles, are billions of tiny granules of sand. The sand comprises eroded bits of the San Juan Mountains and particles of rock left in the valley by alpine glaciers during the Ice Age. For countless centuries, the Rio Grande carried the sand through the San Luis Valley, depositing it in its riverbed and along its shores.

As the Rio Grande changed its course over time, these great deposits of sand were exposed, and high winds blew them across the broad, flat valley and to the base of the steep Sangre de Cristo Mountains. There the winds dropped their load of sand, carrying only the lightest particles up and over the massive barrier. Load by load, over thousands of years, the Great Sand Dunes were created.

Today, the dunes are remarkably stable in spite of winds that continue to blow at 40 miles per hour or more. The moisture contained within the dunes keeps them from blowing away, while the winds work like a sculptor, constantly shaping and contouring them.

The tallest sand dunes in North America continue to shift and change at the base of the Sangre de Cristo Mountains.

Hohokam Pima
National Monument

Evidence of an advanced society of farmers

In the mesquite-studded desert valley southeast of Phoenix, excavations have revealed a surprisingly developed ancient farming culture that lasted from several centuries before the birth of Christ to A.D. 1400 or 1500.

The Hohokam people, named after a modern Pima Indian word meaning "that which has vanished," are believed to have been the first irrigationists in what is now the United States. An ancient system of hand-dug canals—the earliest dating from as far back as 300 B.C.—extends for miles throughout Arizona's Salt River and Gila River valleys.

In 1934 and again 30 years later, archaeologists excavated a site on the Gila River Indian Reservation that the Pima called Skoaquik, or "Place of the Snakes." Snaketown, as the archaeologists called it, contained pit houses, canals, what appears to be a ball court, countless artifacts, and shells decorated with etchings. The houses essentially were shallow pits dug into the ground and covered with mud and brush.

After more than 12 centuries of occupation, Snaketown was abandoned sometime between A.D. 1100 and 1200, but the Hohokam continued to live in scattered, smaller settlements up and down the valley. Today, Snaketown is again underground. After the last dig, archaeologists, using bulldozers, filled the 300-acre site with dirt to protect the remains from weather.

The Snaketown site was designated Hohokam Pima National Monument in 1972, but it remains closed to the public. The Pima Indians, who are thought to be related to the Hohokam people, have made it clear that they do not want non-Indian visitors admitted to the archaeological sites on their reservation. Tourists are welcome to visit other areas of the reservation, however, including the Gila River Indian Arts and Crafts Center, a source of income for local artisans.

Hovenweep
National Monument

Intriguing towers that rise up from the rocks

At Hovenweep, on what is now the Colorado-Utah border, the Anasazi Indians built elegant towers that rose from the rocks. Hovenweep National Monument, proclaimed in 1923, contains the ruins of six clusters of multistory towers located at the heads of canyons.

A self-guiding tour lets visitors explore the prehistoric sites of Square Tower Group. These sites are the best-preserved of the monument's ruins and include square and circular towers, many-roomed pueblos, and small cliff dwellings. Though most of the mortar that held them together has long since crumbled, some of the walls still stand more than 20 feet tall.

Scientists have determined that the Anasazi constructed the towers at Hovenweep—Ute for "deserted valley"—in the 1200s, though their purpose is unclear. They may have been built for food storage, defense, ceremonies, or skywatching. Ports at strategic points in the remaining walls overlook the approaches to buildings, trails, and springs.

The Anasazi were probably the ancestors of the present-day Pueblo tribes. They flourished in the Four Corners region, where Utah, Arizona, New Mexico, and Colorado meet. For nearly 1,500 years, they hunted, gathered wild plants, and raised corn, beans, and squash here. At some point, for reasons unknown, the Anasazi left Hovenweep, abandoning their buildings to the elements.

Prehistoric Pueblo Indians built multistory dwellings and round towers at the heads of canyons. Ports at strategic points in the tower walls allowed the inhabitants to observe their surroundings.

Lava Beds
National Monument

A beautiful place with a turbulent history

The history of this beautiful and desolate place is turbulent, both in geologic and human terms. Hardly had this rugged, northern California landscape cooled from a million years of volcanic activity when it was stained with the spilled blood of those who had learned to make a living here.

Evidence of the geologic violence can be seen everywhere here in the form of spatter and cinder cones, lava flows, and chimneys. Perhaps the most spectacular remnants are the lava tubes, formed when the cooler surface layer of a lava flow solidified while the lava beneath remained fluid, eventually draining out when the eruption stopped. Formed over 30,000 years ago, these tubes run for thousands of feet. Nearly 200 of them are open for exploration by visitors. Lamps are provided by the Park Service (warm clothing and protective head gear is also recommended).

In the thousand years since the last cinder cones were formed, vegetation has grown, from grasslands at lower altitudes (4,000 feet)

One of the most striking features of Lava Beds National Monument is its abundance of lava tube caves—there are nearly 200 within the monument.

For centuries, this rough lava landscape in northern California was home to the Modoc Indians. The government forced the tribe to move to Oregon.

■ ■ ■

to ponderosa pines at higher elevations (the highest point in the monument is 5,493 feet).

The abundance of game and fish, along with the shelter provided by the rugged rock formations, made this a place for human habitation as well. For centuries this area was home to the Modoc Indians, who used the reeds (tules) that grew around Tule Lake to make baskets, boats, and homes.

The arrival of European settlers in the 1850s marked the beginning of the end for the Modoc way of life. In 1864, they were relocated to Oregon. After a few months, the Modocs began returning to their homeland in numbers that continued to increase.

In 1872, the U.S. Army was ordered to return the Modocs to the reservation. This time fighting broke out, and the Modocs used the caves and fissures of the jagged landscape to their advantage, holding out for five months before succumbing to a much-enlarged army force in 1873.

A SAD BETRAYAL

When a wave of gold-seekers swept over California in the mid-1800s, the Modocs, based along the shores of Tule Lake, resisted the intruders.

Then a new chief, Kintpuash, pursued peace with the settlers. After a period of imperfect harmony, though, the settlers pushed for the removal of the Modocs to a reservation in Oregon, where they were forced to share scarce rations with their traditional enemies. Eventually they returned to their ancestral land.

The second attempt to remove them resulted in a war in which the Modocs held off the U.S. Army for five months. Betrayal by a few tribe members finally enabled the Army to capture Kintpuash. He and three others were hanged, and the remaining 153 Modocs were again removed from the Lava Beds, this time for good.

■ ■ ■

Montezuma Castle
National Monument

A palatial dwelling built 800 years ago

Tucked into a cliff recess high above the Verde Valley in Arizona is a multistory dwelling built by the Sinagua more than 800 years ago. The Sinagua, Spanish for "without water," were close neighbors and contemporaries of the Anasazi. They originally occupied the foothills and plateaus near the Verde Valley, where they lived in pithouses and farmed without irrigation, depending on rain to water their crops.

Around 1125, the Sinagua moved into the valley and began using the irrigation system left by the Hohokam, who had lived here earlier. They also adopted the Anasazi style of building homes of stone above ground.

The 20-room dwelling preserved at Montezuma Castle National Monument was begun early in the twelfth century. A short trail along Beaver Creek leads from the visitor center, which displays Sinagua pottery, textiles, and other artifacts, to the ruins, which are closed to exploration. The Sinagua were not as skilled at masonry as the Anasazi, yet this prehistoric structure is one of the best-preserved in the Southwest. A six-story apartment nearby, however, has deteriorated badly.

The monument also contains Montezuma Well, a natural limestone sink fed by artesian springs. This oasis in the desert attracted Hohokam and Sinagua farmers, who irrigated their crops with its water. Traces of irrigation ditches, thickly coated with lime, are still visible throughout the area.

Opposite page: Montezuma Castle National Monument preserves two multistory cliff dwellings built by the Sinagua around the turn of the twelfth century.

Montezuma Well, a natural limestone sink fed by artesian springs, provided water for Hohokam and Sinagua farmers to irrigate their crops. Between A.D. 1125 and 1400, the well supported a community of 150 to 200 residents.

Muir Woods

National Monument

560 acres of redwoods in a fog-filled California canyon

ome 140 million years ago, colossal evergreens covered much of the Northern Hemisphere. As the climate changed, their numbers dwindled, and today their descendants—redwoods and giant sequoias—survive only in pockets in California, southeastern Oregon, and central China.

In 1905, Congressman William Kent and his wife bought 295 acres of one of the Bay Area's last virgin stands of old-growth redwoods and donated it to the Federal Government for protection. Three years later, President Theodore Roosevelt declared the tract a national monument and suggested naming it after Kent, but the congressman wanted the woods named for John Muir, one of the nation's earliest and most eloquent conservationists.

When Muir learned the new redwood preserve would be named after him, he wrote, "This is the best tree-lover's monument that could possibly be found in all the forests of the world."

Right: *Moss carpets the trunks of many trees in Muir Woods, the result of a combined assault by winter rains and summer fog.*

Far right: *In 1908, one of the Bay Area's last uncut stands of old-growth redwoods was preserved in honor of legendary conservationist John Muir.*

Muir Woods National Monument

Camping is not permitted in Muir Woods, but the area is ideal for hiking. Trails wind through groves of majestic coastal redwoods that spire as high as 252 feet.

Muir Woods National Monument, just north of San Francisco in a fog-filled canyon, contains 560 acres of coast redwoods. Cathedral and Bohemian Groves contain the woods' tallest redwoods, spiring as high as 252 feet. The oldest redwood here is at least 1,000 years old. Lush ferns and redwood sorrel carpet the canyon floor, while moss and lichens coat trees and rocks.

Six miles of walking trails cross the monument, including a self-guided, paved nature trail that explains the life cycle of redwoods. Some grow from tiny seeds the size of oatmeal flakes, which generally sprout only if fire has cleared the floor of old pine needles so that seedlings can reach the mineral layer of the soil.

In Muir Woods most trees reproduce by sprouting. Sprouts shoot up from stumps or from roots around the base of a tree. Bark six to 12 inches thick protects the trees from fire, insects, and fungi.

Following the trails that lead deeper into the woods offers more solitude, and it is here that Muir's advice rings true: "Come to the woods, for here is rest."

Although redwoods are the main attraction, Muir Woods is also home to California buckeye, Douglas fir, madrona, and other tree species.

Natural Bridges

National Monument

Impressive formations created by erosion

Three massive natural bridges of stone—the largest and most impressive collection of such formations in the world—can be found at this site in southeastern Utah. The oldest is Owachomo, a 106-foot-high bridge that is only nine feet thick across the top. Though it is no longer being eroded by water, it is susceptible to cracking.

The Sipapu Bridge ("place of emergence" in Hopi), is the largest bridge in both height (220 feet) and span (268 feet). The youngest of the three is Kachina Bridge, named for the symbols that are carved on the bridge and also found on kachina dolls. This bulky bridge is 210 feet high and 93 feet thick. Floodwaters in White Canyon are still eroding and enlarging Kachina.

Water is the force that forms natural bridges (natural arches are formed by other erosional processes). When a river forms a great loop, almost circling back on itself, it can create a thin rock wall in which a natural bridge can form. Running water scrapes away at opposite sides of the thin wall. Eventually, the river breaks through the wall and takes the new, shorter course under the bridge. The river continues to wear down the rock, slowly enlarging the opening.

In addition to the bridges, the monument contains fascinating plant and animal life, as well as prehistoric ruins.

The national monument contains three massive stone bridges built by wind and water—the largest collection of natural bridges in the world.

Navajo
National Monument

Some of the best-preserved ruins in the Southwest

Tucked into the stark walls of Tsegi Canyon are some of the best-preserved ruins in the Southwest. Navajo National Monument preserves three ancient Anasazi villages discovered by Navajos long after the "Ancient Ones" were gone, hence the monument's name. Two of these villages—Betatakin and Keet Seel—are open to visitors willing to make the effort to get there.

The first Anasazi moved into the village called Betatakin around A.D. 1250. The deep, south-facing alcove was a good place to build, and by 1286, the village may have been home to as many as 125 people. It was abandoned within 50 years.

Keet Seel, home to at least 150 people, was the largest of the villages, and it was occupied much longer than Betatakin. Anasazi lived here as early as A.D. 950, but the structures from that period are gone. What remains are the houses and kivas (ceremonial places) from the mid-1200s.

The ruins are not easily accessible. Ranger-led tours of Betatakin take six hours and require the physical equivalent of walking up a 70-story building. The round-trip hike to Keet Seel is 16 miles and can take ten hours or more. Tours are seasonal and participation is limited.

Betatakin, which means "ledge house" in Navajo, was once a bustling center of life for some 125 Anasazi Indians.

Organ Pipe Cactus
National Monument

Spectacular evidence of nature's adaptability

*I*f necessity is indeed the mother of invention, then adversity must be the mother of adaptation, for the cruel heat of the Sonoran Desert has given rise to adaptation in the extreme.

Visitors to Arizona's Organ Pipe Cactus National Monument can see proof of nature's resourcefulness everywhere, from the kangaroo rat, which drinks no water yet thrives in one of the world's most arid climates, to the creosote bush, which manufactures its own natural herbicide to prevent competition for water by encroaching plant life.

The most visible adaptations to this extreme climate are the stunning and sometimes bizarre forms of the monument's 26 species of cactus, including cholla, prickly pear, senita, saguaro, and the towering organ pipe cactus, with its huge vertical arms stretching up to 25 feet high. Although plentiful in Mexico, the organ pipe is rare in the United States, its northern range limited almost exclusively to the monument.

Evidence can also be found of those who failed to adapt. Unmarked graves along old El Camino del Diablo—"The Devil's Highway"—are somber testament to the unforgiving nature of this desert.

Portions of this historic trail are paralleled by the 53-mile Puerto Blanco Drive, one of two scenic loops available to motorists. The Puerto Blanco traverses a stunning array of scenery, from the oasis of Quitobaquito to the heart of the Sonoran Desert, featuring organ pipe cacti, saguaros, and elephant trees. The shorter Ajo Mountain

Nearly 30 species of cactus thrive here, including the multiarmed namesake of the monument, a large cactus rarely found in the United States, although it is common in Mexico.

Organ Pipe Cactus National Monument showcases the country's most pristine tract of Sonoran Desert.

Drive also features impressive desert landscapes and large stands of organ pipe cactus.

Besides these two scenic drives, the national monument also contains a few unimproved dirt roads leading to abandoned mines, empty ranch houses, and other historic sites.

For those wanting a closer look, there are several excellent hiking trails, some with interpretive signs or pamphlets explaining important natural features. The trails offer breathtaking views of nearby mountains and the surrounding terrain. The best months to hike are October through April.

LIFE IN THE DESERT

The passage from day to night in the Sonoran Desert is a transition from one world to another. Jackrabbits, snakes, kangaroo rats, and elf owls emerge from their underground burrows, cactus holes, and other cool and sheltered spots where they have spent the day. Even the organ pipe cactus waits until the sun has set to open its delicate lavender-white flowers, closing them again near sunrise.

Of those animals that prefer daylight, such as lizards, bighorn sheep, and most birds, the majority limit activity to early morning or late afternoon during the summer, seeking shade during the hottest part of the day, when air temperatures can reach 118 degrees and ground temperatures can escalate to a blistering 175 degrees.

Petroglyph
National Monument

An amazing
collection of
rock carvings

Ancient depictions of humpbacked flute players and humanlike "star beings" decorate the volcanic cliffs of New Mexico's Petroglyph National Monument. Established in 1990 on the edge of Albuquerque, the site is owned and managed jointly by the National Park Service, the City of Albuquerque, and the State of New Mexico.

The 7,272-acre park preserves more than 15,000 historic and prehistoric images along the West Mesa escarpment, making it one of the world's largest collections of rock carvings. From prehistoric times, people have recorded the world around them—as well as their

Petroglyph National Monument preserves more than 15,000 petroglyphs, making it one of the world's largest collections of these ancient rock carvings.

Early Americans used rock art in ceremonies and rituals, but also to record time, legends, important events, and even daily happenings.

■ ■ ■

myths and beliefs—on stone. Images carved into the rock are called petroglyphs; painted images are called pictographs. Petroglyphs are the most common type of rock art in North America, occurring by the thousands in the Southwest.

Pueblo artists may have begun carving images into the rocks as far back as 12,000 years ago. Several trails that wind through the site provide a good sampling of their work. A trail guide helps visitors identify the images.

Geometric patterns found along the Canyon Trail are thought to be the oldest petroglyphs in the area. Other common images include human figures, masks, animals, and insects.

After thousands of years of exposure to the elements, the boulder ridge, created by volcanic eruptions some 150,000 years ago, developed a dark layer of clays, minerals, and organic material called "rock varnish." Artists pecked through the dark outer layer with a sharpened stone, exposing the lighter interior and giving contrast to the images.

Rock artists also created petroglyphs by holding a sharpened stone against the rock surface and hitting it with another stone, piece of bone, or sturdy hunk of wood.

In addition to providing the perfect canvas for rock art, the escarpment is a rich habitat for desert plants, grasses, and wildflowers. Hawks, roadrunners, coyotes, foxes, and lizards can be found among the plants.

ROCK ART RITUALS

Archaeologists have spent decades researching rock art and have learned a great deal about how and when early Americans created these mysterious symbols. Why they carved and painted images on rocks is a more difficult question to answer.

It appears that most rock art was created during ceremonies or rituals as a way of asking the gods for their blessings in the form of rain, fertility, a plentiful food supply, and other necessities. Ancient people also used rocks like pages in a history book to record time, territory, legends, important events, and daily happenings.

As archaeologists continue to uncover the secrets of rock art, we continue to learn more about the lives of early Americans.

■ ■ ■

Pinnacles
National Monument

A sanctuary for people and birds of prey

The russet spires and crags of Pinnacles National Monument, south of the San Francisco Bay area, provide an ideal sanctuary, both for people and birds of prey. Raptors are drawn to the tall rocks to nest and raise their young; people come to hike the chaparral country, climb sheer rock walls, and explore caves.

The Pinnacles, which pierce the sky like a collection of spears, are the remains of an ancient volcano that was sculpted by wind, water, and frost. The rest of the volcano has been carried almost 200 miles south by movement along the San Andreas Fault.

The more than 16,000-acre monument has two separate entrances, Bear Gulch on the east and Chaparral on the west. No roads link the two, but 26 miles of hiking trails do. The easy Bear Gulch Caves trek provides views of rock climbers and birds and the opportunity to explore murky caves. Moses Spring Trail climbs steeply through oak and buckeye, and High Peaks Trail has good views of the area's contrasting geology. To the north visitors can see the jagged, volcanic Balconies Cliffs. To the far southwest is the smoothly rounded Gabilan Range, a more typical formation for this area.

The Pinnacles are alive with plant and animal life year-round, but especially in the spring, when colorful wildflowers cover the green hills.

A favorite place for rock climbing, the monument has an endless supply of outcroppings—some of them 600 feet high—connected by 26 miles of trails.

Pipe Spring
National Monument

A memorial to cowboys and early cattle ranches

*I*n 1870, Brigham Young, president of the Mormon Church, visited an oasis in the parched Arizona Strip. He quickly recognized Pipe Spring's potential value as a cattle ranch for the church and made plans to build a fort to protect the valuable water supply.

Called Windsor Castle, the fort—along with barracks and juniper-post corrals—is preserved at Pipe Spring National Monument as a memorial to early cattle ranches and cowboys.

Church members helped pay their tithing by working on the fort. They quarried stone from the red sandstone cliffs to the west and hauled lumber from a nearby sawmill to build the fort. Windsor Castle consisted of two rectangular, two-story houses with connecting walls that formed a courtyard. The structure housed bedrooms, offices, a parlor, the kitchen, the area's first telegraph, and a room for making cheese. The rooms are furnished with original items from the pioneer days. The ranch peaked in 1879, with 2,269 head of cattle and 162 horses worth more than $54,000. The Mormon Church sold the ranch in 1888.

On the grounds, visitors can tour re-created gardens and orchards, the blacksmith shop, harness room, corral, and other historic buildings, including the cabin where explorer John Wesley Powell's survey crew stayed in 1871. A short trail loops through the monument, highlighting historic and natural features of Pipe Spring.

The nineteenth-century fort at Pipe Spring guarded a valuable water supply in the Arizona desert. Mormon settlers established a successful cattle ranch here during the 1870s.

Rainbow Bridge
National Monument

One of the seven wonders of the world

One of the seven wonders of the world can be found in the canyon-lands of southeastern Utah. Rainbow Bridge is the world's largest natural bridge, standing 290 feet tall and spanning 275 feet; the top of the bridge is 42 feet thick and 33 feet wide.

Rainbow Bridge is made of salmon-pink sandstone, with dark red and brown vertical streaks of iron ore. These particles, called "desert varnish," may have leached from the rocks, or they may have been carried by the wind as dust that stuck to the moister areas of the rock. Subtle shades of purple and orange are brought out by the afternoon sunlight, turning the bridge into a rainbow of stone. For many Native Americans, Rainbow Bridge is a sacred place. The Navajo believe rainbows represent the guardians of the universe.

The base of Rainbow Bridge was built by nature hundreds of millions of years ago, as layers of reddish-brown sands and muds, called Kayenta Sandstone, were deposited and compacted. The span of the bridge, composed of Navajo Sandstone, was formed as wave after wave of sand was deposited, forming dunes up to 1,000 feet high. Over the next 100 million years, the base and the dunes were buried under more than 5,000 feet of rock layers. The heat and immense pressure further compacted and hardened the rock of these formations.

Around 60 million years ago, the area now known as the Colorado Plateau began to uplift. Streams cut into and eroded the layers of rock as they lifted above sea level. As these massive layers rose and tilted, streams gained more momentum and force.

Water flowing off Navajo Mountain formed Bridge Creek. As the creek mean-

Remote Rainbow Bridge is hidden among canyons that have been carved by streams making their way to the Colorado River.

Rainbow Bridge, standing 290 feet high with a span of 275 feet, is the largest natural bridge on earth.

■ ■ ■

dered toward the Colorado River, it slowly eroded the sandstone, creating thin rock walls as it nearly looped back on itself. Rushing water during floods pounded away at the walls until the loosely cemented Navajo sandstone gave way, creating a hole. Over the centuries, as the creek flowed through the hole, it continued to work away at the sandstone until Rainbow Bridge was formed.

Most people travel by boat from Lake Powell to the rather remote Rainbow Bridge National Monument, though it is possible to hike a grueling 13 miles to reach the monument. Hikers must get a permit from the Navajo Nation and should carry the topographical "Navajo Mountain Quadrangle Map," available from the Park Service.

Hiking either to and from or just around the 160-acre monument allows visitors to experience some of the spectacular scenery of the Colorado Plateau. Steep rock walls form a labyrinth of canyons—some dry, some alive with cottonwood, ash, western redbud, serviceberry, and other plants.

THE LOST BRIDGE

Before Lake Powell was created, the Rainbow Bridge area was one of the most inaccessible regions in the continental United States. Around the turn of the century, few, if any, white people had seen the bridge, though they heard reports of the bridge from Native Americans.

In 1909, two groups of scientists decided to look for the great stone arch. The two parties, one led by the government surveyor W. B. Douglass and the other led by University of Utah dean Byron Cummings, eventually decided to join forces. Two Indian guides helped lead them over the slick rock surfaces and through the maze of rugged canyons to what is now called Bridge Canyon. There, in the late afternoon sun, they saw the beautifully colored bridge. A year later it was proclaimed a national monument.

■ ■ ■

Salinas Pueblo Missions

National Monument

Where the Franciscans attempted to introduce Christianity

*I*n 1853, Major J. H. Carlton was sent on an expedition to the Salinas Valley in New Mexico. At dusk he came upon some eerie ruins. "The tall ruins standing there in solitude had an aspect of sadness and gloom," he wrote. "The cold wind…appeared to roar and howl through the roofless pile like an angry demon."

Carlton knew that the ruins were once a Christian church, but he did not know that the long heaps of stone nearby marked an ancient pueblo. The pueblo he came across is Abo, one of three included in Salinas Pueblo Missions National Monument.

Franciscan friars began arriving in the high desert of what is now central New Mexico in the 1620s, bringing with them a zealous desire to Christianize the natives of the New World. To the Pueblo Indians, who looked to a number of gods to answer the village's needs, the idea of worshipping just one god was alien. But the Franciscans told them their salvation depended on accepting the Christian God.

The friars were attracted to the Salinas Valley because it was a major trade center and one of the most populous parts of the Pueblo world. The Pueblo Indians, numbering 10,000 or more, had developed a stable agricultural community and lived in apartmentlike complexes called pueblos. Beginning in 1629, the Spanish built colonial missions attached to Abo, Gran Quivira, and Quarai. There the Indians were instructed in religion and European crafts and husbandry, with the goal of making them good Spanish citizens.

Franciscan friars became active in central New Mexico during the 1620s. Shown at right are the ruins of their mission at the Pueblo Indian village of Quarai.

The remains of a corn-grinding room at Gran Quivira. Pueblo women once knelt at these workstations, using the smaller stones to pound corn into meal.

268

Opposite page: An approaching storm darkens the sky behind the church ruins at the Gran Quivira pueblo. The house of worship has withstood the elements better than the pueblo dwellings visible in the foreground.

■ ■ ■

Underground circular kivas, reminiscent of ancestral pit houses, served as sacred chambers for special ceremonies at the pueblos. Some Franciscan friars burned sacred kivas in an attempt to force Pueblo Indians to abandon their traditional religions.

■ ■ ■

To support their settlements, Spanish governors relied on profits from the sale of slaves captured in raids on Plains tribes and from goods produced by Indian labor. The Franciscans tried to ease the burden this placed on the Pueblo villages, but the government did not want to see such a profitable arrangement end.

In addition to the difficulties of cultural change, Apache raids, drought, and epidemics of diseases introduced by Europeans further destabilized the villages. The surviving Indians fled the pueblos in the 1670s, just 50 years after the friars' arrival.

The ruins preserved at the monument, which was established in 1909, are the best examples of seventeenth-century Spanish Franciscan mission churches in the United States. At Gran Quivira, a self-guided walking trail takes visitors from the ruins of the old church courtyard and mission burial ground to a partially excavated pueblo with its five kivas. Quarai is the most complete of the Salinas churches, and Abo features sophisticated church architecture and a large unexcavated pueblo.

The visitor center has slide and film presentations and displays of tools and pottery from the ruins.

KIVA SOCIETIES

Pueblos were divided into religious kiva societies, and every villager was a member of one. When a Pueblo Indian was ill or in need, he or she could turn to members of the group for help.

The Indians held ceremonies in the underground kivas to bring rain, fertile crops, and dependable harvests to the pueblo. Dancers dressed in kachina masks represented the spirits who would bring the Indians' messages to the gods. At first the Pueblo priests were willing to accept the new Christian god into their pantheon, but when the friars tried to make the Pueblo Indians give up their gods by destroying the kachina masks and burning their kivas, some Indians revolted.

In 1692, Spanish officials decided to allow the Indians to practice their religions alongside Christianity, but by then the Salinas pueblos had been abandoned.

■ ■ ■

Sunset Crater Volcano

National Monument

Protecting the region's volcanic treasures

The peaks, cinder cones, and lava flows of Sunset Crater Volcano National Monument represent a long period of volcanic activity. Evidence found here suggests that the eruptions were separated by periods of inactivity during the last two million years.

The last of these eruptions occurred about 900 years ago, forming the symmetrical cinder cone with its summit crater. Lava, cinders, and ash were blown from the volcano, covering the area in a blanket of black ash and cinders.

The region's Sinagua Indians had to leave the area until the volcano quieted and the ash settled. As the eruptions ceased, lava poured out from vents near the cinder cone's base. Minerals contained in vapors that escaped from fumaroles stained the cinders red. The volcano's cinder rim now seems to glow as if lit by a perpetual sunset.

The 3,000-acre monument was proclaimed in 1930 to protect the area's volcanic treasures. A visitor center provides information on the geology of the monument and is the contact point for guided tours.

A self-guided trail with markers leads across a lava flow, where hikers can see a hollow lava tube, squeeze-ups, hornitos, and other volcanic features. The lava tube is 25 feet long and so cold that there is ice in it for most of the year. The Lenox Crater Trail takes visitors for a climb up a cinder cone.

The red rim of Sunset Crater Volcano, dusted with snow, rises 1,000 feet above the desert of north central Arizona.

In 1065, an eruption at Sunset Crater blanketed the region with black cinder. More than 900 years later, pine forests have reclaimed the landscape.

Timpanogos Cave

National Monument

A fantastic arrangement of fragile formations

High on the steep slopes of Utah's Wasatch Range, three limestone caves pierce 11,750-foot Mt. Timpanogos.

On a fall day in 1887, a Mormon settler by the name of Martin Hansen was cutting timber high on the south slopes of American Fork Canyon when he saw a set of mountain lion tracks. He followed the prints to where they ended on a high ledge. There he found an entrance to a small cave. Hansen returned later to explore it, discovering an array of fragile cave formations inside.

In 1915, while their family explored Hansen Cave, two teenagers stumbled upon the opening to a second cave, and in 1921 a third cave was found. The next year, President Warren G. Harding established Timpanogos Cave National Monument to protect the caverns and their spectacular features from vandalism.

The caves were formed 65 million years ago when water hollowed out the subterranean chambers. Over countless years, water trickled through the caves, depositing minerals shaped like tiny crystals on the ceilings, walls, and floors. The crystal deposits built up, forming a variety of stalactites, stalagmites, flowstone, draperies, and helictites, some as fragile as the threads of a spider's web.

Early tourists had to climb the side of the mountain to reach the

The trail to the caves offers an opportunity to explore American Fork Canyon, a rugged gorge slicing through the Wasatch Range. Douglas firs, white firs, maples, and oaks grow on the canyon's slopes.

One of the highlights of the Timpanogos Cave Tour is the Chimes Chamber. Park rangers lead groups of no more than 20 through the subterranean chambers.

■ ■ ■

caves. Today, visitors can walk up a paved trail, though the trip is still strenuous. In the 1930s, tunnels were built to connect the caves, and today a one-hour ranger-led tour explores Hansen, Middle, and Timpanogos caves.

Highlights of the tour include the Chimes Chamber of Timpanogos Cave, with its profusion of brilliant white helictites, and the Great Heart of Timpanogos, a giant cave formation of linked stalactites.

Though the caverns are millions of years old, they are still changing. Drop by drop, water continues to work its magic.

Timpanogos Cave is known for its tremendous amount and variety of helictites, unusual cave formations that do not usually occur in such great numbers.

■ ■ ■

Tonto
National Monument

Hidden cliff dwellings of the Salado Indians

As early as 5000 B.C., the rich floodplain of the Tonto Basin in Arizona attracted settlers. The first were the Hohokam. By 1150, however, the basin inhabitants had developed pottery styles, constructions methods, and other traits different from the traditional Hohokam ways, indicating that a new culture had emerged—the Salado. Tonto National Monument is the only National Park site dedicated to these people.

The Salado, like the Hohokam, were farmers, but they are distinguished by their beautiful pottery and woven cloth, examples of which are on display at the site's visitor center.

The monument includes two cliff dwellings built by the Salado more than 600 years ago, which visitors can walk through. The Salado built their pueblos into the hillside where wind and water had carved out recesses. The pueblos contain several connected rooms that were used for sleeping, storage, cooking, and protection.

The Lower Ruin had perhaps 16 ground floor rooms, some of which had a second story. The Indians used the open spaces of the terraces and rooftops for work and play. A steep trail leads to the Upper Ruin on a nearby ledge, a much larger dwelling with 32 rooms on the ground floor.

When peering into these rooms, visitors can see handprints on the walls and smoke stains on the ceilings, powerful reminders that these ruins were once full of life.

For centuries, until sometime between A.D. 1400 and 1450, the prehistoric Salado people lived in apartment-style buildings built into hillsides above the Tonto Basin.

The Salado relied on wild plants to supplement their cultivated crops. Saguaro cactus provided sweet, red fruit and could be used as a building material.

Tuzigoot

National Monument

A glimpse at life in a Sinagua community

The prehistoric dwellings at Tuzigoot, like those at nearby Montezuma Castle, were built by Sinagua farmers, yet their different styles of architecture are striking. Montezuma Castle is built into a cliff recess, while the Tuzigoot pueblo sprawls along an open ridge 120 feet above the Verde Valley.

The Sinagua began building their pueblo in A.D. 1125 and continued adding on to it until 1425. At first, about 50 people lived in a small cluster of rooms, but during the 1200s, the number increased to as many as 200 people.

The ground floor of the pueblo had 77 rooms, and in some places it stood two stories high. A few exterior doors led into the pueblo, but the Sinagua generally climbed ladders to enter their rooms through openings in the roof. The Park Service has recreated a typical Sinagua room in the visitor center to provide a glimpse of what life was like in a pueblo.

In addition to their day-to-day work in the fields, the Indians prepared food, dried animal skins, and made baskets and other items, some necessary, some decorative. They also made tools out of stone and bone, wove cloth out of locally grown cotton, and created attractive ornaments out of shells, turquoise, and a local red stone.

In the early 1400s, for reasons not fully understood, the Sinagua abandoned the Verde Valley, never to return.

The remains of the ancient Sinaguan village at Tuzigoot National Monument crown the summit of a long ridge above the Verde Valley.

Tuzigoot National Monument contains the remains of a Sinaguan village that flourished between 1125 and 1425. The original pueblo had 77 ground floor rooms.

Walnut Canyon

National Monument

A community of Sinagua Indian cliff dwellings

Nine hundred years ago, the eruptions at what is now called Sunset Crater created rich farmland in northern Arizona. A rush of people converged on the volcano area, so a group of Sinagua moved south of the volcano to a canyon where there was room to build and raise crops.

Between A.D. 1125 and 1250, the Sinagua built more than 300 small rooms of stone and mud into the limestone cliffs of Walnut Canyon. A rugged trail in Walnut Canyon National Monument leads to the ruins of 24 cliff dwellings, offering intimate views of the rooms. Visitors who look closely can see an 800-year-old fingerprint left in plaster by one of the builders.

From the trail it is possible to see 100 other dwellings across the canyon, and a short walk around the rim provides views of even more. The canyon provided the Sinagua with a good livelihood for almost 150 years. The canyon floor had a dependable source of water, and both rims provided fertile land to grow corn, beans, and squash.

The Sinagua also benefited from the diverse plant and animal life found in the canyon. The former included black walnuts, Douglas fir trees, cacti, and grapes; the latter comprised deer, foxes, and bears.

The Sinagua left Walnut Canyon for reasons that are not clear. Some anthropologists believe their descendants live today among the region's Pueblo Indians.

Nearly 800 years ago, Sinagua Indians used their masonry skills to build homes into the ledges of Walnut Canyon.

White Sands

National Monument

Snow-white dunes in the New Mexico desert

Like a blizzard on the windswept northern plains, snow-white dunes build and shift on the hot, dry New Mexico desert. The wind-sculpted hills of sand, which rise up to 60 feet high in some places, make up the world's largest gypsum desert. White Sands National Monument, proclaimed in 1933, contains 275 square miles of this unique dunefield.

The creation of the dunes began millions of years ago when a shift in the earth's crust exposed mountains and highlands containing layers of gypsum rock. For centuries, wind, rain, and melting snow dissolved the thick layers of gypsum and washed them into Lake Lucero, an ancient lake that filled part of the Tularosa Basin of south-central New Mexico.

About 10,000 years ago, the climate became hotter and drier. Eventually, Lake Lucero dried up, leaving behind a dry lake bed of large gypsum deposits that baked in the wind and sunshine of the basin. Powerful winds pounded the gypsum crystals into snowlike particles and whipped them into drifts. The process continues to this day.

Strong winds continue to push and build the dunes. As each dune grows and shifts away from the dried-up lake, a new one forms to take its place. As a result, the dunes are moving northeast as much as 30 feet per year.

The visitor center near the entrance to the site has exhibits and a sound and light program that help explain the formation of the

At White Sands National Monument, the footprints that visitors leave are slowly swallowed by drifting sand.

SURVIVAL OF THE FITTEST

Hardy plants and animals of the gypsum sand dunes have developed interesting features that allow them to survive in this harsh environment.

Some animals, like the Apache pocket mouse and an earless lizard, are as pale as the dunes themselves, allowing them to blend in with their surroundings. The camel cricket has gone one step further—it is so translucent that the outlines of its internal organs are visible.

Plants like the skunkbush develop long root systems that can reach deep into the dunes for nutrients. Others grow very tall—some up to 30 feet—in order to keep their "heads" above sand.

■ ■ ■

dunes and introduce the plants and animals that make their home here. A paved road, with markers that are explained in a guide book, leads into the dunes. Visitors can climb the dunes, which stay amazingly cool even on the hottest days, and explore them on a self-guiding nature trail.

Lake Lucero, where the gypsum crystals formed, is only accessible by a ranger-led car caravan. The lake lies within the White Sands Missile Range, site of the first atomic bomb test. The monument is surrounded by the missile range and Holloman Air Force Base.

Great dunes of snow-white gypsum sand cover 275 square miles of the northern end of the Chihuahuan Desert, forming the world's largest gypsum dune field.

■ ■ ■

Wupatki
National Monument

A former domain of the Sinagua Indians

Before the eruption of Sunset Crater Volcano in A.D. 1064, the Sinagua Indians of the region lived in earth lodges at the edges of large open meadows where they farmed. The eruption forced them to leave the area, relocating to villages in and around Arizona's Verde Valley.

Here the Sinagua found red Moenkopi sandstone, an excellent building material. They cut the sandstone into slabs and carefully stacked them, reinforcing structures with mud mortar. Pueblos were typically built on rock outcrops that were protected from erosion and provided good views of the surrounding lands.

Wupatki National Monument, proclaimed in 1924, has more than 35,000 acres of archaeological ruins. The main ruin at Wupatki is a three-story pueblo. Named after the Hopi word for "tall house," Wupatki Pueblo contained as many as 100 rooms during the 1100s. Some of the rooms have been excavated to reveal the clay firepits the occupants used for cooking and heating.

Near the pueblo are the remains of a ball court built of stone—a feature introduced by the Hohokam to the south—and an open-air amphitheater. The oval structure, with its smooth earthen floor, may have been used for tribal meetings and ceremonial dances.

Nearby is a fissure, or "blow hole," in the ground that works as a natural barometer—it expels or inhales air depending on the surface atmospheric pressure.

Wupatki National Monument includes the remnants of several pueblos, as well as a ball court and amphitheater.

Wupatki National Monument

Lomaki was one of several pueblos built by Sinagua Indians around A.D. 1065, after the eruptions at Sunset Crater to the south.

Archaeologists believe Wupatki was part of a major prehistoric trading network between the Indians of North America and those of Mexico and Central America. The Sinagua made their home here until about 1225.

The visitor center has exhibits detailing the history of the Walnut Canyon area and is the starting point for the Wupatki Ruins Trail, a self-guiding tour of the largest pueblo, the ball court, and the amphitheater. Other trails provide access to panoramic views and some of the monument's other pueblo ruins.

Yucca House

National Monument

Abandoned ruins of a prehistoric settlement

On the gently sloping base of southwestern Colorado's Sleeping Ute Mountain—so named because its silhouette against the horizon from the northeast resembles a person sleeping—is a cluster of mounds and ruins marking a prehistoric village.

The ruins were first described by Professor William H. Holmes in 1877, who named the two most conspicuous mounds the Upper House and the Lower House. The Upper House is the most prominent mound, rising 15 to 20 feet above its foundation. It contains the ruins of a three- or four-story building and is surrounded by many smaller mounds. To build the village, Indians hauled limestone a mile or more from the base of the Mesa Verde tableland.

Despite being one of the oldest national monuments, Yucca House, designated in 1919, is also one of the least developed. The site has no manmade features, and the mounds have yet to be excavated, though the Park Service expects they will yield much archaeological information.

One important question that remains unanswered, not only at this site, but also at other early Indian settlements in the region, is: What happened during the period between the twelfth and fourteenth centuries that caused so many of these communities to be abandoned? Theories abound, but no one knows for sure. Perhaps future excavations—here or at other sites that have yet to be studied—will finally solve the mystery.

Located about 15 miles south of Cortez, Colorado, the Yucca House is not for the casual visitor; the ten-minute drive from the highway is almost impassable in wet weather. Those who do make the journey can sign the visitor book, explore the ten-acre site, and witness the beauty of the area. There are no exhibits or interpretive signs as of this writing, so visitors will have to imagine what life might have been like in this village hundreds of years ago.

Bent's Old Fort

National Historic Site

An important way station on the Santa Fe Trail

*I*n southeastern Colorado near the Arkansas River stood an important way station along the Santa Fe Trail. Two brothers from Saint Louis, William and Charles Bent, and their partner Ceran St. Vrain, built a trading post in 1833 where the Santa Fe Trail met the Navajo Trail. It was known as La Junta, or "the junction."

The adobe fort, which measured 135 feet by 180 feet and had walls 15 feet high, contained living quarters, an Indian council room, a billiard room, warehouses, workshops, a trade room, and a dining room. Cacti planted along the top of the walls and two corner bastions with openings for cannons and muskets provided some security for the fort.

The Bent brothers employed what were then unheard-of methods to attract the Cheyenne, Arapaho, and other tribes to their trad-

Bent's Old Fort on the Santa Fe Trail has been reconstructed and furnished to approximate its appearance in 1845, when it was a center of commerce and politics.

Before the U.S. Army arrived in the 1840s, the fort was considered a friendly meeting place where even rival Indian tribes could gather to trade in peace.

■ ■ ■

Mountain men not unlike these contemporary interpreters routinely came to Bent's Fort to be outfitted before embarking on their trapping expeditions.

■ ■ ■

ing outlet: Instead of trying to cheat the Indians, they dealt with them fairly. They also refused to trade much in whiskey.

In 1837, William Bent married Owl Woman, the daughter of a Cheyenne medicine man, further cementing the good relations between the fort and the Indians. As a result, Bent's Fort became the trading hub of the Southwest. Indians brought buffalo robes and furs to trade for American manufactured goods hauled overland from Missouri and Mexican shipments coming north from Santa Fe.

For nearly two decades the trading post operated peacefully. But the Mexican-American War brought many soldiers to the area, as the fort became a military staging post for the U.S. invasion of New Mexico. The Indians stopped coming to the fort, and William Bent, disgusted by the federal government's use of his property, packed all his goods and blew the fort up in 1849.

The Park Service took over the ruins in 1976 and reconstructed Bent's Old Fort. Nowadays, it is always 1845 at the fort, where several rooms are furnished with antiques and reproductions, and rangers in period costumes play the roles of traders, trappers, and native peoples.

FOR SALE

The main items of trade at Bent's Fort were buffalo robes, beaver pelts, and horses that Cheyenne and Arapaho Indians, as well as Mexicans and mountain men, exchanged for factory-made items.

The fort's store also carried an unusual array of goods to sell to trappers and travelers. William Bent's son, George, remembered "such unusual luxuries as butter crackers, Bent's water crackers, candies of various sorts, and most remarkable of all, great jars of preserved ginger…."

■ ■ ■

Eugene O'Neill
National Historic Site

Home to one of America's greatest playwrights

Overlooking the San Ramon Valley and distant Mount Diablo in California, Tao House was once home to Eugene O'Neill, one of America's greatest playwrights. Today, it is a national historic site dedicated to O'Neill's life and work.

O'Neill was born in New York City in 1888 to actor parents who lived a vagabond life. O'Neill left his troubled home early and traveled the world. He lived for a time in a flophouse in Manhattan, drank heavily, and tried to commit suicide. At age 24, he went into a sanitarium to be treated for tuberculosis. While recovering, he began to write plays, and his life changed forever. Four years later, a group of amateur actors in Provincetown, Massachusetts, first staged one of his plays. Four years after that, he received the first of his four Pulitzer Prizes for the tragedy *Beyond the Horizon.*

O'Neill soon became known as America's most exciting playwright, and he was awarded the Nobel Prize for Literature in 1936. With the stipend, he and his wife Carlotta were able to build Tao House, which O'Neill called his "final harbor." Carlotta decorated the 28-room cinder block house with deep blue ceilings, red doors, black-stained floors, and Chinese furniture.

Though the O'Neills often entertained friends and family, Carlotta kept visitors away when her husband was working. O'Neill wrote what are generally considered his finest works here, including *The Iceman Cometh* and *Long Day's Journey into Night.*

A worsening tremor in his hands slowly robbed O'Neill of the ability to write, and he did not complete another play after 1943. He died in Boston ten years later.

Playwright Eugene O'Neill's beloved Tao House, where he wrote The Iceman Cometh *and* Long Day's Journey into Night, *is open for guided tours.*

288

Fort Bowie

National Historic Site

Where our government waged war on the Apaches

A footpath weaves through Fort Bowie National Historic Site, roughly paralleling a historic military wagon road past ruins and reminders of the bloody fight for control of Apache Pass.

Apache Spring—an important source of water in this pass through the Chiricahua Mountains of Arizona—attracted settlers to the area. First came the Apaches, probably in the early sixteenth century. A few centuries later, white emigrants, prospectors, and soldiers began arriving in ever-increasing numbers.

As settlers moved farther west, a mail and stage route was needed through the mountains. The unfailing water supplied by

Nestled between the Chiricahua and Dos Cabezas mountains, Fort Bowie National Historic Site includes the ruins of the fort, Apache Springs, a stagecoach station, and a cemetery.

Fort Bowie National Historic Site

Little remains of Fort Bowie, a once-substantial Army post built to protect travelers and mail coaches from Apache raids.

■ ■ ■

Apache Spring made Apache Pass the logical place for a stage station, even though it was in the heart of the Chiricahua Apaches' homeland. A station for the Butterfield Overland Stageline was built in Apache Pass in 1858, and its ruins can still be seen there.

The national historic site, which was established in 1964, also contains the ruins of Fort Bowie, built after the peace between the Apaches and whites ended when the Apache leader Cochise was wrongly accused of kidnapping a rancher's stepchild.

By 1869, a second, larger fort was built to serve as a base for more ambitious military operations against the Apaches. The fort's cemetery is evidence of the difficult life at the isolated fort, where the food was generally bad and the soldiers were often sick. After the surrender of Apache leader Geronimo at the fort in 1886, the Indian wars ended, and the fort was soon abandoned.

The backdrop of scenery today is little changed since the days of the fort. Apache Pass separates the Chiricahua Mountains to the south from the Dos Cabezas range to the north. Desert grasses and chaparral cover the lower slopes, giving way to oaks, junipers, and pinyon pine on the upper slopes. Willows and cottonwoods follow water sources, and wildflowers explode with color after good winter rains.

A simple, weathered tombstone marks the final resting place of one of Geronimo's sons.

Fort Point
National Historic Site

A fortress weakened by advances in weaponry

Guarding the narrow entrance to San Francisco Bay, Fort Point National Historic Site stands as a reminder of a time when ordinary brick walls sufficed as protection from the weapons of war.

Built from 1853 to 1861 on the site of an earlier Mexican adobe fortification, the fort had outer walls five to seven feet thick. More than eight million bricks were used in its construction, which cost about $2.8 million.

At its peak strength, the fort held 102 cannons, including a number of Rodman guns, named for their designer, Brigadier General Thomas Rodman. These powerful guns could fire 128-pound projectiles more than three miles.

During the Civil War, the fort held up to 456 enlisted men and 15 officers. In 1886, however, its vulnerability to newer, larger weapons made the fort obsolete, and it was abandoned.

In 1933, the fort was given new life as the center of operations for the construction of the Golden Gate Bridge. Initial plans for the bridge called for the demolition of the fort, but engineers were eventually able to preserve it by spanning it with a steel arch.

In 1941 and 1943, the fort was again put to use, this time by the 6th U.S. Coastal Artillery Regiment. After the war, interest grew in preserving the fort, and in 1970 Congress designated it a national historic site.

Despite its outstanding architecture, the brick fortress that once protected San Francisco Bay became obsolete when newer, more powerful cannons were invented.

Golden Spike
National Historic Site

A symbolic meeting of our nation's railroads

On May 10, 1869, workers from the Union Pacific and Central Pacific railroads met at Promontory Summit in Utah and drove the golden and silver spikes that both symbolically and literally connected the East to the West. The joining of the two railroads is celebrated at Golden Spike National Historic Site, which was designated in 1957.

America's first railroads began operation in the 1830s, and by the Civil War the Eastern states were linked by more than 30,000 miles of rail. The country west of the Missouri River, however, remained virtually unserved by railroads.

In 1862, Congress realized the political and economic gains to be had by a transcontinental railroad, so it authorized the Central Pacific to build a rail line eastward from Sacramento, and the Union Pacific to build one westward from Omaha. The Central Pacific crew immediately faced the rugged Sierras, while the Union Pacific had to contend with the Plains Indians.

East meets West again as full-size replicas of the Central Pacific Jupiter *and the* Union Pacific 119 *locomotives re-create the first joining of the rails at Promontory Summit.*

292

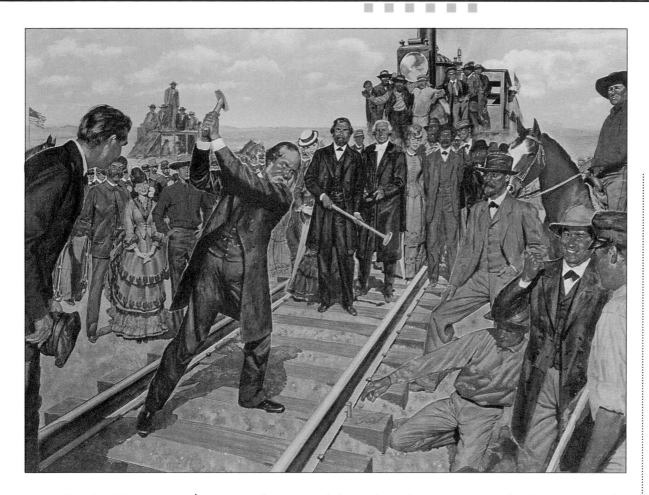

Railroad officials met at Promontory Summit, Utah, in May of 1869 to hammer in the final spikes that created the country's first transcontinental railroad.

As they neared the end, each company raced to lay more tracks and claim more land. They actually worked right past each other, laying more than 200 miles of parallel grades. Finally, Congress intervened and forced them to meet at Promontory Summit. In all, the Central Pacific laid 690 miles of track, while the Union Pacific tally came to 1,086 miles.

The visitor center at the site has exhibits and films, including one on photographer A. J. Russell, who captured the event on film. Displays feature replicas of the famous golden and silver spikes, a segment of the original track, and a sculpture honoring the Chinese laborers who worked hard to complete the railroads but were mistreated and paid little more than slave wages.

The Park Service has relaid almost two miles of track on the original railroad bed and operates exact replicas of two steam engines, the Central Pacific's *Jupiter* and the Union Pacific's *119* during the summer season.

A FALSE ALARM

Engineers planning the route for the railroad bed used spyglasses to help scout the land ahead, though they soon learned they couldn't always trust what they saw through this tool.

According to one report, a civil engineer issued an order to charge when he saw an Indian's feather standing up in his headband. The warrior was apparently trying to hide behind some tall grass. Four men charged, blasting away with their revolvers. When they reached their target, they found a dead skunk with an erect tail like a feather.

Hubbell Trading Post

National Historic Site

A source of income for Navajo craftspeople

Scattered throughout the West are remains of various frontier outposts. Once part of a thriving trade and military engine that fueled westward expansion, they survive now as remnants of the past. One exception is the Hubbell Trading Post National Historic Site in Arizona; the 1878 post is still doing business.

John Lorenzo Hubbell, of American and Spanish descent, was one of the first men to recognize the artistic merit of Navajo silversmiths and rug makers. He knew there was a market for these items, so he established a trading post on the Navajo Reservation in 1878. Eventually, his empire would grow to encompass 24 trading posts.

The Navajos were still adjusting to life on a reservation when Hubbell arrived, and he became their trusted friend. Known as Don

On the Navajo Reservation in Arizona, the trading post established by John Lorenzo Hubbell in 1878 is still doing business today.

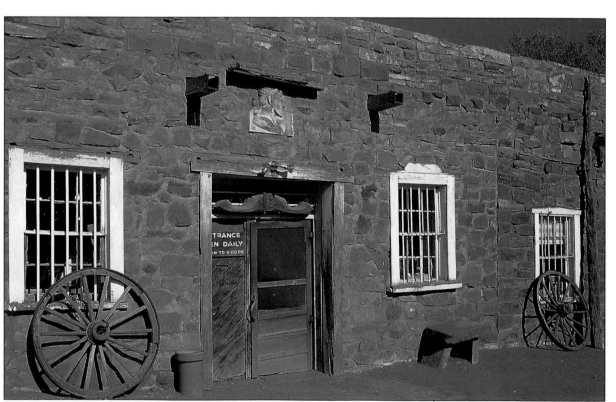

The frontier store became part of a network of 24 trading posts operated by Hubbell and his sons throughout the Southwest.

Lorenzo to whites and "Old Mexican" or "Double Glasses" to the Navajo, Hubbell translated and wrote letters for the Indians, explained government policy, and cared for the sick and dying when smallpox swept the reservation in 1886. Hubbell's immunity to the disease, due to a boyhood bout with smallpox, was a sign of higher power to the Navajo.

Rangers lead tours of Hubbell's home and the trading post compound, where visitors can participate in the business activities of a trading post. Members of Southwest tribes still come here to sell and trade jewelry, baskets, pottery, and other crafts.

Hubbell Trading Post is typical of frontier stores of the era. A stove stands in the center of the long rectangular building, where, in the winter, Navajos talked and gossiped around its warmth. Behind

AN HONEST TRADER

John Lorenzo Hubbell was, first and foremost, a businessman, but he was just as famous for his wise counsel and honest dealings with the Navajo. According to Hubbell:

"The first duty of an Indian trader, in my belief, is to look after the material welfare of his neighbors; to advise them to produce that which their natural inclinations and talent best adapts them; to treat them honestly and insist upon getting the same treatment from them . . . to find a market for their products and vigilantly watch that they keep improving in the production of same, and advise them which commands the best price. This does not mean that the trader should forget that he is to see that he makes a fair profit for himself, for whatever would injure him would naturally injure those with whom he comes in contact."

Hubbell Trading Post National Historic Site

Abandoned wagons from an earlier era serve as a reminder of the important commerce conducted here during frontier times.

the massive counters, stained with many years of use, shelves hold coffee, flour, sugar, candy, Pendleton blankets, tobacco, calico, pocketknives, and canned goods.

The Hubbell rug room contains stacks of beautiful hand-woven rugs for sale, and visitors can watch weavers at work on rugs in a separate building. At sheep-shearing time, visitors may see wool being weighed and stacked for shipment, just as it was during Hubbell's day.

The adobe Hubbell Home appears as it did when Don Lorenzo lived there, complete with original furnishings and Navajo floor rugs and basketwork. He entertained many artists and politicians here. Hubbell died in 1930 and is buried next to his wife and closest Navajo friend on a hill overlooking the trading post.

John Muir
National Historic Site

Honoring the man who started the conservation movement

Muir hiked all over the West before settling in this Victorian house in northern California's Alhambra Valley.

As John Muir wrote to his sister in 1873, "The mountains are calling and I must go." Even after marrying, having two children, and building a successful fruit-ranching business in the Alhambra Valley, now part of the John Muir National Historic Site, the call of wilderness was too strong for Muir to ignore.

Before eventually settling into a Victorian house in Martinez, California, Muir logged several thousand miles on foot, often carrying little more than a change of underwear. On his first trip to Yosemite Valley in California's Sierra Nevada Mountains, he was appalled to find hordes of sheep, which he called "hoofed locusts," grazing the valley bare. An eloquent speaker who used facts to back up his arguments, Muir successfully lobbied to have Yosemite declared a national park. He also helped establish Petrified Forest, Mt. Rainier, and Grand Canyon national parks.

In 1903, he and President Theodore Roosevelt went on a three-day camping trip in Yosemite. One night, Muir set fire to a dead pine tree, and as the fire blazed, Roosevelt yelled enthusiastically, "This is bully! Hooray for Yosemite!" During his tenure, Roosevelt doubled the number of national parks to ten.

Muir returned periodically to his house in Martinez to write the influential books and magazine articles that helped establish conservation as a national movement. "Thousands of tired, nerve-shaken, over-civilized people are beginning to find out that going to the mountains is going home, that wilderness is a necessity...," he wrote in the *Atlantic Monthly*.

The estate is little changed from when Muir lived here from 1890 until 1914. The 17-room home is furnished with period pieces and some originals, including a portrait of Muir painted by his sister.

A TRUE CRUSADER

John Muir came to national attention when he challenged professional geologists who said that glaciers did not create Yosemite Valley.

The prevailing theory was that a sudden collapse of the earth's surface had formed the valley. Muir discovered 65 living glaciers in Yosemite and numerous scars from moving ice sheets to support his now-accepted argument.

Muir worked tirelessly to have Yosemite Valley declared a national park, and then put his heart into the battle to save the park's spectacular Hetch Hetchy Valley from being dammed and flooded as a municipal reservoir. Muir lost and, heartbroken, died a year later.

Hetch Hetchy became a rallying cry for a new direction in preservation, and in 1916, two years after Muir's death, the National Park Service was created.

Manzanar
National Historic Site

A wartime detention camp for Japanese Americans

At the base of the Sierra Nevadas, an empty guard post stands along a lonely stretch of desert highway. It is one of the few remnants of the War Relocation Center at Manzanar, one of ten such camps that once detained Americans who were neither charged with nor convicted of a crime.

In 1992, 50 years after President Franklin Roosevelt signed the wartime decree that allowed the forced evacuation of Japanese Americans living on the West Coast, Congress designated Manzanar a national historic site.

By the spring of 1942, just months after the Pearl Harbor attack, Manzanar was a city of more than 10,000 people, most of whom were from Los Angeles County. Half of Manzanar's population were women and one-fourth were children. Infants and some elderly, barely able to walk, were also brought here. Though the government maintained that the Nisei (ethnic Japanese living in America) were brought here for their own protection, the inmates were painfully aware that the guns in the guard towers pointed inward, not outward.

When the Nisei arrived, they found their new homes to be 576 tar paper barracks, divided into "apartments." Families averaging eight people were assigned to a 20-foot by 25-foot or smaller room. The rooms were furnished with iron cots, three blankets per person, and bags they could fill with straw to sleep on. The barracks had so many cracks in the walls that the residents would wake up covered with a fine layer of dust.

The 560-acre camp was divided into residential blocks, each with a communal kitchen

A monument honors the more than 10,000 Japanese Americans who were interned at Manzanar from 1942 to 1945.

Little remains of the detention camp, which once housed 10,000 people, and the Park Service has decided not to rebuild it.

and bathhouses. The residents stood in long lines in the hot, dry summers and the bitter cold winters, waiting to eat or to use the bathrooms.

Despite the harsh climate, lack of privacy, and the inescapable dust, the Nisei lived with as much dignity as possible, turning Manzanar into a very American community, complete with churches, schools, Boy Scout troops, baseball tournaments, community theater, and a newspaper.

In September of 1945, after more than three years at Manzanar, the prisoners were set free. Without ceremony or fanfare, each was given $25 and a bus ticket home.

Visiting Manzanar now, it is hard to believe that it was once a busy community. Only three buildings remain: a sentry post, a guard post with a slightly pagodalike style, and a large wood-frame building that once served as the camp's auditorium and gymnasium. But by walking the dusty streets, visitors will discover traces of former rock gardens and the remains of buildings and utility systems.

The Park Service has decided not to rebuild the camp, opting instead to leave Manzanar in its current state.

THE LAST WORD

Like any American town, Manzanar published its own newspaper, the *Manzanar Free Press*.

The final editorial of the *Free Press* summed up the Nisei's hopes and fears as they prepared to leave Manzanar: "In just three months, Manzanar, one-time 'home' to more than 10,000 people, will be only a memory—a memory of joy and heartache, happiness and fear, of love and hate.... But now the time has come when we must find a place for ourselves in a normal community. Our children must know what life is beyond the barbed wire.... But wherever we go, we must begin again with a renewed faith to build for ourselves and those of our heritage a place of security in this great nation so that our children will never be forced to experience the loss and hardships that we have known these last few years."

Puukohola Heiau

National Historic Site

Ruins of the temple of Hawaiian king Kamehameha

Hawaiians built the massive temple known as Puukohola Heiau around 1790 by carefully assembling lava rocks, stones, and boulders. No mortar was used in the construction.

■ ■ ■

History and legend come together at Puukohola Heiau National Historic Site, which preserves the last major religious structure of the ancient Hawaiian culture built in the islands.

According to legend, before Kamehameha was born, it was said that a "killer of chiefs" would appear one day. Hawaiian chiefs, fearing that the baby Kamehameha might be the prophesied one, tried to kill him, but his mother sent him away to safety. He grew up to be a feared warrior.

In 1782, he became ruler of the northwest half of the island of Hawaii and warred with other chiefs for control of all the islands. Eventually he had only one rival left, his cousin Keoua Ku'ahu'ula. A famous prophet told Kamehameha's aunt that he could conquer the whole island if he built a large temple to his family war god atop Puukohola, "the hill of the whale."

In 1790, Hawaiians began to build the massive temple platform without the use of mortar by setting lava rocks and boulders together. One year later, the temple was complete, and Kamehameha dedicated the temple by sacrificing his rival cousin to his war god. The prophecy was fulfilled in 1810, after years of war, when Kamehameha became ruler of all the Hawaiian Islands. After Kamehameha's death in 1819, his son abandoned the past religious ways and had the temple destroyed.

Broken pieces of stone are all that remain of the cliffside leaning post that allowed a high priest to observe sharks in the sea below before offering them a human sacrifice.

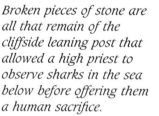

■ ■ ■

Visitors can reach the remains of Kamehameha's temple, as well as all other historical sites in the 77-acre park, on foot. The foundation of Puukohola measures 224 feet by 100 feet and has long narrow terrace steps across the side facing the sea so that people in canoes floating offshore could see the interior of the temple. The platform has survived major earthquakes over the years, but the walls are beginning to crumble, so visitors are no longer allowed to climb onto it.

On the hillside between Puukohola Heiau and the sea is the foundation of Mailekini Heiau—all that remains of the temple used by Kamehameha's ancestors.

The Hale-o-ka-puni Heiau, a temple to the shark god, is believed to be submerged just offshore of Puukohola. Nearby is the stone leaning post, where the high priest watched sharks circle about the temple before devouring his latest offering to them.

Along the coast is Pelekane, the royal residence. It was here that Kamehameha's son, King Kamehameha II, prepared to rule all of the Hawaiian Islands.

The foundation of Puukohola Heiau, which means "the hill of the whale" is approximately 224 feet by 100 feet. None of the structures that once stood upon it have survived.

■ ■ ■

SMOOTH SAILOR

In 1790, a British sailor named John Young was stranded on the island of Hawaii. In time, he became Kamehameha's trusted adviser. Kamehameha named him Olohana and eventually made him a chief.

Olohana was governor of Hawaii from 1802 to 1812, at the same time serving as the king's business agent. His former home is just north of Puukohola Heiau. Little is left of the dwelling, but historians believe it was built of stone and mortar and was probably the first European-style house on the islands.

■ ■ ■

USS Arizona

National Memorial

Honoring the soldiers who died at Pearl Harbor

Early in the morning on December 7, 1941, a Japanese attack fleet of 33 warships arrived undetected at Pearl Harbor. The coded messages "To, To, To" and "Tora, Tora, Tora" alerted the fleet about 7:55 A.M. that the sneak attack had begun. At approximately 8:10 A.M., a 1,760-pound armor-piercing bomb slammed through the deck of the USS *Arizona*. In less than nine minutes, 1,177 members of her crew went down with the ship.

In addition to Pearl Harbor, the Japanese attacked other targets on Oahu, including Hickam, Wheeler, and Bellows airfields. The purpose of the Japanese attack was to destroy America's Pacific fleet. Though the U.S. fleet suffered heavy losses, the attack was not a total success. As a result, the United States joined the Allies to defeat Japan and Germany in World War II.

The National Park Service leads tours out to the gleaming white USS *Arizona* Memorial, which spans the sunken battleship. The ship is visible from the memorial, and a Vermont marble wall lists the names of the sailors and marines who died onboard.

The shoreside visitor center includes a museum and a brief film on the attack. Nearby is Bowfin Park, where visitors can tour the submarine USS *Bowfin,* which was active during World War II.

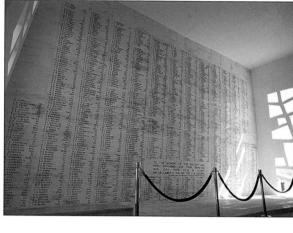

In the shrine room of the memorial, the names of all who went down with the Arizona *are engraved on a marble wall.*

■ ■ ■

The 184-foot-long USS Arizona *Memorial spans the sunken battleship, a casualty of the Japanese attack on Pearl Harbor on December 7, 1941.*

■ ■ ■

Opposite page: *Park Service boats bring visitors to the gleaming white memorial.*

■ ■ ■

The Northwest

National Monuments and Historic Sites

The national monument legacy began in the Northwest in 1906, when President Theodore Roosevelt gave the first such designation to Devils Tower, an unusual, 850-foot column of rock in northeastern Wyoming.

Since then, seven more of the region's natural wonders—and one very famous battlefield—have been preserved as national monuments, while five places of special historic interest have been designated national historic sites.

The region's geological story is told by its caves and fossil beds and intriguing rock formations; the story of human settlement is revealed, in part, through its forts and missions, its trading posts and cattle ranches.

Rising above the black pine trees and red soil of northeastern Wyoming, Devils Tower was formed millions of years ago when molten rock surged up from the earth.

The main house of the former Grant-Kohrs Ranch, one of the giant cattle ranches of the Old West. The historic site is located in Montana.

Aniakchak
National Monument and Preserve

One of the world's great dry calderas

Aniakchak National Monument and Preserve, midway down the wild and roadless Alaska Peninsula, includes one of the world's great dry calderas, as well as lava flows, cinder cones, and explosion pits.

The six-mile wide, 2,000-foot deep caldera was formed when a 7,000-foot volcanic mountain erupted about 3,500 years ago. The mountain collapsed, leaving a relatively flat-floored, ash-filled bowl. The remaining rim of the mountain ranges from 3,000 to 4,500 feet in elevation.

That, however, was not Aniakchak's last hurrah. It has erupted more than 20 times since that first monster explosion, the last time in 1931. That eruption scattered ash over villages up to 40 miles away and added a small but impressive explosion pit to the already pockmarked caldera floor. Still considered active, Aniakchak is part of the so-called Ring of Fire, a volcanic area along the Pacific Ocean rim.

Visitors can hike, climb, and explore the caldera's windswept plains, cinder cones, and lava fields. Though much of Aniakchak looks like a desolate moonscape, wildlife is abundant and easy for visitors to see. Brown bears, caribou, wolverines, red foxes, and the occasional wolf, among others, are found here. Bald eagles, one of 40 species in the monument, roost on the caldera rim. Meanwhile, Sockeye salmon fight their way up the Aniakchak River into Surprise Lake, the river's shallow headwater lake inside the caldera.

To the east, rugged bays and inlets and offshore islands in the Pacific provide habitat for sea mammals and sea birds. Mosses, grasses, and flowering plants have invaded sheltered spots in the caldera, and scattered meadows of grasses and wildflowers add a splash of color to the landscape.

Aniakchak National Monument and Preserve on the wild Alaska Peninsula preserves a six-mile-wide, 2,000-foot-deep caldera formed by the collapse of a 7,000-foot mountain.

Cape Krusenstern
National Monument

Protecting Alaska's northwestern wildlands

Although it has been a national monument since 1978, Alaska's Cape Krusenstern continues to sustain native Eskimos, who hunt, fish, and trap within the monument's 660,000 acres, as they have done for thousands of years.

Cape Krusenstern's bluffs and 114 beach ridges along the Chukchi Sea contain archaeological evidence of 6,000 years of prehistoric human use of the coastline. Some artifacts here are older than well-known remains of ancient Greek civilizations on the Mediterranean Sea. The coastal people of Cape Krusenstern lived mainly on sea mammals, but they also ranged inland to hunt caribou and other land mammals.

Caribou still roam in large numbers through the wild and undeveloped monument, foraging the tundra in a constant search for food. During the summer months, caribou feed on grasses and grasslike sedges, small shrubs, berries, and twigs. In the winter, they dig through the snow to find lichen, called reindeer moss.

Many other animals make Cape Krusenstern their home, including wolves, moose, grizzly bears, wolverines, foxes, and eagles. This rich coastal area also supports huge numbers of nesting birds and abundant sea life. In the summertime, wildflowers bloom on the treeless plain, and hordes of biting insects descend on the area.

Cape Krusenstern is a coastal plain, broken by lagoons and gently rolling hills. Shifting sea ice, ocean currents, and waves have formed—and continue to form—spits and lagoons, which can be explored by kayak or on foot. Combined with adjacent Kobuk Valley National Park and Noatak National Preserve, the monument protects more than 9,000,000 acres of subarctic and arctic wildlands in northwest Alaska.

Cape Krusenstern National Monument preserves bluffs and beach ridges along the shorelines of northwestern Alaska.

Craters of the Moon

National Monument

Lava flows created this weird lunar landscape

Fifteen thousand years ago, a great wound opened in the surface of the earth in southern Idaho, and lava spewed out. This explosive activity continued until about 2,000 years ago, creating a weird lunar landscape. For centuries, people generally avoided this area.

The Shoshone Indians hunted here but chose to live elsewhere, while pioneers in covered wagons skirted the molten land, and miners avoided staking claims nearby. The area was virtually unknown until the 1920s, when geologist Harold T. Stearns suggested that a national monument be established here.

Stearns was the first to use the name Craters of the Moon because he thought "the dark craters and the cold lava, nearly destitute of vegetation" were similar to the surface of the moon as seen through a telescope. The name stuck, and in 1924, Craters of the Moon National Monument was established.

Craters of the Moon—a dormant, but not extinct, volcanic area—encompasses 85 square miles of ancient lava flows twisted, molded, and splattered into tubelike caves, tree molds, steep-sided cones, and solid bombs. The lava caves were formed when fluid, molten lava spilled out of the ground and flowed downhill like a stream of water. The surface of this stream soon cooled and hardened, but the molten lava inside continued to flow, leaving the crust as the walls of a tube or cave.

Jagged fields of basalt lava, capable of shredding the footwear of unwary hikers, are a reminder of volcanic activity that occurred here thousands of years ago.

Sagebrush and other hardy native plants have taken root in the dark, volcanic soil. Brightly colored wildflowers accent the landscape during spring and summer months.

Some of the caves contain stalactites that were created by the dripping of molten lava before cooling, and tree molds mark where living trees once stood before being surrounded by molten lava. Bombs are pieces of lava that were blown out of craters and solidified while airborne, falling to the ground in spindle, ribbon, and breadcrust shapes.

A seven-mile-long road leads past the monument's major formations, including Big Cinder Butte, one of the world's largest cinder cones. Self-guiding trails allow visitors to explore shiny lava flows, spatter cones, lava caves, and the surrounding wilderness.

Though this area has been described as barren, desolate, and destitute of life, it is home to 2,000 insect species, 148 birds, 47 mammals, eight reptiles, and a lone toad species. Hardy native plants, such as sagebrush, mock orange, and tansybush, grow right on the lava flows, their roots reaching into cracks and crevices. In the spring and summer, brightly colored wildflowers bloom against the backdrop of red rock and shiny black lava.

TWO KINDS OF LAVA

The black rocks at Crater of the Moon are lava flows, basaltic rocks that formed from magma originating deep in the earth. The two most common types at the monument were named for their appearances: Pahoehoe (pronounced pa-hoy-hoy), meaning "ropey," and a'a, (pronounced ah-ah), meaning "rough."

More than half the park is covered by pahoehoe flows, which are relatively smooth. Pahoehoe lava emerged as fluid, hardening into pleats, billows, and hummocks. A'a flows are much more rugged and can quickly chew up hiking boots. A'a lava was more viscous on emerging, and its surface contains rubble and stubbly spines, making it almost impossible to walk on.

Devils Tower

National Monument

The unusual core of an ancient volcano

For many people, Devils Tower is the place where alien beings landed and made friendly contact with Earth in the movie *Close Encounters of the Third Kind.* To American Indians, it is *Mateo Tipi,* or Bear Lodge. To geologists it is the core of an ancient volcano. But for all people, including future generations, Devils Tower is notable as the first national monument, so proclaimed by President Theodore Roosevelt in 1906.

Scientists believe that Devils Tower, thrusting 1,267 feet above the Belle Fourche River in northern Wyoming, was formed 60 million years ago. A flow of magma pushed up into a layer of sedimentary rock, where it cooled and shrank, separating into columns, or flutes. Over millions of years, the sedimentary rock eroded to expose the volcanic mass of igneous rock that forms the tower. The diameter of the base is 1,000 feet, and its tear-drop-shaped top is 1½ acres.

Scientists say Devils Tower is the remnant core of an extinct volcano. Kiowa legend says it is a giant tree stump created to save seven sisters from a huge bear, which scored the stump with its massive claws.

Devils Tower is a pillar of igneous rock rising 867 feet above rolling grasslands. It is a sacred site for several Plains Indian tribes.

Devils Tower National Monument

A popular Fourth of July gathering place for area ranchers a century ago, Devils Tower still draws large crowds of sightseers, hikers, and climbers.

The unusual formation was formed millions of years ago, when a flow of magma pushed into a layer of sedimentary rock, which eventually eroded.

■ ■ ■

In 1875, Colonel Richard Dodge named the formation, slightly altering the Indian moniker, which translated to Bad God's Tower. Eighteen years later, amid much fanfare from more than 1,000 spectators, two local men made the first climb to the summit on the Fourth of July, planting a flag atop the tower. They used a wooden ladder they had built for the first 350 feet, and their wives made money during the event by selling refreshments and pieces of the flag as souvenirs.

A couple of years later, one of the wives used her husband's ladder to become the first woman to reach the summit. Today, more than 5,000 climbers come here from all over the world every year to climb on the massive formation, and there are more than 120 routes to the summit.

There is plenty to see and do on the ground, too. A museum in the park's visitor center contains exhibits on the area's history, geology, and animals. A tour on the 1¹⁄₄-mile trail around the base of Devils Tower reveals more of the area's geology and wildlife.

More than 90 species of birds, including bald and golden eagles, prairie falcons, and American kestrels, live here, where the pine forests of the Black Hills meet the grasses of the prairie. Whitetail deer, mule deer, rabbits, chipmunks, and porcupines are common inhabitants of the monument, and a large prairie dog town covers the grasslands below the tower.

THE KIOWA LEGEND

According to Kiowa legend, a boy and his seven sisters once played at the site of Devils Tower. Suddenly, the boy was mysteriously transformed into a bear: his fingers became claws, his body became covered with fur, and he began to run on his hands and feet.

The seven sisters ran in terror from the bear, who followed them to the stump of a great tree. The tree spoke to them, telling the girls to climb upon it. As they did, the stump began to rise into the air. The bear clawed at the bark but could not reach them. The sisters were carried into the heavens, where they can be seen as seven bright stars in the Big Dipper. Meanwhile, the stump turned to stone, covered by the deep gouges of the bear's claws.

■ ■ ■

Fossil Butte
National Monument

The entombed remains of prehistoric plants and animals

Some 50 million years ago, during the Eocene Epoch of the Cenozoic Era, Fossil Butte National Monument in southwestern Wyoming was submerged under a lake 50 miles long and up to 20 miles wide.

Palms, figs, cypress, and other subtropical trees and shrubs grew along Fossil Lake's shorelines, while willows, beeches, oaks, maples, and ferns covered the lower slopes of nearby mountains. Six-foot gars, paddlefish, bowfins, mooneyes, stingrays, turtles, and more than 20 other freshwater species lived in the tributaries, shallows, and deep water of the lake. Crocodiles patrolled the lakeshore, and birds and bats flew overhead.

As these creatures died, they sank to the bottom of the lake. Eventually the lake dried up, leaving behind a flat-topped remnant of rock that stands where the center of the lake once was. Imbedded in the butte are the fossils of more than 20 kinds of fish, 100 varieties of insects, and an unknown number of plants.

Two different trails await visitors. One leads to old quarries on the butte; the other, to a quarry site where fossils can be viewed in the field.

Limestone cliffs of the Green River formation at Fossil Butte National Monument contain the fossilized remains of birds and plants.

■ ■ ■

These fossils are among the most perfectly preserved remains of ancient plant and animal life in the world. Not just the skeletons of fish are visible, but their teeth, delicate scales, and skin as well. Among the fossils preserved here are the fragile bones of a bat, the oldest ever found in North America, and a remarkably complete fossil snake.

While most of Fossil Lake's plants and animals died natural deaths, occasionally huge numbers of fish were killed suddenly. These die-offs are recorded in "mass mortality" layers. A sudden change in temperature or an invasion of blue-green algae may have contributed to these die-offs. A large "mass mortality" slab is on display at the visitor center, along with many other fossils.

Several short hiking trails with exhibits allow visitors to see the fossils in their natural condition and learn about some of the history of fossil-collecting in the area. The Fossil Lake Trail winds through the aspen groves and high desert landscape that surround the butte.

Fossil Butte contains a rare deposit of fossilized fish that lived some 50 million years ago, when this area was covered by a huge lake.

■ ■ ■

315

Hagerman Fossil Beds

National Monument

An amazing collection of horse remains

Imbedded in the banks of the Snake River in south-central Idaho is a nearly intact 3.5-million-year-old ecosystem. These fossil beds, located in the town of Hagerman, reveal an extraordinary variety and abundance of animal fossils from the Pliocene epoch.

More than 100 species of vertebrates have been found at Hagerman, including 18 fish, four amphibians, nine reptiles, 27 birds, and 50 mammals. The collection of ancient animals ranges from swans and saber-toothed tigers to rabbits and snails.

Hagerman is best known, however, for its high concentration of horse fossils. The horse quarry has more than 150 individual fossils of *Equus simplicidens,* one of the earliest known representatives of the modern horse. The quarry contains horses of all ages, from yearlings to old adults, and some nearly complete skeletons. This site may have once been a bog or watering hole, where great numbers of horses would have come to drink. Some may have died and been buried in the mud surrounding the watering hole, accounting for the high concentration of bones here.

Hagerman Fossil Beds National Monument, established in 1988, is still in the development stage, though the Park Service is beginning to offer visitor services. A temporary visitor center in town has exhibits, and a boardwalk in the monument provides a great view of the fossil beds.

Hagerman Fossil Beds contains the world's largest deposit of fossil horses, including a zebralike animal known as the Hagerman Horse, the oldest known horse species in North America.

Hagerman Fossil Beds National Monument is located on the west bank of the Snake River near Hagerman, Idaho.

John Day Fossil Beds

National Monument

An ancient record of life on Earth

A tour through John Day Fossil Beds National Monument is like taking a trip back in time. While fossil beds that extend over five million years are considered rare, the three units of this monument preserve a 45-million-year record of plant and animal life.

Over millions of years, in what are now the desert hills of eastern Oregon, plants and animals fell into lakebeds and sinkholes where they were buried by river sediments or volcanic debris and transformed into fossils.

Twenty-five million years ago, the John Day site was a warm, temperate-climate forest with birch, oak, sweetgum, chestnut, and beech trees. The important fossils at the Sheep Rock unit are mammals, including the oreodont, a pig-sized creature that grazed in small herds.

Thirty million years ago, the climate was slowly changing from subtropical to temperate, as evidenced by the fossil leaves found in large quantities at the Painted Hills unit. Forty million years ago, the subtropical climate was more like that of countries such as India or Sri Lanka. Fossilized leaf imprints and whole leaves at Painted Hills and Clarno indicate that a variety of plants grew here, including palm, fig, cinnamon, cycad, and tree ferns.

The visitor center features fossils recovered from the John Day Basin, and outdoor trails lead past fossil beds and through the monument's scenic landscape.

Fossils as much as 45 million years old have been uncovered in the scenic John Day River Valley.

Little Bighorn Battlefield

National Monument

The site of Custer's Last Stand

A stone tablet marks the spot where Custer fell during the Battle of Little Bighorn.

uster's Last Stand, called "the Battle of Greasy Grass Creek" by American Indians, took place on June 25, 1876. Lieutenant Colonel George A. Custer and some 260 soldiers of the 7th U.S. Cavalry attacked a Sioux and Cheyenne village in southeastern Montana. The Indian defenders, led by Sitting Bull and Crazy Horse, greatly outnumbered the soldiers, none of whom survived.

Five years later, the government erected a monument to honor the soldiers killed in the battle. One hundred years later, in 1991, Native Americans received recognition for *their* losses at the battle, and the Park Service site's name was changed from Custer Battlefield to Little Bighorn Battlefield National Monument.

The monument contains 765 acres of prairie where the Sioux, Nez Perce, and Kiowas rode their horses and hunted buffalo for centuries. As white miners and settlers began to arrive and the buffalo began to disappear, the Indians tried to hold on to their traditional way of life. In 1868, a treaty guaranteed the Black Hills to the Sioux. Considered a wasteland by whites, the hills, which were called "Paha Sapa," were sacred to the Sioux.

Four years later, a rumor spread that gold could be found in the hills. In 1874, Custer illegally led a team of soldiers into the Black Hills and reported that they were full of gold "from the roots down." When the Sioux refused to

A memorial honors George Armstrong Custer and the soldiers of the 7th U.S. Cavalry who were killed at "Custer's Last Stand."

Opposite page: Sitting Bull and Crazy Horse dealt the U.S. Army its biggest defeat in the Indian Wars. The site is preserved as the Little Bighorn Battlefield National Monument.

Little Bighorn Battlefield National Monument

RUMORS AND MYTHS

A few romantic myths surrounding "Custer's Last Stand" have been slow to die. Custer did not ride into battle with his long blond curls streaming. He had purposely cut them short to make his scalp less attractive to Indian warriors. And according to some historians, only one officer, Lieutenant Charles DeRudio, brandished a sword. The others left theirs behind because they were too heavy to carry.

■ ■ ■

sell the land, the War Department labeled them as "hostile" and started a war against them.

In June of 1876, the Sioux discovered that Custer was approaching their camp on Greasy Grass Creek, and they prepared to meet him. Though the battle at Little Bighorn was a victory for the Sioux, it proved to be their downfall, as outraged white Americans accelerated their war against them.

Self-guided trails lead through the battlefield and down ravines, past grave markers, by the rifle pits where soldiers huddled, and past the grassy bench on the west bank of the Little Bighorn where the Sioux village once stood.

Markers show where Custer's men fell. The bodies were reinterred and placed in a common grave in 1881.

■ ■ ■

Oregon Caves
National Monument

A stunning array of geological formations

Few caves in the National Park System offer a more stunning array of geological formations than Oregon Caves. Known as the "marble halls of Oregon," the rare marble cave was proclaimed a national monument in 1909.

All six of the world's major rock types are found in the cave, along with a crystalline substance called "moonmilk." The substance, which looks and feels like cottage cheese, is composed of the same type of bacteria used to make antibiotics. People in the nineteenth century discovered that smearing moonmilk on wounds made them heal almost magically.

Many different types of ever-changing formations fill the cave. Pendant decorations hanging from the ceiling are called stalactites. Formations growing up from the floor are stalagmites. Sometimes the two meet and fuse, forming a column. Dripstones decorate the walls where water drips into the cave. Graceful formations called flowstone were slowly deposited as water seeped quietly over walls and floors.

Oregon Caves were discovered in 1874 when local rancher Elijah Davidson followed his dog into an opening in the mountains while chasing a bear. The cave quickly became a popular spot for tourists.

Tours provide a look into the cave's geology, ecology, and inhabitants. Cave creatures include the Townsend's big-

Oregon Caves National Monument is located beneath the lush Siskiyou National Forest in southwestern Oregon. Elijah Davidson discovered the caves in 1874.

SAVING THE CAVES

For a century after the Oregon Caves were discovered, tour operators with good intentions nearly destroyed the cave. To accommodate very large numbers of tourists, they laid down asphalt paths and installed bright lights in the cave.

Unfortunately, their efforts were harming the cave's environment. For several years now, the Park Service has been working to restore the cave to its original condition.

Because asphalt attracts exotic organisms as it decays, all the old paths are being replaced with high-tech walkways, and lower-wattage lights will replace the bright bulbs that encourage moss and fungus growth.

The changes will improve airflow in the cave so stalactites and stalagmites won't freeze and break in the winter, and cave creatures can move about more freely.

◼ ◼ ◼

eared bat and numerous blind, colorless insects. A grasshopperlike species found here in 1989 is believed to be unique to Oregon Caves. To find out what kind of creatures live in the cave, Park rangers set out traps baited with Limburger cheese.

Wildlife also abounds outside the cave. Black-tailed deer, porcupines, and giant Pacific salamanders inhabit the lush Siskiyou National Forest that surrounds the cave. Nature trails lead past mountain streams, mossy cliffs, fields of wildflowers, and a 1,500-year-old Douglas fir that is 40 feet around. The Cliff Nature Trail, which climbs to an elevation of 4,000 feet, provides panoramic views of the countryside.

At the turn of the century, the caves were known as the "marble halls of Oregon" for their spectacular array of formations.

◼ ◼ ◼

Fort Laramie
National Historic Site

The earliest of white settlements in Wyoming

Fort Laramie National Historic Site, near the confluence of the North Platte and Laramie rivers, preserves the earliest permanent white settlement in Wyoming, known officially as Fort William.

When the American Fur Company bought the post in 1836, it became a major fur-trading center. The company replaced the rotting log structure with one of adobe, adding bastions and other fortifications. They changed the name to Fort John on the Laramie, soon shortened to Fort Laramie.

In the 1840s, the fort became an oasis for pioneers following the Oregon Trail. It was the first contact with civilization in more than 300 miles, and it marked the end of the long plains crossing and the beginning of the mountain crossing. The fort capitalized on its strategic location by selling provisions and fresh draft animals—at outlandish prices—to the weary travelers.

Fort Laramie provided rest and a bit of civilization for trappers, traders, miners, missionaries, Pony Express riders, and others who traveled through the area.

Fort Laramie National Historic Site

Officers' quarters and barracks housed soldiers as well as civilians. Guests at Fort Laramie have included such notables as Buffalo Bill, Wild Bill Hickok, Calamity Jane, and Mark Twain.

Early relations between Indians and whites were peaceful, but as immigration increased, relations were strained. In 1849, the federal government bought the fort and made it a military outpost. Soldiers built quarters, stables, and other buildings around a central parade ground. The fort was an important spot for peace councils, and sometimes up to 100 tipis surrounded it.

The fort was a bustling center, described by one female traveler in 1866 as "a scene of seeming confusion not surpassed in any popular, overcrowded store of Omaha itself."

When the Park Service acquired the 833-acre site in 1938, many of the buildings were dilapidated or in ruins. A dozen of these structures have been restored to their historic appearance, including the trader's store, the surgeon's quarters, and the cavalry barracks. The most handsome building is "Old Bedlam," a white, balconied structure built in 1849 to house the bachelor officers. It was the center of social life at the fort and a popular site for parties, which probably accounts for the nickname "Bedlam."

Historical interpreters playing the role of Union soldiers help bring the past to life at Fort Laramie National Historic site.

GHOST RIDER

Some people believe that Fort Laramie has a ghost. A young woman in an old-fashioned green riding habit has been seen there riding a horse. Sometimes she is inside the fort, riding through the parade grounds; at other times she is galloping through the hills. But when someone approaches, she always vanishes.

It is said that the young woman in green was the daughter of an officer at the fort. One day she rode out on the plains alone, despite her father's warnings. She was never seen again.

Fort Vancouver

National Historic Site

The Pacific headquarters of Hudson's Bay Company

*F*ort Vancouver is where it all began for the Pacific Northwest. Built in 1825 as the headquarters for the British-owned Hudson's Bay Company's fur-trading operation on the Pacific Coast, it became the economic, social, and cultural hub of the Oregon Country.

Narcissa Whitman, who stayed in the fort along with her missionary husband in 1836, described Fort Vancouver as "the New York of the Pacific." The fort was named for the famous British sea explorer Captain George Vancouver, whose discovery of the Columbia River led to the establishment of the outpost.

At its height in 1844–46, the fort included 22 buildings surrounded by a stockade of upright logs. A U.S. Army camp was established nearby in 1849, and soldiers relaxing between the Indian Wars played polo at the fort. The Treaty of 1846 between the United States and Great Britain left Fort Vancouver on American soil, and 14 years later, the Hudson's Bay Company moved out.

The present Fort Vancouver is a reproduction of the original wooden fort, which burned to the ground in 1866. One hundred years later, after painstaking archaeological excavations revealed the site of the fort, the Park Service began to rebuild Fort Vancouver, which joined the National Park System in 1948.

Now a spiked wooden stockade surrounds six acres of buildings, including the blacksmith's shop,

The bastion, built to protect Fort Vancouver against American threats, was three stories high and had eight cannons on the top floor.

Fort Vancouver once boasted 22 major structures, as well as 30 to 50 wooden buildings outside the stockade walls. Since 1966, the stockade and five major buildings have been reconstructed.

At the Indian Trading Store, Indians and settlers traded for items that were imported from Britain.

During the summer months, costumed interpreters help visitors imagine what life here was like in the nineteenth century.

where iron and steel items needed for the fur trade industry were made; the bakery, where four men baked bread and biscuits for up to 300 people; and the Indian trade shop and dispensary, which housed the fur-trading operations, as well as the hospital and doctor's office and residence.

The house of Dr. John McLoughlin, the administrator of the fort who later became known as the "Father of Oregon," is a roomy and elegant house with white-clapboard siding and a large front veranda. Costumed interpreters bring the fort to life, occasionally firing up the ovens and baking sea biscuits or forming iron tools at the blacksmith's shop.

The visitor center has exhibits, a small store, and a film depicting the fort's early history. Near the fort is Officer's Row, a tree-lined street of 21 beautiful homes built between 1849 and 1906 for the officers of the fort. Two of the most impressive homes, the Marshall House and the Grant House, are open to the public.

WHIMS OF FASHION

Fort Vancouver's success was built—and doomed—by the changing world of fashion. In the 1830s and 40s, beaver-felt hats were all the rage among the fashion-conscious. The Hudson's Bay Company sent brigades of 50 to 200 men, women, and children out from Fort Vancouver to trap the thick-furred animal. Most of the trapping was done in the winter, when the pelts were thickest, requiring trappers to stand in ice cold water to set traps.

Once a year, the trappers came to Fort Vancouver to sell their furs and socialize. Then hatmakers turned the soft underfur of the pelt into hats. But by the 1860s, silk hats had replaced beaver felt, the demand for beaver pelts declined, and trapping came to an end.

Grant-Kohrs Ranch
National Historic Site

This former cattle ranch was one of the biggest

The Grant-Kohrs Ranch National Historic Site in western Montana, once one of the largest cattle ranches in the United States, recalls the days when the range was unfenced and seemingly endless.

The Grant-Kohrs Ranch began in the 1850s when Johnny Grant, a Canadian trapper and hunter, settled in Deer Ranch Valley, where he raised cattle and built the largest home in Montana Territory. A newspaper reported that the house looked as if "it had been lifted by the chimneys from the banks of the St. Lawrence and dropped down in Deer Lodge Valley."

In 1866, Johnny Grant sold his cattle ranch—farmhouses, furniture, cattle, and all—for $19,200. Under the new owner's management, the ranch grew to 25,000 acres and became a center for stock breeding.

Conrad Kohrs, a butcher and Danish immigrant, bought the ranch in 1866 and expanded the operation. At one point, Kohrs and his partner ran their cattle on more than a million acres of land in four states and Canada. For nearly a quarter of a century, Kohrs brought between 8,000 and 10,000 cattle to market a year.

Today, rangers carry on the early ranch life, tending cattle, mending fences, and taking care of horses and equipment on the now 1,500-acre ranch. Visitors can tour several ranch buildings, including the handsome ranch house and the bunkhouses where cowboys and ranch hands slept, ate, and spun yarns. Kohrs' wife Augusta filled the home with the finest Victorian furniture and objects available, bringing a touch of culture to the otherwise primitive surroundings.

Johnny Grant built this home in 1862. Conrad Kohrs, who bought the farm from Grant, added a brick wing in 1890 and his wife, Augusta, furnished the home with splendid Victorian pieces.

McLoughlin House

National Historic Site

The pioneer home of the "Father of Oregon"

Thirteen miles south of Portland, in Oregon City, stands the McLoughlin House, one of the few remaining pioneer homes in the former Oregon Country, a region that once stretched from Alaska to California and from the Pacific to the Rockies.

Built in 1845–46 by the "Father of Oregon," Dr. John McLoughlin, the home was known locally as "the house of many beds" due to the hospitality he extended to immigrants and others passing through Oregon City. Employed by British-owned Hudson's Bay Company as chief broker at Fort Vancouver, McLoughlin's job included discouraging American immigration to the region. He defied this policy openly, foreseeing that the declining fur trade and the unstemmable tide of American settlers would eventually doom Britain's claim over the Oregon Country.

McLoughlin House is one of the few remaining pioneer dwellings in the region once known as Oregon Country.

After a falling-out with Governor George Simpson, the Company's top official in North America, McLoughlin resigned in 1845. He moved to Company land along the Willamette River, and purchased the title for $20,000. There he built his home and, in 1851, was granted American citizenship. A generous supporter of newcomers to the region, he helped them by providing food, supplies, credit, and land for schools and churches.

Furnished to look as it did in McLoughlin's time, the home is owned and operated by the McLoughlin Memorial Association.

Whitman Mission

National Historic Site

A memorial to a family of true pioneers

Whitman Mission National Historic Site preserves the site of an early mission and a piece of the Oregon Trail.

In 1836, Marcus and Narcissa Whitman, the Rev. Henry and Eliza Spalding, and William Gray successfully crossed the North American continent from New York to the largely unknown land called Oregon Country. The trail they followed was later known as the Oregon Trail. Narcissa and Eliza were the first white women to achieve this feat, and the Whitman's baby, Alice Clarissa, was the first child born of U.S. citizens in the Pacific Northwest.

The Whitmans settled among the Cayuse and Nez Perce Indians and established the first mission on the Columbia Plateau at Waiilatpu, near present-day Walla Walla, Washington. The site is preserved as the Whitman Mission National Historic Site, though only wagon ruts and stones in the lawn, marking the outlines of buildings, remain.

Trails and wayside exhibits lead visitors past the mission, the Whitmans' graves, and the Whitman monument. The visitor center has artifacts from the days of the mission, including tools, clothes, and the bible that Marcus Whitman brought with him from the East.

The Whitmans helped guide other immigrants traveling the Oregon Trail and offered the mission as a way station. Their efforts to convert the Indians ended in 1847 when a band of Cayuse attacked the mission and killed the Whitmans and 11 others, whom they thought were responsible for a measles epidemic that had wiped out half the tribe.

A memorial honors Marcus and Narcissa Whitman, who worked with local Indians and weary travelers on the Oregon Trail for 11 years before being killed by Cayuse warriors in 1847.

Appendix
America's Monuments, Memorials, and Historic Sites

THE NORTHEAST

National Monuments

**Castle Clinton
National Monument**
c/o Federal Hall National Memorial
26 Wall Street
New York, NY 10005
(212) 344-7220
Days/Hours: 9 A.M. to 5 P.M. daily
except Christmas
Admission: Free

**Fort McHenry
National Monument and
Historic Shrine**
End of East Fort Avenue
Baltimore, MD 21230-5393
(410) 962-4290
TDD (301) 962-4290
Days/Hours: 8 A.M. to 5 P.M. daily
except Christmas and New Year's
Day; hours extended in summer
Admission: $2

**Fort Stanwix
National Monument**
112 East Park Street
Rome, NY 13440
(315) 336-2090
Days/Hours: 9 A.M. to 5 P.M. daily,
April 1 through December 31;
closed Thanksgiving and
Christmas
Admission: $2

**Statue of Liberty—Ellis Island
National Monument**
Liberty Island
New York, NY 10004
(212) 363-3200
Days/Hours: 9 A.M. to 5 P.M. daily;
hours extended in summer
Admission: Free

National Historic Sites

**Adams
National Historic Site**
135 Adams Street
P.O. Box 531
Quincy, MA 02269-0531
(617) 773-1177
Days/Hours: 9 A.M. to 5 P.M., April
19 to November 10
Admission: $2

**Allegheny Portage Railroad
National Historic Site**
P.O. Box 189
Creston, PA 16630
(814) 886-6100
Days/Hours: 9 A.M. to 6:15 P.M.
daily
Admission: Free

**Boston African-American
National Historic Site**
46 Joy Street
Boston, MA 02114-4025
(617) 742-5415
Days/Hours: Call for times of
conducted tours
Admission: Free

**Clara Barton
National Historic Site**
5801 Oxford Road
Glen Echo, MD 20812
(301) 492-6245
Days/Hours: 10 A.M. to 5 P.M.
daily except Thanksgiving,
Christmas, and New Year's Day
Admission: Free

**Edgar Allan Poe
National Historic Site**
c/o Independence National
Historical Park
313 Walnut Street
Philadelphia, PA 19106
(215) 597-8780
Days/Hours: 9 A.M. to 5 P.M. daily

except Thanksgiving, Christmas,
and New Year's Day
Admission: Free

**Edison
National Historic Site**
Main Street and Lakeside Avenue
West Orange, NJ 07052
(201) 736-0550 or
(201) 736-5050
Days/Hours: The visitor center is
open 9 A.M. to 5 P.M. daily; lab
tours offered Wednesday through
Saturday; Glenmont tours offered
Wednesday through Sunday
Admission: $2

**Eisenhower
National Historic Site**
P.O. Box 1080
Gettysburg, PA 17325
(717) 334-1124
Days/Hours: Hours vary; call
before visiting
Admission: $2, plus $1.25 shuttle
bus fare

**Eleanor Roosevelt
National Historic Site**
519 Albany Post Road
Hyde Park, NY 12538
(914) 229-9115
Days/Hours: Open daily from May
through October; closed from
Thanksgiving through the last day
of February; open Saturday and
Sunday only the rest of the year
Admission: Free

**Ford's Theatre
National Historic Site**
c/o National Capital Parks, Central
900 Ohio Drive, SW
Washington, DC 20242
(202) 426-6924
Days/Hours: 9 A.M. to 5 P.M. daily
Admission: Free

**Frederick Douglass
National Historic Site**
1411 W Street, SE
Washington, DC 20020-4813
voice or TDD (202) 426-5961
Days/Hours: 9 A.M. to 5 P.M. daily,
April through October; 9 A.M. to 4
P.M., October through April; closed
Thanksgiving, Christmas, and
New Year's Day
Admission: Free

**Frederick Law Olmsted
National Historic Site**
99 Warren Street
Brookline, MA 02146
(617) 566-1689
Hours/Days: 10 A.M. to 4:30 P.M.
Friday, Saturday, and Sunday;
other times by appointment
Admission: Free

**Friendship Hill
National Historic Site**
RD 2, Box 528
Farmington, PA 15437
(412) 329-5512
Days/Hours: 8:30 A.M. to 5 P.M.
daily except Christmas
Admission: Free

**Gloria Dei Church
National Historic Site**
Delaware Avenue and Christian
Street
Philadelphia, PA 19106
(215) 389-1513
Days/Hours: Gloria Dei is an
active religious congregation;
please call for hours before visiting
Admission: Free

**Hampton
National Historic Site**
535 Hampton Lane
Towson, MD 21286
(410) 962-0688
Days/Hours: The grounds are
open 9 A.M. to 5 P.M. daily except

Thanksgiving, Christmas, and New Year's Day; the mansion is open 9 A.M. to 4 P.M.
Admission: Free

Home of Franklin D. Roosevelt
National Historic Site
519 Albany Post Road
Hyde Park, NY 12538
(914) 229-9115
Days/Hours: 9 A.M. to 5 P.M. daily, April through October; Thursday through Monday, November through March
Admission: $4

Hopewell Furnace
National Historic Site
2 Mark Bird Lane
Elverson, PA 19520
(610) 582-8773
TDD (610) 582-2093
Days/Hours: Open daily except Thanksgiving, Christmas, and New Year's Day
Admission: $2

John Fitzgerald Kennedy
National Historic Site
83 Beals Street
Brookline, MA 02146
(617) 566-7937
Days/Hours: 10 A.M. to 4:30 P.M. Wednesday through Sunday; by guided tour only
Admission: $2

Longfellow
National Historic Site
105 Brattle Street
Cambridge, MA 02138
(617) 876-4491
Days/Hours: Open daily except Thanksgiving, Christmas, and New Year's Day
Admission: $2

Martin Van Buren
National Historic Site
P.O. Box 545
Kinderhook, NY 12106
(518) 758-9689
Days/Hours: Open daily from May through October; closed from December 6 to April 30; hours vary
Admission: $2

Mary McLeod Bethune
Council House
National Historic Site
1318 Vermont Avenue, NW
Washington, DC 20005
(202) 332-1233
Days/Hours: 10 A.M. to 4 P.M. weekdays
Admission: Free

Pennsylvania Avenue
National Historic Site
c/o Pennsylvania Avenue Development Corporation
Suite 1220N
1331 Pennsylvania Avenue, NW
Washington, DC 20004-1703
(202) 724-9091
Days/Hours: The different sites have different hours
Admission: Free

Sagamore Hill
National Historic Site
20 Sagamore Hill Road
Oyster Bay, NY 11771
(516) 922-4788
Days/Hours: 9:30 A.M. to 5 P.M. daily except holidays
Admission: $2; 16 and under, free

Saint-Gaudens
National Historic Site
Route 3, Box 73
Cornish, NH 03745
(603) 675-2175
Days/Hours: The buildings are open 8:30 A.M. to 4:30 P.M. and the grounds from 8 A.M. until dusk daily, Memorial Day weekend through October
Admission: $2

Saint Paul's Church
National Historic Site
c/o Federal Hall National Memorial
26 Wall Street
New York, NY 10005
(914) 667-4116
Days/Hours: Open Tuesday through Saturday; hours vary
Admission: Free

Salem Maritime
National Historic Site
174 Derby Street
Salem, MA 01970

(508) 740-1660
Days/Hours: 9 A.M. to 5 P.M. daily
Admission: Free

Saugus Iron Works
National Historic Site
244 Central Street
Saugus, MA 01906
(617) 233-0050
Days/Hours: 9 A.M. to 5 P.M. daily in summer; 9 A.M. to 4 P.M. in winter; closed Thanksgiving, Christmas, and New Year's Day
Admission: Free

Sewall-Belmont House
National Historic Site
144 Constitution Avenue, NE
Washington, DC 20002
(202) 546-3989
Days/Hours: 10 A.M. to 3 P.M. Tuesday through Friday; noon to 4 P.M. weekends and most holidays
Admission: Free

Springfield Armory
National Historic Site
One Armory Square
Springfield, MA 01105
(413) 734-8551
Days/Hours: 10 A.M. to 5 P.M. daily except Thanksgiving, Christmas, New Year's Day, and Mondays between Labor Day and Memorial Day
Admission: Free

Steamtown
National Historic Site
150 South Washington Avenue
Scranton, PA 18503-2018
(717) 340-5200
Days/Hours: Open daily except Thanksgiving, Christmas, and New Year's Day
Admission: Free; fee for excursion and museums

Theodore Roosevelt Birthplace
National Historic Site
28 E. 20th Street
New York, NY 10003
(212) 260-1616
Days/Hours: Call for visiting hours
Admission: $2

Theodore Roosevelt Inaugural
National Historic Site
641 Delaware Avenue
Buffalo, NY 14202
(716) 884-0095
Days/Hours: 9 A.M. to 5 P.M. Monday through Friday; noon to 5 P.M. on Saturday and Sunday. Same schedule for museum except January through March, when it is closed on Saturdays; both are closed New Year's Day, Good Friday, Memorial Day, July 4, Labor Day, Thanksgiving, and December 24, 25, and 31
Admission: $2; free for organized groups

Thomas Stone
National Historic Site
6655 Rose Hill Road
Port Tobacco, MD 20677
(301) 934-6027
Days/Hours: 9 A.M. to 5 P.M. Wednesday through Sunday, September through May, and daily during June, July, and August; closed on Christmas and New Year's Day
Admission: Free

Touro Synagogue
National Historic Site
85 Touro Street
Newport, RI 02840
(401) 847-4791
Days/Hours: This is an active place of worship; call before visiting
Admission: Free

Vanderbilt Mansion
National Historic Site
519 Albany Post Road
Hyde Park, NY 12538
(914) 229-9115
Days/Hours: The mansion is open 9 A.M. to 5 P.M. daily except Thanksgiving, Christmas, and New Year's Day and two days a week in winter; the grounds are open from dawn to dusk year-round
Admission: $2

Weir Farm
National Historic Site
735 Nod Hill Road
Wilton, CT 06897

(203) 834-1896
Days/Hours: Call for information about programs and scheduled tours
Admission: Free

WASHINGTON, DC

Thomas Jefferson Memorial
c/o National Capital Parks, Central
900 Ohio Drive, SW
Washington, DC 20242
(202) 426-6841
Days/Hours: Open daily, 8 A.M. to midnight
Admission: Free

Korean War Veterans Memorial
c/o National Capital Parks, Central
900 Ohio Drive, SW
Washington, DC 20242
(202) 426-6841
Days/Hours: Open 24 hours a day
Admission: Free

JFK Center for the Performing Arts
Washington, DC 20242
(202) 416-8000
Hours: 10 A.M. to 11 P.M. (tours: 10 A.M. to 1 P.M. daily)
Admission: Free

LBJ Memorial Grove on the Potomac
c/o George Washington Memorial Parkway
Turkey Run Park
McLean, VA 22101
(703) 285-2598
Days/Hours: Open daily, 8 A.M. to dusk
Admission: Free

Lincoln Memorial
c/o National Capital Parks, Central
900 Ohio Drive, SW
Washington, DC 20242
(202) 426-6841
Days/Hours: Open 24 hours a day
Admission: Free

National Mall
c/o National Capital Region
1100 Ohio Drive, SW
Washington, DC 20242

(202) 755-7798
Days/Hours: Open 24 hours a day
Admission: Free

Theodore Roosevelt Island
c/o George Washington Memorial Parkway
Turkey Run Park
McLean, VA 22101
(703) 285-2598
Days/Hours: Open daily, 8 A.M. to dusk
Admission: Free

U.S. Capitol
Capitol Hill
Washington, DC 20242
(202) 224-3121
Hours: 9 A.M. to 4:30 P.M. daily (8 A.M. to 8 P.M., Memorial Day through Labor Day)
Admission: Free

Vietnam War Veterans Memorial
c/o National Capital Parks, Central
900 Ohio Drive, SW
Washington, DC 20242
(202) 426-6841
Days/Hours: Open 24 hours a day
Admission: Free

Washington Monument
c/o National Capital Parks, Central
900 Ohio Drive, SW
Washington, DC 20242
(202) 426-6840
Days/Hours: 9 A.M. to 5 P.M. daily (8 A.M. to midnight, April through Labor Day)
Admission: Free

White House
c/o White House Visitor Center
Washington, DC 20242
(202) 456-7041
Days/Hours: 7:30 A.M. to 4 P.M.
Admission: Free; call number above for details about guided and walk-through tours of the White House

THE SOUTH

National Monuments

Booker T. Washington National Monument
Route 3, Box 310
Hardy, VA 24101
(703) 721-2094
Days/Hours: 8:30 A.M. to 5 P.M. daily except Thanksgiving, Christmas, and New Year's Day
Admission: $2

Alibates Flint Quarries National Monument
P.O. Box 1460
Fritch, TX 79036
(806) 857-3151
Days/Hours: Open daily, weather permitting; tours available from 10 A.M. to 2 P.M. daily, Memorial Day to Labor Day; by appointment during the rest of the year
Admission: Free

Buck Island Reef National Monument
P.O. Box 160 Christiansted
St. Croix, VI 00821-0160
(809) 773-1460
Days/Hours: Concessioners offer trips to Buck Island from St. Croix between 9 A.M. and 4 P.M.
Admission: Free

Castillo de San Marcos National Monument
1 Castillo Drive
St. Augustine, FL 32084
(904) 829-6506
Days/Hours: 9 A.M. to 6 P.M. in summer; 9 A.M. to 5:15 P.M. in winter; closed Christmas
Admission: $2

Congaree Swamp National Monument
200 Caroline Sims Road
Hopkins, SC 29061
(803) 776-4396
Days/Hours: 8:30 A.M. to 5 P.M. daily except Christmas
Admission: Free

Fort Frederica National Monument
Route 9, Box 286-C
St. Simons Island, GA 31522
(912) 638-3639
Days/Hours: 8 A.M. to 5 P.M. daily
Admission: $4 per car or $2 per person

Fort Matanzas National Monument
c/o Castillo de San Marcos National Monument
1 Castillo Drive
St. Augustine, FL 32084
(904) 471-0116
Days/Hours: 8:30 A.M. to 5:30 P.M. daily except Christmas
Admission: Free

Fort Pulaski National Monument
P.O. Box 30757
Savannah, GA 31410-0757
(912) 786-5787
Days/Hours: The visitor center is open 8:30 A.M. to 5 P.M. daily; fort from 8:30 A.M. to 5:15 P.M. daily
Admission: $4 per vehicle or $2 per person

Fort Sumter National Monument
1214 Middle Street
Sullivan's Island, SC 29482
(803) 883-3123
Days/Hours: The Fort Sumter schedule varies from season to season; Fort Moultrie is open 9 A.M. to 6 P.M. in the summer and 9 A.M. to 5 P.M. the rest of the year
Admission: Free, but visitors must pay if using concessioner-operated transportation

George Washington Birthplace National Monument
Route 1, Box 717
Washington's Birthplace, VA 22443
(804) 224-1732
Days/Hours: Open daily except Christmas and New Year's Day
Admission: $2

Ocmulgee National Monument
1207 Emery Highway
Macon, GA 31201

(912) 752-8257
Days/Hours: 9 A.M. to 5 P.M. daily
except Christmas and New Year's
Day
Admission: Free

Poverty Point
National Monument
c/o Poverty Point State
Commemorative Area
P.O. Box 276
Epps, LA 71237
(318) 926-5492
Days/Hours: 9 A.M. to 5 P.M. daily
except Thanksgiving, Christmas,
and New Year's Day
Admission: $2; free for visitors 12
and younger or 62 and older

Russell Cave
National Monument
Route 1, Box 175
Bridgeport, AL 35740
(205) 495-2672
Days/Hours: 8 A.M. to 5 P.M. daily
except Christmas
Admission: Free

National Historic Sites

Andersonville
National Historic Site
Route 1, Box 800
Andersonville, GA 31711
(912) 924-0343
Days/Hours: 8 A.M. to 5 P.M. daily
Admission: Free

Andrew Johnson
National Historic Site
P.O. Box 1088
Greeneville, TN 37744
(615) 638-3551
Days/Hours: 9 A.M. to 5 P.M. daily
except Christmas
Admission: $2

Carl Sandburg Home
National Historic Site
1928 Little River Road
Flat Rock, NC 28731
(704) 693-4178
Days/Hours: 9 A.M. to 5 P.M. daily
except Christmas
Admission: $2

Charles Pinckney
National Historic Site
c/o Fort Sumter National

Monument
1214 Middle Street
Sullivan's Island, SC 29482
(803) 883-3123
Days/Hours: Not yet open to the
public

Christiansted
National Historic Site
Box 160 Christiansted
St. Croix, VI 00821
(809) 773-1460
Days/Hours: 8 A.M. to 5 P.M. daily
except Christmas
Admission: $2

Fort Davis
National Historic Site
P.O. Box 1456
Fort Davis, TX 79734
(915) 426-3224
Days/Hours: 8 A.M. to 5 P.M. daily
Memorial Day through Labor Day;
8 A.M. to 6 P.M. the rest of the
year; closed Christmas
Admission: $2; free for visitors 16
or younger, educational groups,
and holders of Gold Eagle, Golden
Age, or Golden Access Passports

Fort Raleigh
National Historic Site
c/o Cape Hatteras National
Seashore
Route 1, Box 675
Manteo, NC 27954
(919) 473-5772 or
(919) 473-2111
Days/Hours: 9 A.M. to 5 P.M. daily
except Christmas
Admission: Free

Jamestown
National Historic Site
c/o Colonial National Historical
Park
Yorktown, VA 23690
(804) 898-3400
Days/Hours: 8:30 A.M. to 6 P.M.
daily in summer; 8:30 A.M. to
5:30 P.M. in winter
Admission: $4 per car or $2 per
person

Jimmy Carter
National Historic Site
P.O. Box 392
100 Main Street
Plains, GA 31780

(912) 824-3413
Days/Hours: The visitor center is
open daily from 9 A.M. to 5 P.M.;
The Presidential Library is open
Monday through Saturday from 9
A.M. to 4:45 P.M. and on Sundays
from noon to 4:45 P.M.
Admission: The historic site is
free; there is a fee for the
Presidential Library

Maggie L. Walker
National Historic Site
3215 East Broad Street
Richmond, VA 23223
(804) 780-1380
Days/Hours: 9 A.M. to 5 P.M.
Wednesday through Sunday
except Thanksgiving, Christmas,
and New Year's Day
Admission: Free

Martin Luther King, Jr.
National Historic Site
526 Auburn Avenue, NE
Atlanta, GA 30312
(404) 331-3920
Days/Hours: The visitor center is
open from 9 A.M. to 6 P.M. daily;
Dr. King's Birth Home from 10
A.M. to 5:30 P.M. daily; both are
closed on Christmas and New
Year's Day
Admission: Free

Ninety Six
National Historic Site
P.O. Box 496
Ninety Six, SC 29666
(803) 543-4068
Days/Hours: The visitor center is
open 8 A.M. to 5 P.M. daily except
Thanksgiving, Christmas, and
New Year's Day; trails remain
open after the visitor center closes
Admission: Free

Palo Alto Battlefield
National Historic Site
1335 East Washington Street
P.O. Drawer 1832
Brownsville, TX 78522
(210) 548-2788
Days/Hours: Not yet open to the
public

San Juan
National Historic Site
Box 712

Old San Juan, PR 00902
(809) 729-6777
Days/Hours: 8 A.M. to 6 P.M. daily
Admission: Free

Tuskegee Institute
National Historic Site
P.O. Drawer 10
Tuskegee Institute, AL 36087
(334) 727-3200
Days/Hours: The Carver Museum
is open from 9 A.M. to 5 P.M. daily
except Christmas and New Year's
Day; guided tours of The Oaks
begin on the hour
Admission: $2

THE MIDDLE WEST

National Monuments

Agate Fossil Beds
National Monument
P.O. Box 27
Gering, NE 69341
(308) 668-2211
Days/Hours: 8:30 A.M. to 5:30
P.M. daily except major holidays
Admission: Free

Effigy Mounds
National Monument
151 Highway 76
Harpers Ferry, IA 52146
(319) 873-3491
Days/Hours: 8 A.M. to 5 P.M. daily;
hours extended to 7 P.M. during
summer weekends; closed
Thanksgiving, Christmas, and
New Year's Day
Admission: $4 per vehicle or $2
per person; 16 and younger, free

George Washington Carver
National Monument
P.O. Box 38
Diamond, MO 64840
(417) 325-4151
Days/Hours: 9 A.M. to 5 P.M. daily
Admission: $2

Grand Portage
National Monument
Box 668
Grand Marais, MN 55604
(218) 387-2788
Days/Hours: The stockade is open

8 A.M. to 5 P.M. daily from mid-May through mid-October; outdoor areas are open year-round
Admission: $2

Homestead
National Monument of
America
Route 3, Box 47
Beatrice, NE 68310
(402) 223-3514
Days/Hours: 8:30 A.M. to 5 P.M.; until 6 P.M. in summer; closed Christmas
Admission: Free

Jewel Cave
National Monument
Route 1, Box 60AA
Custer, SD 57730
(605) 673-2288
Days/Hours: Monument is open year-round but times of tours vary; visitor center is open from 8 A.M. to 7 P.M.
Admission: Tour fees range from $2 to $15

Pipestone
National Monument
P.O. Box 727
Pipestone, MN 56164
(507) 825-5464
Days/Hours: 8 A.M. to 5 P.M. daily except Christmas and New Year's Day; hours extended in summer
Admission: $2

Scotts Bluff
National Monument
P.O. Box 27
Gering, NE 69341-0027
(308) 436-4340
Days/Hours: Open daily; closed on federal holidays during the off-season; hours vary according to season
Admission: $4 per car or $2 per person

National Historic Sites

Abraham Lincoln Birthplace
National Historic Site
2995 Lincoln Farm Road
Hodgenville, KY 42748
(502) 358-3137
Days/Hours: 9 A.M. to 4:45 P.M. in winter; 9 A.M. to 5:45 P.M. in

spring and fall; 9 A.M. to 6:45 P.M. in summer; closed Christmas
Admission: Free

Brown v. Board of Education
National Historic Site
424 S. Kansas Avenue, Suite 332
Topeka, KS 66603-3441
(913) 354-42743
Days/Hours: Not yet open to the public

Chicago Portage
National Historic Site
c/o Cook County Forest Preserve
Cummings Square
River Forest, IL 60305
(708) 366-9420
Days/Hours: Open 24 hours a day
Admission: Free

Chimney Rock
National Historic Site
P.O. Box F
Bayard, NE 69334
(308) 586-2581
Days/Hours: Open 24 hours a day; there are no facilities at the site
Admission: Free

Fort Larned
National Historic Site
Route 3338
Larned, KS 67550
(316) 285-6911
Days/Hours: 8 A.M. to 5 P.M. daily except Thanksgiving, Christmas, and New Year's Day
Admission: $2

Fort Scott
National Historic Site
Old Fort Boulevard
Fort Scott, KS 66701-1471
(316) 223-0310
Days/Hours: 8 A.M. to 6 P.M. daily, Memorial Day to Labor Day; 8 A.M. to 5 P.M. the rest of the year
Admission: $2; 16 and younger, plus seniors holding Golden Age, Eagle, or Access passes, free

Fort Smith
National Historic Site
Box 1406
Fort Smith, AR 72902
(501) 783-3961

Days/Hours: 9 A.M. to 5 P.M. daily except Christmas
Admission: $2

Fort Union Trading Post
National Historic Site
Route 3, Box 71
Williston, ND 58801
(701) 572-9083
Days/Hours: 9 A.M. to 5:30 P.M. except Thanksgiving, Christmas, and New Year's Day
Admission: Free

Harry S Truman
National Historic Site
223 North Main Street
Independence, MO 64050-2804
(816) 254-7199
Days/Hours: 8:30 A.M. to 5 P.M. daily; closed Thanksgiving, Christmas, New Year's Day, and Mondays between Labor Day and Memorial Day
Admission: $2

Herbert Hoover
National Historic Site
P.O. Box 607
West Branch, IA 52358
(319) 643-2541
Days/Hours: 9 A.M. to 5 P.M. daily except Thanksgiving, Christmas, and New Year's Day
Admission: $2

James A. Garfield
National Historic Site
c/o Western Reserve Historical Society
8095 Mentor Avenue
Mentor, OH 44060
(216) 255-8722
Days/Hours: 10 A.M. to 5 P.M. Tuesday through Saturday; noon to 5 P.M. Sunday
Admission: Free

Knife River Indian Villages
National Historic Site
P.O. Box 9
Stanton, ND 58571
(701) 745-3300
Days/Hours: 9 A.M. to 6 P.M., June through Labor Day; 9 A.M. to 4:30 P.M. the rest of the year
Admission: Free

Lincoln Home
National Historic Site
413 South Eighth Street
Springfield, IL 62701
(217) 492-4150
Days/Hours: 8:30 A.M. to 5 P.M. daily except Thanksgiving, Christmas, and New Year's Day; hours extended during summer
Admission: Free, but tickets must be obtained from the Lincoln Home Visitor Center at 426 South Seventh Street

Ulysses S. Grant
National Historic Site
7400 Grant Road
St. Louis, MO 63123
(314) 842-1867
Days/Hours: Not yet open to the public

William Howard Taft
National Historic Site
2038 Auburn Avenue
Cincinnati, OH 45219
(513) 684-3262
Days/Hours: 10 A.M. to 4 P.M. daily except Thanksgiving, Christmas, and New Year's Day
Admission: Free

Jefferson National Expansion
National Memorial
11 North Fourth Street
St. Louis, MO 63102
(314) 425-4465
Days/Hours: Open daily, 8 A.M. to 10 P.M. in summer; 9 A.M. to 6 P.M. in winter (visitor center); closed Thanksgiving, Christmas, and New Year's Day
Admission: $1 per person; $3 per family. Tram ride is $2.50 for adults, 50 cents for children.

Mount Rushmore
National Memorial
P.O. Box 268
Keystone, SD 57751
(605) 574-2523
Days/Hours: Open daily, 8 A.M. to 10 P.M. from mid-May to mid-September; 8 A.M. to 5 P.M. from mid-September to mid-May
Admission: Free

THE SOUTHWEST

National Monuments

Aztec Ruins
National Monument
P.O. Box 640
Aztec, NM 87410
(505) 334-6174
Days/Hours: 8 A.M. to 5 P.M. daily;
longer in summer; closed
Christmas and New Year's Day
Admission: $2

Bandelier
National Monument
HCR 1, Box 1
Los Alamos, NM 87544
(505) 672-3861
Days/Hours: Visitor center open
from 8 A.M. to 6 P.M. daily in
summer; hours vary the rest of
the year; closed Christmas
Admission: $5 per vehicle or $3
per person

Black Canyon of the Gunnison
National Monument
2233 East Main, Suite A
Montrose, CO 81401
(303) 249-7036
Days/Hours: The visitor center is
open daily throughout the summer
and intermittently during spring
and fall
Admission: $4 per vehicle

Cabrillo
National Monument
P.O. Box 6670
San Diego, CA 92106
(619) 557-5450
Days/Hours: 9 A.M. to 5:15 P.M.
daily; Bayside Trail closes at 4 P.M.
Admission: $4 per vehicle or $2
per person

Canyon de Chelly
National Monument
P.O. Box 588
Chinle, AZ 86503
(520) 674-5500
Days/Hours: 8 A.M. to 6 P.M. daily,
April 30 through September 30; 8
A.M. to 5 P.M. daily, October 1
through April 30

Admission: A free permit must be
obtained at the visitor center
before entering the canyon

Capulin Volcano
National Monument
P.O. Box 40
Capulin, NM 88414
(505) 278-2201
Days/Hours: 8:30 A.M. to 4:30
P.M. daily, but hours vary
seasonally; open year-round,
weather permitting, except major
holidays
Admission: $4 per vehicle

Casa Grande Ruins
National Monument
1100 Ruins Drive
Coolidge, AZ 85228
(602) 723-3172
Days/Hours: 7 A.M. to 6 P.M. daily
Admission: Free

Cedar Breaks
National Monument
P.O. Box 749
Cedar City, UT 84720
(801) 586-9451
Days/Hours: The visitor center is
open daily from early June to mid-
October
Admission: $4

Chiricahua
National Monument
Dos Cabezas Route, Box 6500
Willcox, AZ 85643
(602) 824-3560
Days/Hours: 8 A.M. to 5 P.M. daily;
closed Christmas
Admission: $4 per vehicle or $2
per person

Colorado
National Monument
Fruita, CO 81521
(303) 858-3617
Days/Hours: Monument and
visitor center are open every day;
hours vary
Admission: $4 per vehicle or $2
per person

Devils Postpile
National Monument
P.O. Box 501
Mammoth Lakes, CA 93546
(209) 565-3341

Days/Hours: 7:30 A.M. to 5:30
P.M., late June to early September;
closed in winter
Admission: Free

Dinosaur
National Monument
P.O. Box 210
Dinosaur, CO 81610
(303) 374-2216
Days/Hours: The quarry is open 8
A.M. to 4:30 P.M. daily; hours
extended in summer; the visitor
center is closed weekends and
holidays in winter
Admission: $5 per vehicle or $3
per person; visitor center, free

El Malpais
**National Monument and
Conservation Area**
P.O. Box 939
Grants, NM 87020
(505) 285-5406
Days/Hours: Visitor center open 8
A.M. to 5 P.M., Memorial Day to
Columbus Day; 8 A.M. to 4:30 P.M.
the rest of the year; closed
Thanksgiving, Christmas, and
New Year's Day
Admission: Free

El Morro
National Monument
Route 2, Box 43
Ramah, NM 87321-9603
(505) 783-4226
Days/Hours: 9 A.M. to 7 P.M. in
summer; 9 A.M. to 5 P.M. the rest
of the year; closed Christmas and
New Year's Day
Admission: $2

Florissant Fossil Beds
National Monument
P.O. Box 185
Florissant, CO 80816
(719) 748-3253
Days/Hours: 8 A.M. to 4 P.M. daily;
until 7 P.M. in summer; closed
Thanksgiving, Christmas, and
New Year's Day
Admission: $2 per person or a
maximum of $4 per family

Fort Union
National Monument
Watrous, NM 87753
(505) 425-8025

Days/Hours: 8 A.M. to 5 P.M. daily
except Christmas and New Year's
Day
Admission: $2

Gila Cliff Dwellings
National Monument
Route 11, Box 100
Silver City, NM 88061
voice or TDD (505) 536-9344
Days/Hours: Hours at the visitor
center and ruins vary seasonally;
closed Christmas and New Year's
Day
Admission: Free

Hohokam Pima
National Monument
c/o Casa Grande Ruins National
Monument
P.O. Box 518
Coolidge, AZ 85228
(602) 723-3172
Days/Hours: Closed to the public

Lava Beds
National Monument
Box 867
Tulelake, CA 96134
(916) 667-2282
Days/Hours: The visitor center is
open from 9 A.M. to 6 P.M.,
Memorial Day through Labor Day;
8 A.M. to 5 P.M. the rest of the
year; closed Thanksgiving and
Christmas
Admission: $4 per vehicle or $2
per person

Montezuma Castle
National Monument
P.O. Box 219
Camp Verde, AZ 86322
(520) 567-3322
Days/Hours: 8 A.M. to 5 P.M. daily;
hours extended in summer;
Admission: $2

Muir Woods
National Monument
Mill Valley, CA 94941
(415) 388-2595
TTD (415) 556-2766
Days/Hours: Open year-round
from 8 A.M. to sunset
Admission: Free

Navajo
National Monument
HC 71, Box 3
Tonalea, AZ 86044-9704
(602) 672-2366
Days/Hours: 8 A.M. to 6 P.M. in summer; 8 A.M. to 5 P.M. the rest of the year; closed Thanksgiving, Christmas, and New Year's Day; Keet Seel open from Memorial Day to Labor Day
Admission: Free; permit required to visit Keet Seel

Organ Pipe Cactus
National Monument
Route 1, Box 100
Ajo, AZ 85321
(602) 387-6849
Days/Hours: The visitor center is open 8 A.M. to 5 P.M. daily
Admission: $4 per vehicle or $2 per person

Petroglyph
National Monument
123 Fourth Street, NW
Albuquerque, NM 87102
(505) 766-8375
Days/Hours: 8 A.M. to 5 P.M. in winter; 9 A.M. to 6 P.M. in summer
Admission: Free

Pinnacles
National Monument
Paicines, CA 95043
(408) 389-4485
Days/Hours: 24 hours a day, year-round; visitor center hours vary
Admission: $4 per vehicle or $2 per person

Pipe Spring
National Monument
HC 65, Box 5
Fredonia, AZ 86022
(602) 643-7105
Days/Hours: 8 A.M. to 4 P.M. daily
Admission: $2

Rainbow Bridge
National Monument
c/o Glen Canyon National Recreation Area
Box 1507
Page, AZ 86040
(602) 645-8200
Days/Hours: The monument is open year-round; the visitor center

at Glen Canyon is open 8 A.M. to 5 P.M., Labor Day to Memorial Day; 7 A.M. to 7 P.M. the rest of the year; closed Christmas
Admission: Free; permit required to hike trails

Salinas Pueblo Missions
National Monument
P.O. Box 496
Mountainair, NM 87036-0496
(505) 847-2585
Days/Hours: Open daily, year-round
Admission: Free

Sunset Crater Volcano
National Monument
Route 3, Box 149
Flagstaff, AZ 86004
(520) 556-7042
Days/Hours: The visitor center is open 8 A.M. to 5 P.M. daily except Christmas; hours may be extended in summer; monument is open from dawn to dusk
Admission: $4 per vehicle or $2 per person (fee includes entrance to Wupatki National Monument)

Tonto
National Monument
P.O. Box 707
Roosevelt, AZ 85545
(602) 467-2241
Days/Hours: 8 A.M. to 5 P.M. daily except Christmas; hours may be extended in summer
Admission: $2

Tuzigoot
National Monument
P.O. Box 219
Camp Verde, AZ 86322
(602) 634-5564
Days/Hours: 8 A.M. to 5 P.M. daily; hours extended in summer; closed Christmas
Admission: $2

Walnut Canyon
National Monument
Walnut Canyon Road #3
Flagstaff, AZ 86004
(520) 526-3367
Days/Hours: The visitor center is open 8 A.M. to 5 P.M. daily except Christmas; Island Trail closes at 4 P.M.; park gate closes at 5 P.M.;

hours may be extended during summer
Admission: $4 per vehicle or $2 per person

White Sands
National Monument
P.O. Box 1086
Holloman AFB, NM 88330
(505) 479-6124
Days/Hours: 8 A.M. to 4:30 P.M. daily; hours extended in summer
Admission: $4 per vehicle or $2 per person

Wupatki
National Monument
HC 33, Box 444A
Flagstaff, AZ 86004
(520) 556-7040
Days/Hours: The visitor center is open 8 A.M. to 5 P.M. daily except Christmas; hours may be extended in summer; the ruins are open from dawn to dusk
Admission: $4 per vehicle or $2 per person (fee includes entrance to Sunset Crater National Monument)

Yucca House
National Monument
c/o Mesa Verde National Park, CO 81321
(303) 529-4461
Days/Hours: open daily; no visitor facilities
Admission: Free

National Historic Sites

Bent's Old Fort
National Historic Site
35110 Highway 194 East
La Junta, CO 81050-9523
(719) 384-2596
Days/Hours: 9 A.M. to 5 P.M. daily
Admission: $2

Eugene O'Neill
National Historic Site
P.O. Box 280
Danville, CA 94526
(510) 838-0249
Days/Hours: Visits to the site are by reservation only
Admission: Free

Fort Bowie
National Historic Site
P.O. Box 158
Bowie, AZ 85605
(602) 847-2500
Days/Hours: Ruins and trail open from sunrise to sunset; visitor center open 8 A.M. to 5 P.M. daily except Christmas
Admission: Free

Fort Point
National Historic Site
P.O. Box 29333
Presidio of San Francisco, CA 94129
(415) 556-1693
Days/Hours: 10 A.M. to 5 P.M. daily
Admission: Free

Golden Spike
National Historic Site
P.O. Box 897
Brigham City, UT 84302
(801) 471-2209
Days/Hours: 8 A.M. to 6 P.M. in summer; 8 A.M. to 4:30 P.M. in winter; closed Thanksgiving and Christmas
Admission: $4 per vehicle or $2 per person

Hubbell Trading Post
National Historic Site
Box 150
Ganado, AZ 86505
(602) 755-3475
Days/Hours: 8 A.M. to 5 P.M. daily except Thanksgiving, Christmas, and New Year's Day; 8 A.M. to 6 P.M. in summer
Admission: Free

John Muir
National Historic Site
4202 Alhambra Avenue
Martinez, CA 94553
(510) 228-8860
Days/Hours: 10 A.M. to 4:30 P.M. Wednesday through Sunday; closed Thanksgiving, Christmas, and New Year's Day
Admission: $2

Manzanar
National Historic Site
c/o Death Valley National Monument

Death Valley, CA 92328
(619) 786-2331
Days/Hours: 24 hours a day
Admission: Free

Puukohola Heiau
National Historic Site
P.O. Box 44340
Kawaihae, HI 96743
(808) 882-7218
Days/Hours: 7:30 A.M. to 4 P.M.
daily
Admission: $2

USS *Arizona*
National Memorial
National Park Service
1 Arizona Memorial Place
Honolulu, HI 96818
(808) 422-2771
Days/Hours: 7:30 A.M. to 5 P.M.
(visitor center); tours from 8:00
A.M. to 3:00 P.M. daily
Admission: Free

THE NORTHWEST

National Monuments

Aniakchak
National Monument and
Preserve
P.O. Box 7
King Salmon, AK 99613
(907) 246-3305
Days/Hours: Open year-round
Admission: Free

Cape Krusenstern
National Monument
Northwest Alaska Areas
P.O. Box 1029
Kotzebue, AK 99752
(907) 442-3760 or
(907) 442-3890
Days/Hours: The visitor center is
open 8 A.M. to 5 P.M. Monday
through Friday; hours extended in
summer
Admission: Free

Craters of the Moon
National Monument
P.O. Box 29
Arco, ID 83213
(208) 527-3257
Days/Hours: 8 A.M. to 6 P.M. daily

until September 16, then 8 A.M. to
4:30 P.M.; closed on winter
holidays
Admission: $4 per vehicle or $2
per person

Devils Tower
National Monument
P.O. Box 8
Devils Tower, WY 82714-0008
(307) 467-5283
Days/Hours: The monument is
open year-round; the visitor center
is open April through October
Admission: $4 per vehicle or $2
per person

Fossil Butte
National Monument
P.O. Box 592
Kemmerer, WY 83101
(307) 877-4455
Days/Hours: 8 A.M. to 7 P.M. daily
in summer; 8 A.M. to 4:30 P.M. the
rest of the year; closed for winter
holidays
Admission: Free

Great Sand Dunes
National Monument
11500 Highway 150
Mosca, CO 81146
(719) 378-2312
Days/Hours: Visitor center open 8
A.M. to 5 P.M. daily except on
federal holidays; hours extended
from Memorial Day to Labor Day
Admission: $4 per vehicle or $2
per person

Hagerman Fossil Beds
National Monument
P.O. Box 570
Hagerman, ID 83332
(208) 837-4793
Days/Hours: 8 A.M. to 5 P.M.
weekdays, Memorial Day through
end of September; 8:30 A.M. to 5
P.M. Thursday through Sunday the
rest of the year
Admission: Free

Hovenweep
National Monument
McElmo Route
Cortez, CO 81321
(303) 529-4461
Days/Hours: Open year-round
Admission: Free

John Day Fossil Beds
National Monument
420 W. Main
John Day, OR 97845
(503) 987-2333
Days/Hours: 8:30 A.M. to 5 P.M.
daily; not open on weekends
during winter
Admission: Free

Little Bighorn Battlefield
National Monument
P.O. Box 39
Crow Agency, MT 59022
(406) 638-2621
Days/Hours: 8 A.M. to 6 P.M.
spring and fall; 8 A.M. to 8 P.M.,
Memorial Day through Labor Day;
8 A.M. to 4:30 P.M. winter; closed
Thanksgiving, Christmas, and
New Year's Day
Admission: $4 per vehicle or $2
per person during summer months

Natural Bridges
National Monument
Box 1
Lake Powell, UT 84533
(801) 259-5174
Days/Hours: Monument is open
24 hours a day; the visitor center
is open 8 A.M. to 4:30 P.M. daily;
closed Thanksgiving, Christmas,
and New Year's Day
Admission: $4 per vehicle or $2
per person

Oregon Caves
National Monument
19000 Caves Highway
Cave Junction, OR 97523
(503) 592-3400
Days/Hours: Open daily except
Thanksgiving and Christmas; call
for times of tours
Admission: Cost of tours varies

Timpanogos Cave
National Monument
Route 3, Box 200
American Fork, UT 84003
(801) 756-5239
Days/Hours: open 7 A.M. to 5:30
P.M., Memorial Day through Labor
Day
Admission: $5 for visitors 16 and
older; $4 for visitors ages 6 to 15;
5 years old and younger, free

National Historic Sites

Fort Laramie
National Historic Site
P.O. Box 86
Fort Laramie, WY 82212
(307) 837-2221
Days/Hours: 8 A.M. to 4:30 P.M.
daily except Thanksgiving,
Christmas, and New Year's Day;
hours extended in summer
Admission: $2

Fort Vancouver
National Historic Site
612 East Reserve Street
Vancouver, WA 98661
(360) 696-7655
Days/Hours: 9 A.M. to 5 P.M.,
Memorial Day to Labor Day; 9
A.M. to 4 P.M., Labor Day to
Memorial Day; closed
Thanksgiving, Christmas Eve and
Day, and New Year's Day.
Admission: $2

Grant-Kohrs Ranch
National Historic Site
Box 790
Deer Lodge, MT 59722
(406) 846-3388
Days/Hours: Open daily except
Thanksgiving, Christmas, and
New Year's Day
Admission: $2

McLoughlin House
National Historic Site
713 Center Street
Oregon City, OR 97045
(503) 656-5146
Days/Hours: 10 A.M. to 4 P.M.
Tuesday through Saturday; 1 P.M.
to 4 P.M. Sunday; closed on
Mondays, holidays, and the
month of January
Admission: $3 adults; $2.50
seniors; $1 children ages 6-17

Whitman Mission
National Historic Site
Route 2, Box 247
Walla Walla, WA 99362
(509) 522-6360
Days/Hours: Open daily except
Thanksgiving, Christmas, and
New Year's Day
Admission: $2

Index
America's Monuments, Memorials, and Historic Sites

343